STORIES FROM THE ROAD

MY YEARS AS A LONG HAUL TRUCKER

DON TAYLOR

 FriesenPress

One Printers Way
Altona, MB, R0G 0B0
Canada

www.friesenpress.com

ISBN
978-1-03-911863-8 (Hardcover)
978-1-03-911862-1 (Paperback)
978-1-03-911864-5 (eBook)

1. BIOGRAPHY & AUTOBIOGRAPHY, PERSONAL MEMOIRS

Distributed to the trade by The Ingram Book Company

TABLE OF CONTENTS

INTRODUCTION

This book is not a linear story. It is a collection of my experiences as a professional driver, spanning a career that started in March 1985 as a taxi driver, progressing to my years driving "turnpike doubles" (a pair of 53 foot trailers, commonly referred to simply as "pikes"). They are one version of long combination vehicles, or "lcv" as they are more commonly known. You may find some of my experiences absolutely hilarious; others totally unbelievable. I can assure you, however, they are all true.

Over the years I've been laughed at, spit at, spit on, robbed, threatened by gun and knife point, swindled, and shot at. People sometimes ask me: "Why do you stay at a job that is so inherently dangerous, and keeps you away from home for so long at a time?" The answer is simple, and complex. The simple answer is, I enjoy doing it. Where else can a high school drop-out earn between $80,000 and $100,000 a year driving someone else's vehicle while getting to see North America? The complex answer is that it takes a special kind of person to become a long haul tractor-trailer driver. Most wash out within six months. But if you make through that first year, you're pretty much a lifer. You won't be able to walk away. It gets into your blood. It becomes a lifestyle. Not a job, not a career, but a way of life.

Due to the fact that trucks routinely cross the border between Canada and the United States, the industry uses the imperial system for measurements. Even the trucks built and sold for use in Canada still use imperial gauges for everything except the speedometer and odometer, Air pressure is measured in PSI, and temperature gauges are in Fahrenheit. Therefore, to eliminate confusion, I have stayed with the imperial units.

Grab your duffle bag and camera, and let's get this show on the road. Because if the tires ain't turning, I ain't earnin'.

DEDICATIONS

This book is dedicated to the countless drivers who spend countless days and weeks, driving countless miles to deliver all the goods that keep the world economy going. It is, for the most part, and long, tiring, lonely thankless job, but almost every driver will tell you, there's nothing else they'd rather do.

The thought of writing a book never really occurred to me. But in sitting around talking with friends and family, and relating some of the stories found herein, more than a few suggested I should write a book. I kind of laughed it off, thinking; "who would be interested in this?" But it did get my wondering if anyone WOULD be interested. So I talked to a few acquaintances, who I assumed would give me honest answers as to whether they would be interested in such a book. I received about a 70% favourable response, so I decided it was time to get started.

The writing of a book, ANY book, requires one to descend into the warm embrace of a word processor for many long hours. As I'm still actively driving all over North America, I would have to squeeze writing time into my much valued time off at home.

I'd like to thank those who were instrumental in getting me moving on this project. First off, my lovely wife, Sue. Her love, tolerance, and patience while I pounded away on this book have known no end. Thanks also go to the following, in no particular order, for reviewing the manuscript, and pointing out areas that needed clarification for non trucking people to understand: Beverly Kouhi-Soloway, Maureen McKeown-Tsuchida, Fiona Odlum, and Greg Mackling. Thanks also go out to countless others who indirectly helped by jolting some memories from the recesses of my memory.

With few exceptions, the names of people have been changed to protect their anonymity. It has not been my intention to paint any of the companies I worked for in a bad light. All trucking companies have their good points, and their bad points. The perfect company doesn't exist, due to drivers wanting different perks. The best you can do, is pick a company that fits your personal needs. My current company's "home time" policy is that you will be home for your booked time off, even if it means parking the truck, and flying you home. For the record, I've been flown home (and back) three times in two years, once because the transmission went as I was loading to come home.

Getting on the Road

The Journey Starts

Before we start exploring my journeys as a long-haul driver across North America, let's take a look at my personal route to this adventure. I don't come from a family with a trucking history. Far from it. Mom (Annette) was in the medical field. Dad (Donald) was a general labourer.

My parents met on a blind date which is a bit ironic, since my father was legally blind. He only had six percent vision. As I've been told, he'd been awaiting a date one night when the lady stood him up. Instead, she chose to go on a date with another fellow. On the spur of the moment, a mutual friend of parents set the two of them of up on a last-minute night out. During the date, my future-parents went to his sister's place. At his sister's place, was the woman who stood dad up, and her "new" date. Turned out, the young woman was one of my father's friends. She didn't know that her "new" date was friends with her "old" date. Awkward much? Dad being Dad, carried on as if he didn't know the young lady at all. That was Dad. Calm and cool as a cucumber.

Dad never really talked much about his childhood, probably because he thought it unremarkable. Since his death, I've learned a fair bit about him. My love and respect for him has grown even more. As a child, he had contracted polio, spent time in an iron lung, and had to learn how to walk again. Due to his limited vision, he attended a school in Southern Ontario, where he learned to read Braille.

My father never let his near-blindness slow him down, let alone stop him. When he met my mother met in the late 1950s or early 1960s, he drove himself around. Yeah. A blind dude driving a car. To the best of my knowledge, he only had one accident. If I recall correctly, alcohol may have played a part. Dad was also a pretty decent cook. My father was always active. He was a recreational five-pin bowler and he curled regularly each winter. In the summer, he loved swimming, especially snorkeling. I remember one time when we were snorkeling together. When we came to the surface, he asked me if I had seen the turtle on the lake bottom. I hadn't. I dove back down to investigate. Sure enough, there was a turtle, almost invisible. Dad had seen the slight difference in colour between the bottom of the lake and the turtle's shell. Blew me away how he could do stuff like that. In some way, I swear he could "see" better than I could.

I was born in December of 1962, the fourth of five children, and the only boy. Some say I was a bit of a trouble maker. I have few memories of my pre-school years, however one that stands out happened when I was about three or four years old. I'd uttered some "dirty word" or another. Dad asked me what I had said. Me being me, sat where I was, pulling grass out of the ground, innocently replied: "nothing?" He didn't buy that. Dad decided to do what many of a 1960s parent did to insolent children: Wash my mouth out with soap. He went in the house to get a bar of soap. As he stuffed the bar of soap in my mouth, I just bit down, probably thinking he wouldn't be able to reach my tongue to rub the soap if I clenched it in my teeth. Stupid, stupid, stupid! Dad just pulled it, leaving more than enough soap caked on the back of my teeth. To this day, I can still taste the soap.

Growing up, we were far from being rich or even affluent. Mom worked part-time as a physiotherapy assistant. Dad was a track shed foreman (supervising the loading and unloading of rail cars) for Saskatchewan Wheat Pool. Work at the elevators slowed down during the winter when shipping on Lake Superior and the rest of the Great Lakes ended. Lay-offs in elevators were massive. For the first eighteen years Dad worked at the elevators (1950 to 1968) he was laid off every winter. Still, we lacked for nothing. There was always food on the table, heat in the winter (no small detail in that part of the country), and we always had clean clothes to wear. Some of our clothes came from a store, others Mom made for us. For a number of years, my grandmother (Mom's mom) lived with us as part of our large family. Granny did all the cooking, cleaning, and watching over all five of us children while our parents worked. I can only imagine the willpower that took. My oldest sister, Susan, was born in 1954 while Debi, the youngest, arrived in 1965. In between, were the middle-ones: Dianne made her appearance 1955, Sharron in 1956, and myself in 1962. To see all five of us together, you could see the resemblance between Susan and Debi, but the three of us in the middle don't look alike at all. I look, sound and act a lot like Dad.

In 1960s Ontario, children started kindergarten the September of the year you turned five. Someone born in January started the same time as someone born in December. As a late-in-the-year baby, I was still four years old when I started school in the fall of 1967. Some of my classmates were almost a year older than I was. I was at a distinct disadvantage, in more than one way. I was always a small child, something I did not outgrow until well into my twenties. Years later, when I started high school, I was still tall, lanky, and under 100 lbs. Perfect to be picked on right from my first school days. My situation was made even worse with two mental health issues that still persist: dyslexia and attention deficit hyperactivity disorder (ADHD). In the 1960s, these mental health issues were non-existent as far as explaining a child's behavior. ADHD was unknown. Instead, it was called "day dreaming". The cure was a rap across the knuckles with a pointer or a yard stick, or a slap upside the head to get you back to reality. As I can personally attest, physical punishment was still okay in Ontario (and Canadian) schools well into the 1990s.

As I was younger and smaller than everyone is my class, my parents unsuccessfully begged the school board to hold me back a year. Since I had completed the required learning for the next grade their request was denied. True, I had managed to complete the grade, but only by the narrowest of margins. My second-grade teacher was particularly brutal towards me. Often I didn't understand the material because I had difficulty concentrating and figuring out what the rest of the class seemed to easily understand. Instead, my six-year-old mind would become distracted by my imagination. My "go to" happy places included playing rocket ship with my pencil, or using the old trapezoid-shaped eraser and my ruler to play truck driver. Yup. You guessed it. Knuckles smacked again. Finally, after my parents diligent campaigning, the school board relented a bit, suggesting the then-popular solution to educational difficulties: change schools. Obviously, this was not going to work. Same issues, just a different school. During my early school years, I was sent for psychiatric assessments, had a three-sided wall put around my desk, had my desk moved into the hall, and even had a special teacher for some subjects. You name it, they tried it. Still, I managed to keep a high enough grade to continue to advance through each grade on schedule.

During the school years, I had very few friends. In the second grade I met a new boy whose family had recently moved from the Toronto area. He beat the living snot out of me, and left me hanging in a tree. Years later, we would meet again under more mature circumstances. We became friends, however it wasn't until a few years later that we both put two and two together about our first meeting. We shared a good chuckle about it, and we're still close friends to this day. Finally, as Grade 8 came to an end, the school board realized that I was still struggling and was not ready to take on the challenges of high school. I would have to repeat Grade 8. I remember the principal calling me to the office to break the news to me. I was totally crushed. I ran home, crying my eyes out. The few friends I had made were moving on to high school, and I wasn't. My second version of Grade 8 wasn't much different from the first. I was still bullied like there was no tomorrow. I've never been a fighter. Back then, it was just easier and less painful to take the abuse, and carry on.

I had hoped that high school would provide a new learning experience but I was still at the mercy of the school bullies. Some of the abuse from my high school classmates was pretty bad. I was almost run over two or three times by guys trying to show off to their girlfriends. They thought it was funny to try and tag me with their vehicles. I was gagged, bound hand-and-wrist, and stuck butt- first in a garbage can in the girl's washroom. Then I was tickled to the point of tears until I lost control of my bladder. I was left there for two hours. The physical abuse (getting beat up) continued in the gym class locker room as well as during my daily walks to and from school. Many of my school books were destroyed. Rented band instruments were stolen or damaged beyond repair. Needless to say, the bullying and the learning disorders played havoc with my education. As I started my third try at Grade 11, my younger sister finally caught up to me. I didn't last much longer, and dropped out of school in 1979 when I was seventeen.

After ditching high school, I left for an eight-month stint in the Canadian Naval Reserves in Esquimalt, British Columbia, just outside of Victoria. I had been involved in the Navy through the Sea Cadet youth program and the Naval Reserves since about 1977. In addition to the Sea Cadets/Naval Reserve, I was also in the Boy Scouts of Canada. I was again bullied somewhat in the Naval Reserves, but no physical abuse. Nonetheless, the emotional bullying and humiliation was often just as difficult. Finally, in early 1980, I'd had enough. It was time to pull the plug and return to Thunder Bay. I started looking for work as soon as I was home. I had applied to the Canadian Coast Guard, Saskatchewan Wheat Pool, and a few other places. My two top choices were Saskatchewan Wheat Pool, and the Coast Guard. With the memories of Naval Service still fresh in my mind, however, I took the job offer from Saskatchewan Wheat Pool.

Saskatchewan Wheat Pool (or "the elevators" as we called it) operated huge grain terminals on the shores of Lake Superior where they shipped grains from Western Canada through the St Lawrence Seaway. The grain came in by rail, was stored in the "elevator" (grain terminal), and then loaded onto lakers (inland ships) and salties (ocean-going ships). For Thunder Bay residents, this was just a normal day job. We worked eight hours a day, 40 hours a week, and over time after that. It was hard work, and the work environment was brutally hot in the busy summer shipping season. As I was low man on the "whiskers list", I was laid off every winter for at least five or six months. The pay when I was working, however, was awesome! $11.99 an hour when the 1980 minimum wage in Ontario was just over $3.00. I was living at home, paying room and board, riding my bicycle everywhere I went. I was about six feet two inches tall by this time, weighing about 220 lbs. Around that time, I'd read someplace that for my age and height I should weigh 180 lbs. By watching what I ate and spending even more time riding my bike, I managed to lower my weight to 185.

Then I went for a routine medical appointment. My doctor threatened to hospitalize me on the spot. Not only were my ribs prominently showing, but he could even see some of the tendons. Apparently, I was carrying about nine or ten percent body fat (fifteen to twenty percent is normal for a seventeen to eighteen-year-old boy).

There are two interesting stories from my days at Saskatchewan Wheat Pool. While racism wasn't rampant per se, the various ethnic groups stayed to themselves for the most part both at work and afterwards. We had a good number of Polish, French, Italian, Ukrainian, Finnish, and British people working there. Some were newcomers while others were second or third generation Canadian. Ironically, both stories involve the same instigator. This character was of Italian descent, but in all fairness, his personality had nothing to do with his heritage. He was an arrogant, bossy, and condescending fellow. For these stories, I'll call him "Giovanni". And in both cases, looking back, I can see how the circumstances developed.

One day I was in the lunch room, when the timekeeper came through with a tour group from Japan. The tourists were doing what tourists do. Taking pictures of everything. The timekeeper was telling them that the workers at the elevator are a very tight knit family, everyone gets along, and it operates like a well-oiled machine. No sooner had the translator translated this for the group, when the door flew open, and Giovanni came running through as fast as he could. Legs and arms pumping as if he was trying to set a world record. His face was beet red. He was huffing and puffing, with the wildest, most terrified look on his face I had ever seen. Not ten feet behind him was one of the track-shed dumper operators, wielding a fire ax over his head, screaming "You greasy mother-XXXXX! I'm gonna XXXXXX kill you!". They both carried on through the lunch room, and out the door, onto the dock, and headed to the parking lot. Giovanni survived this encounter, and to the best of my knowledge, no charges were ever filed.

I'm not sure who Giovanni provoked the next time as I only caught the very end of it. I was walking up the dock towards the lunchroom to punch in. Directly behind the lunchroom, also along the dock, was the office for the cleaner deck. As I got close to the door for the lunchroom, I heard a yell, a scream, then breaking glass, followed by Giovanni flying across the dock (six feet) right into the slip where we loaded ships. The slip is a good 100 feet wide, about half a mile long, and 39 feet deep. Had there been a ship in the slip, he wouldn't have survived. It was anyone's guess as to who tossed him out the window. There would have been seven or eight people close enough to have been suspects, but nobody claimed to have seen anything.

My journey through life, at least up until this point, provided me with experiences that would shape the adult I would become. Little did I know as I left my elevator work behind me that I would start on a new path that would become more than just a job. I was about to start the route that led me to becoming a long-haul truck driver delivering goods across North America.

Building a Trucking Career

Becoming a Professional Driver

My professional driving career officially began when I was twenty-two years old. On March 15, 1985 I went to work for Roach's Taxi in Thunder Bay, Ontario. The previous November, I along with many others, was laid off from my position as a general labourer with Saskatchewan Wheat Pool as they anticipated the winter grain shipment slowdown. They were also starting to computerize the elevators, and the writing was on the wall, that most of those being laid off would not be called back in the spring. I had always loved driving, and mom once told me the only car seat she could put me in where I wouldn't cry was one with a steering wheel. I, of course, have no memory of this. I started driving taxi not thinking of it as a start to a trucking career. Instead, I just figured it would do until "something better comes along". It would be nine years of "making do" before I made the jump to being a full-time truck driver.

My test drive with Roach's was with one of their big commercial customers, mainly to see how I'd treat the vehicle on rough roads. The owner's brother was the road tester, meaning, of course, that I was gentle with the car. Taxi drivers in Thunder Bay at the time were paid on commission:

Forty percent of the metered rate, plus tips. If my memory is right, in 1985 the meter started at $1.30 and went up ninety cents for each kilometer. Waiting time was a dime a minute. Cracking $100 ($40 for the driver) a day was a challenge. Ontario minimum wage in 1985 was $4.35 (equal to just over $8 in today's money) at the time, and a full day's work for those earning that was around $35 (in that day's financial system).

The day after I started driving taxi, the local transit union went on strike. Talk about being thrown to the wolves! With no buses running, taxis were extremely busy. During the transit strike a busy cab driver could easily earn $200 a day. While the income was great, my stress level was off the charts. "Busy" was a massive under-statement. Traffic was chaos. For the first few days I vividly remember getting home, shaking and almost crying from the stress of a ten or twelve-hour shift.

After the strike was over, things started slowing down. Every cabbies' income dropped. I was still living at home, however, paying minimal room and board. I helped out taking care of the lawn and snow removal, along with some handyman jobs around the house. My most important function was, as always, being available to pop home to let Mom into the house. She had a real habit of locking herself out. Once she even managed to lock herself out of the house and out of the car while it was running. I can't count the times I'd get a message over the taxi radio asking me to go let mom in the house. It got to the point the dispatcher would say: "Number #46, you know the drill," or "#46, your mom called". This was in the days before cell phones. My mother would then go to the neighbour's house, calling Roach's herself, or having the neighbour call. I asked her more than once why she did not just give the neighbours a house key. Mom replied that it wasn't THAT often she'd locked herself out. Not really. Only once a week or so.

One day, after about a year of driving taxi for Roach's, I walked into the dispatch office, heading to the washroom. This took me past the owner's office. As I passed his open door, he called out to me, asking me when I was going to stop wearing "that God-awful jacket". Said jacket was my much-loved, very well worn, heavy leather biker-style jacket, with a chain going over the right shoulder under the arm. I'd say it weighed about five lbs. Those days I wore it everywhere. On a spur of the moment, I replied,

"When you put me in a new car, not just new to me but a brand-new car, I'll give you the jacket to do with as you please". Two weeks later, I had the keys to a brand new 1986 Ford LTD taxi cab. I surrendered the jacket. No idea what ever became of it.

On another occasion, I was sent to a local bar for a fare. The gentleman got in the car, seeming to be fairly sober, and off we went. I came to a stop sign with a huge snowbank blocking my view. I inched ahead to see around it. Nothing was coming, allowing me to make my turn. Almost immediately, I saw the flashing lights of an Ontario Provincial Police (OPP) car in my mirrors. I pulled over, and the officer said I had failed to stop at the stop sign. I explained that I had stopped. I couldn't see around the snowbank. Then I inched ahead to see if the road was clear. He wasn't impressed. I got a ticket. Well, there goes THAT day's pay to cover a bogus ticket. All the time my passenger was silent, looking straight ahead. After the police car left, my passenger asked if I was considering fighting the ticket. I said I wasn't planning to, as it would come down to his (police officer's) word against mine. There was a snowball's chance in hell that I'd win. He said that he would be happy to appear in court with me as a witness. I thanked him, saying "with all due respect, I doubt that will help me much." He then identified himself as the Chief of Police for the City of Thunder Bay. My mood improved considerably. I advised the court that I would be contesting the ticket, arriving at the appointed hour. The OPP officer was there. It was clear he had no clue what was about to happen. My case was called, and the officer presented his case. I was then called to present my defense. When the judge asked if I had anything else, I said yes, I have a witness. When the chief of police walked forward, in full uniform, the look on the OPP officers face was worth a million dollars! He knew then and there that the case was lost. The judge heard the Chief's story confirming what I had said. He tossed the charges out of court. The judge then suggested that the OPP officer show a little common sense when presented with a believable excuse.

Then there was the summer day when I was sent to a local golf course for a fare. The gentleman literally threw his bag of clubs into the trunk. When he got in, it was obvious he had had a very bad round of golf. When we arrived at his destination, the fare was about $8.50. He turned to me and said: "How about you keep the damn clubs, and we call it even?" I had never golfed in my life to that point, but a few of my co-workers golfed. I thought: "Why not?" After all, it's not every day you get a set of clubs with a bag for under $10.00.

One less enjoyable "ride barter" I was offered (and didn't accept) occurred during a night shift. It was about two a.m., towards the tail-end of the nightly bar rush. I picked up what I assume was a husband and wife from a bar in the area we called "The Bronx". To say it was a rough and tumble part of Thunder Bay would be an understatement. The area they were going to wasn't much better, but I didn't expect much trouble. Both were extremely intoxicated, where as I was sober as a judge. I also out-weighed him by a good 50 lbs. When we got to the destination, the meter was under $10, and he said: "We don't have any money, but you can have a round with my wife to cover the meter." YUCK! She was fine with the idea, complete with a smile, less 7 or 8 teeth, and an invitation to "do with me as you please"! Double YUCK! I ordered them out, and he left, but she stayed, trying to convince me to change my mind. Not happening. I told her, in no uncertain or polite, language to get out of the cab. Nope, she wasn't getting out until the fare was "paid". I ended up having to physically remove her from the car. Unfortunately, when I hauled her out, my thumb hooked on one of her belt loops, breaking a bone in my wrist, which then required a cast. That sucked for a couple of reasons. First, I was off work until the cast came off. Second, I was in a wedding party in four weeks. Tuxedos and plaster-of-Paris casts don't mix very well. Fortunately, the cast came off a week before the wedding, but I had to practice writing again to sign the marriage certificate. That marriage is still together to this day.

The Roach's Taxi owner and I weren't what you'd call friends, but we did share a mutual respect. When we were short staffed, he knew he could count on me to put in extra hours. I certainly did put them in. There were times I'd work a twenty-one-hour day, go home, sleep for six or seven hours, then get back in the car again. My boss learned to see the signs I was burning out long before I did. More than once, after two or three weeks of burning the candle from both ends (as well as in the middle), some stupid little thing would set me off. I'd storm into his office, tear a strip off him, telling him, in no uncertain terms, what he could do with his company, his cars, along with which ever dispatcher had just pushed me over the edge. My tirade would last ten or fifteen minutes, during which time he would just turn in his chair to face me, intertwine his fingers, and rock gently. I'd storm out of the office trailing smoke from my ears, muttering a string of expletives that would make a sailor blush, and go golfing for a week to clear my head. About a week later, he'd call asking if I was ready to return to work. I'd humbly reply "Yes" along with an apology. He'd laugh it off, telling me it wasn't a big deal. He knew the blow-up was coming. He'd just sit through it (I don't even know if he was listening or not). He knew that if I had a week to play golf and decompress, I'd be ready to go again. We eventually normalized my schedule to a seventy-four-and-a-half-hour work week. Instead of the seven in the morning until eight in the evening I was currently working, my new schedule was from seven a.m. to six p.m., Monday to Thursday. On Friday I was in the car by eight in the morning, driving until half-past-two-thirty Saturday morning. After a few hours' sleep, I was on duty for another twelve-hour shift. This time I started at two-thirty in the afternoon, ending at half-past-two-thirty Sunday morning. I was then off the clock until Monday morning, when the routine started all over again. This schedule lasted until I found an opportunity to pursue another passion of mine, music.

Sometime in 1986, a friend of mine called told me his band was looking for a drummer. They played country, country-rock, and oldies-rock. I had been playing drums recreationally since I was a teen. I jumped at the opportunity. Off I went to an audition, where we ran through three songs. The only one I recall was Kenny Roger's Lucille. The only reason I remember that, was because of the time signature (a time signature tells the musician what beats and notes to play). Lucille was a 3/4 whereas most songs are 4/4. For a musician, the unusual time signatures can be difficult to play. To challenge me, they threw me a more difficult song. This however, was not a problem. Because I could also sing (or more accurately, caterwaul in key), I got the job.

Our band played in a few local bars as well as some of the Canadian Legions in the city. Then we headed out on the road for a brief spell. My boss at Roach's was kind enough to give me a leave of absence for a few weeks to pursue this venture. We were gone about a month playing bars in Saskatchewan and Manitoba. There were some ups and downs. Our adventures included me almost killing (literally) our bassist in a laundromat. We were doing laundry some place in Saskatchewan, and he said "I bet I could fit in that dryer." I told him I'd give him $10 if he could squeeze himself in there. He did squeeze into the dryer, and I immediately closed the door, inserted a quarter, and turned it on. I only let him tumble twice before I opened the door to let him out. He wasn't very impressed, but eventually saw the humour in it. He also had the scare of his life when one of his evening "conquests" left before he woke up, but not before writing "Welcome to the world of AIDS" on the mirror in lipstick. Turned out to be a false alarm, but it didn't stop him from chasing waitresses, bar patrons, or any other suitable female he spotted.

After we returned from our "tour", I went back to driving for Roach's again. Later in 1986, another friend of mine told me he had taken a truck driving course, and had received his licence. I was extremely interested. I had always wanted to be a truck driver, but the opportunities in Thunder Bay to get proper training at the time were somewhere between slim and none. The school he attended was, as I recall, "GHA Truck Driving School". They offered both in-class (usually the instructors living room) and in-cab training. Back in 1986, the $1,800 course ran for two weeks of evenings and weekends. Fortunately, Mom and Dad were very supportive, loaning me the money for the course. I'm not one-hundred percent sure I ever repaid them. As I remember, the in-class portion was just enough to teach you how to pass the road test. Back then, you didn't need a separate air brake endorsement. All we really learned about air brakes was how to tell if they needed adjusting, and how to adjust them. The in-cab training was also just enough to qualify for a Class 1 vehicle. It was a cab-over Mercedes single axle tractor with an 8 speed manual transmission, with a twenty-eight-foot single axle trailer loaded with some scrap metal to give it some weight. At the time, it seemed long enough to stretch into the next time zone. The day of the road test, was miserable. Snow, windy, slushy roads, a typical late-November day in Thunder Bay. Despite the weather, I passed the road test, earning my coveted Class A licence. I was ready to go forth, and join the glamorous life. Or so I thought. It would be eight years before that happened.

After a few months of diligently filing out applications, and receiving just as many "Sorry, no experience, no job" replies, I stayed with the taxi job. A life-changing event occurred when I met the woman who I would eventually marry. She, too, worked for Roach's. When work was slow, we'd have chat sessions as we got to know each other better. Then one day, she invited me to dinner. On the way to her place, I stopped to pick up a bottle of wine. I wasn't a wine drinker then (I'm still not), but, as far as I knew, it was the "gentlemanly" thing to do. While she served her homemade Chicken Parmesan, I opened the wine. Of course, the cork went ballistic (it was several months before we found the damned thing), along with about a quarter of the wine following it. There was wine on the ceiling, floor, walls, table, dinner, even on her eight-year-old son. I stood there, frozen in shock thinking: "Way to make a good first impression, asshole!" Then I realized she was actually licking it off my arm! (Okay, maybe not such a bad deal after all!) The rest of the evening was fairly unremarkable.

The next morning, I managed to almost break my neck getting out of her bed. She had a waterbed, without a pedestal, which meant that the sleeping surface was eight inches from the floor. Getting up (I learned later) was best accomplished by rolling over the padded side to the floor, getting up from there. Not that morning. I sat up, swinging my legs over the side. With a mighty heave ho, got myself to a vertical position. Sort of. In my efforts, I pushed too hard, toppling forward into the wall, almost knocking myself out in the process. She, of course, laughed her head off. After a few minutes, I was laughing at myself. As time passed, we became more attached as a couple, eventually moving in together, much to the dismay of my family, who really didn't care for her. When we announced we were getting married in 1991, my younger sister immediately turned to my fiancée, asking "Are you knocked up?"

During my time at Roach's, there was one dispatcher I didn't get along with very well. My future-wife got along with her even less. About 1988 my fiancée got into a particularly nasty disagreement with the dispatcher resulting with her quitting. I followed her out the door to Oikonen's Taxi, a rival company in Thunder Bay. It was here that I met someone who was destined to become a very good, and life-long, friend. There were times, however, when we almost killed each other in pure hatred, but that's a story for later. The first time I met Pete, he had his mouth wired shut, as he had fallen off a roof, and broken his jaw.

Pete was then, and still is, a good sounding board, non-judgmental, and always ready with an ear to listen. A one-in-a-million-type friend. Kenny Oikonen, one of the dispatchers, nicknamed him "Perfecto". This same dispatcher tagged me "Tora Tora", for my intimate interest and knowledge of the December 1941 Japanese surprise attack on Pearl Harbor. During slow times, Kenny and I would discuss the attack, from every angle. What each side did right, along with where they went wrong.

A few years later, Oikonen's was sold to a local garage owner. More than a few people didn't get along with the new manager he installed, me included. Over time, I eventually ended up driving the worst vehicle in the fleet. Similar to the rest of the fleet, it had been converted to dual fuel (gasoline or propane) with the preference being to use propane. There was little room to install a propane tank in a Dodge Diplomat. In their wisdom, they put the large canister in the trunk. The trunk on a late 1980s Dodge Diplomat is ridiculously small to begin with. Once the propane tank was installed, there was hardly enough room for the spare tire. On top of that, the propane system was never fully debugged, requiring refilling the tank two or three times a day. Needless to say, I wasn't exactly impressed. Time better spent with customers was instead spent refuelling.

The next change at Oikonen's Taxi saw the purchase of wheelchair accessible taxis. These much-needed forms of transportation for Thunder Bay were modified mini-vans with lowered floors that used tie-downs to hold the wheelchairs in place. Since I wanted out of the propane-tanked Diplomat, I was intrigued about the mini vans. In Ontario, however, you needed a class F licence to drive a "bus" of up to ten passengers. Over the past couple of years, without any luck finding a truck-driving job, I'd let my Class A license slide missing the mandatory medical testing. In order to get the necessary Class F, I'd have to get my medical & physical testing completed, and take a road test. I arrived at the MTO (Ministry of Transportation Ontario) with my required documents, ready to take the written exam and arrange for a road test. I received some welcome news. Since I had already passed a road test in a tractor trailer, I didn't need another road test, saving me time plus the $75 for a road test. I also learned that all I needed to regain my Class A (truck driving licence) was to produce my medical certificate from the doctor. I also discovered that I should forget about earning a Class F licence. If I wrote the Class C (bus over ten passengers) exam, I could walk out with an Ontario Class AC licence. That is what I did! I was now licensed to drive anything but a motorcycle and a school bus. But the province had recently introduced the requirement of a "Z" endorsement to operate air brakes. I could now legally drive a tractor trailer, but I was unauthorized to use the brakes. What's wrong with this picture?

As it turned out, my wife was attending college working towards her electrical engineering degree (she never made it), and told me about a weekend course to earn my air brake endorsement. I took the course, passing it with flying colours. I was now, once again, fully qualified to operate a tractor trailer. After a few more months of "no experience, no job", Shaw Trucking, a small Thunder Bay company (five trucks plus seven or eight ancient rented trailers) accepted my application. As expected, I started at the bottom, doing some local P&D (pick up & delivery) runs with an experienced local driver. While I was working for the trucking company during the day, I was still driving taxi at night. Again, burning the candle from both ends.

At first, I did very little driving, mostly I was hand-bombing goods all day.

Hand-bombing (also known as "finger printing") involves manually unloading trailers. There are many reasons why this task exists. Grocery warehouses, for example, store products by size, type and weight. If the warehouse orders, 34 cases of salmon-flavoured cat food in 5 oz cans, 54 cases of 7 oz cans, and another 100 cases in 10 oz cans, the plant where they make the cat food places it all on a single pallet. Once it arrives at the warehouse, it must be separated to allow each pallet to contain only one size and flavour. Each pallet has a maximum height to allow it to fit into the slot in the warehouse. Even a full load of the same product might need to be hand bombed to meet the requirements for the warehouse storage area. This may be as simple as removing the top layer of each pallet. Some hand bomb loads are simple, some are a total nightmare. One of the worst I ever saw, and thankfully I didn't have to hand bomb, was a load I delivered to a warehouse in Brantford, Ontario. Whoever loaded this trailer should have been taken out and flogged for about six hours. The company had arranged for a local swamping service to hand-bomb the trailer. I'll stop here, and explain how trailers are usually loaded.

A 53 ft trailer can hold up to 26 pallets on the floor. To accomplish this, the pallets need to be "chimney blocked". One pallet on the left in straight, the other sideways beside it, then one on the right in straight, and the one beside it sideways. A standard pallet is 48 inches by 40 inches. The interior of a refrigerated trailer is about 99 inches wide. If the pallets are put in straight, you can get twenty-six pallets in the trailer. Turned sideways instead, you'll get thirty. When all are turned sideways, however, they can be hard to get out, due to the construction of the pallet, and the risk of serious damage to the freight.

Back to the worst-ever story. The trailer had the pallets chimney blocked. Tricky to get them out, but not impossible. Even worse, they had pallets stacked on top of pallets. A total of 92 pallets were on this trailer that was a real mixed bag of freight. Toilet paper, deodorant, shampoo, hair conditioner, hair spray, toothpaste, mouth wash, and similar goods. All health care and beauty products. There was no rhyme or reason to how it was loaded, and the bill of lading ran to six pages. At the destination, it all had to be sorted out by product, size, weight, scent and flavour. This was such a disaster, that the guys unloading it had to have every pallet removed before they could start sorting everything out. There were 75 cases of Mennen Speed Stick deodorant on the trailer. 25 were in the front, 25 in the centre, and another 25 in the back. Those poor guys (there were five of them) spent seven hours sorting and stacking what came off that trailer. As I said, this was one of the worst I ever saw. I'm glad it wasn't me who had to deal with it.

After three weeks of dealing with my own hand-bombing issues, I finally told the boss I hadn't busted my ass getting a truck-driving licence to unload trailers. He then set me up with an experienced driver to get some on-road driving experience. I instantly quit the taxi business for good.

I was ready to start my career in trucking. We left Thunder Bay and loaded 45,000 lbs of rolled newsprint in Red Rock, Ontario, heading east to Toronto. I did none of the driving on this trip, but my logbook showed otherwise. From Toronto, we were to reload for Pennsylvania, but I'd had more than enough of this instructor, who wasn't interested in teaching anyone anything. He barely spoke English, making the trip extremely boring. I bailed in Toronto, taking a bus back home. The boss said I was giving up too quickly on trucking. I said I wasn't giving up on trucking, I was giving up on that instructor. A few days later, he put me with another driver. Now the real trucking started.

Let it Roll!

How to Scare the Tar Out of a Rookie

My new, more-experienced, and much friendlier instructor, and I headed out in our truck. We picked up a preloaded trailer in the Thunder Bay yard and headed to Lawrenceburg, Tennessee. We shared the driving all the way down. When we arrived at the customer where we were to deliver, I was sound asleep in the bunk. After delivering, it was my turn to drive. The problem was, that having been in the bunk, I had no clue how to get back to the interstate. We were scheduled to head to Dixon, Tennessee, for a load of windshields going to the Ford assembly plant in Oakville, Ontario.

I consulted the Rand McNally Road Atlas (a truck driver's Bible in those day. Long before GPS, Google Maps, and cell phones were available). This gave me a pretty good idea how to get to where I was going. I then asked one of the workers what was the best way from the plant to the interstate, as not all roads are truck routes. That wasn't a mistake I wanted to make. I wrote down the directions as he gave them to me. They were good ones. I followed them to the letter. "Turn right at the gas station, then left at the McDonald's" type of directions. Perfect! Almost. What happened was NOT my fault!

I was on a city and state designated truck route in a semi-urban area. A local resident had decided local cable TV prices were too high, so the night before, he had strung a line across the street to his house, down the wall, and in through the window frame across the room to his thirteen-inch TV that he had on a wheeled TV stand. Except, he didn't string it high enough. Wires are supposed to be a minimum of 14 feet from the ground at their lowest point to allow proper clearance. Trucks, unless under an oversized permit, can be no more that 13 ft 6 in at their highest point. Plenty of room if done properly. I saw the line, figured it must be high enough, as this was an authorized truck route.

My first indication of trouble was hearing glass breaking. I immediately stopped, getting out to see what had happened. Apparently, I had hooked the cable with the exhaust stack, pulling his TV, along with the wheeled stand across the floor towards the outside wall, where the stand stopped. The TV, however, exited through the window and onto the lawn. To say he was upset is an understatement. From a legal standpoint, there was nothing he could do. He couldn't very well call the police, telling them I had broken his window by snagging his illegal cable. To this day, I chuckle when I imagine the look that must have been on his face as his TV took off across the floor and sailed through the window.

When we arrived at the Oakville Ford plant to deliver the load of wind-shields, I learned what "JIT freight" is. It stands for "just in time" and it can be one of the biggest pains in the butt for a driver. The manufacturer keeps very little stock on hand, setting up delivery appointments for specific parts to arrive at a time when they are needed on the assembly line. If you arrive too early, you sit until the parts are needed. If you're late, they may have to stop the assembly line. We arrived with the windshields 26 hours early. With no other option, we sat, waiting for the time to pass.

After delivering the windshields, we were sent to Atlantic Packaging in one of the Toronto suburbs. My instructor decided to give me a learning experience and let me back the truck in, as it's a hard place to back into even though you have plenty of room. To back in requires a 180-degree "blind side" back-up. What this means, is, as you back in, you have to make a complete U-turn, in reverse to the right, using only your mirrors. The problem is, you can't really see anything down the right side with your passenger side mirror when backing up around a corner. You can use the convex mirror to a point, but it gives a distorted view, and once the trailer exceeds a certain angle, you can't see the back end of the trailer or anything beside you. To make it as easy as possible, my instructor was kind enough to act as spotter to be sure I didn't hit anything while blindsiding in. I was slow, meticulous, and very careful. As luck would have it, and yes, it was ALL luck, I managed to hit the dock dead straight, and perfectly square. The shipper, who was watching, said he'd never seen anyone hit the dock so perfectly in one shot. He then asked if I was still a rookie. I was surprised, saying that yes, I was. I'd only been driving less than a week. He smiled, replying: "I can tell. You forgot to open the doors before you backed in." I dropped my head and shoulders in total embarrassment. Well, I'll just pull ahead six feet, open the doors, and back in. Straight line, no maneuvering, how hard could it be? Twenty minutes later, I was back in the door.

That load was bottled water, going to Baltimore, Maryland. What a thrill! I hadn't travelled much before this, and my travels in the USA were limited to northern Minnesota, specifically Duluth. I may have ventured into Superior, Wisconsin, but I don't really recall. I had no idea what Baltimore would be like, just that it was a big city. I was finally going to see some a bit more of the country. Off we went. Before getting there, we called the customer for directions to his warehouse. Along with the instructions, we were told to be there about three a.m. Soon we were on our way, following their directions. Unfortunately, the receiver left out one small detail on the directions. We strayed from the route. Easy to fix. Just get back to the highway to resume the desired route. Suddenly, we saw flashing lights behind us, along with a police car siren. We stopped. The officer walked up to the door (my instructor was driving), saying: "I don't know where you're supposed to be, but it's nowhere near here. Get going, and do NOT stop for ten blocks. If someone walks out in front of you to get you to stop, run their ass over, we'll clean it up later. MOVE!" With that, he turned around, returning to the cruiser. We looked at each other, then continued driving until we got to a safer area. Thankfully, no one tried to get us to stop. We eventually found the place, making the delivery with no further excitement. I can't recall what the reload was or where it went, but most likely Toronto. From there, we would frequently load cores for paper rolls or we take on a food warehouse load headed for either Northern Grocers (who supplied the local A&P stores) or Western Grocers (Safeway stores).

My next few trips with Shaw Transport were with a driver who became somewhat of a friend, Evan. Evan and I had similar personalities. We hit it off wonderfully, which is a definite plus when running team. The combined living -working area of a truck is about 64 square feet. If you run team, this is your world 24/7 for upwards of four weeks at a time. As there is really no getting away from the other person, you'd better get along! Even if you do get along great with each other, there is often still some friction. Fist fights between the best of friends have been known to happen. You also need to establish some safety rules, otherwise people can get seriously injured, or killed.

One of the rules that is common when running team is that whenever you are in the sleeper berth, leave your footwear on the floor on the passenger side. ALWAYS leave your footwear on the passenger side. Though it never happened to me, I've heard stories of a driver pulling into a truck stop, fuelling up, then going in to use the facilities. The co-driver, sensing the truck has stopped, gets dressed, going into the truck stop for personal reasons, then coming out only to see the back of the trailer turning onto the highway. In the days before cell phones and satellite communications, this was a major bummer. Drivers were required to call in to dispatch once every 24 hours to update their progress. In the event of a breakdown or other emergency, you could call in at any time. In reverse, the dispatcher had no way to alert a driver of anything. I had it drilled into me, in turn I drilled it into everyone I drove with: leave your footwear on the floor on the passenger side. If you're the driver, every time you get back in the truck, check that the footwear is there before you go anywhere. Thankfully, I was never left anywhere, nor did I ever leave anyone behind. Well, not by accident, but more on that later.

The next few trips were kind of a blur. One that stands out was a load of flour we picked up at a now-defunct mill in Thunder Bay. It was heading for a bakery in Mexico. We were only taking it as far as Laredo, Texas. From there, it was cross-docked to a Mexican carrier. Since the load was travelling through the United States, but not staying in the USA, customs clearance was a bit different. Normally, for loads that originate in Canada for delivery in the USA (or the other way around), duties and taxes are paid on the goods. This is just like when you go across the border, bringing home items you've purchased outside the country. In the case of commercial goods, the process is a bit different. Customs brokers handle the inner workings, as well as "fronting" the duties and taxes required. The brokers then bill whomever is responsible for the fees, usually the buyer (receiver). These days, the process is extremely streamlined. The total time a driver spends at the border, barring any unforeseen issues, or specialty loads (such as something too large or heavy to travel on one truck) is measured in seconds. Prior to electronic clearance, it could take days to clear a load through customs. My personal record was four days to clear a load. Yes, it sucked. No, there was no way to speed up the process.

The load going to Mexico travelled differently, however. It was on what is called a Transportation and Exportation Bond (or a T&E). The T&E manifest is a four-page document. Page One stays with the port where the bond was originally opened (Grand Marais, Minnesota, in this case). Part Two stays with the driver, showing the opened bond, as well as the closed bond at the exit point (in this case Laredo, Texas). Part Three stays with customs at the exit port (in this case, Laredo again). Part Four stays with the shipment. It is presented to the entry port into the next country (Mexico, in this case). No taxes or duties are paid, but the broker has to post a $25,000 bond to ensure the load does in fact exit the country in the same condition it entered. Customs may inspect the load as it enters, but usually doesn't. They then attach a tamper-resistant seal, recording the seal number on the T&E manifest. When we got to Laredo, before delivering the load to the freight forwarding warehouse, we first had to report to US Customs to have the bond cancelled. The customs official inspects the seal, and if it is intact, he stamps and signs our copy of the T&E. We're then free to deliver to the freight forwarder.

In Laredo, we loaded wet lap (shredded paper fibre mulch) going back to Thunder Bay. Wet lap is heavy, messy, and smells worse than any frat house bathroom after a three-day weekend keg party. Seriously, it is disgusting. Beyond disgusting. It was more than 20 years ago, and I can still smell it to this day. Off we went, heading for the paper mill in Thunder Bay. Running team, we could normally knock the run out in 48 hours. Since this wasn't travelling on a T&E bond, we had to stop at Canada Customs at Pigeon River (Minnesota/Ontario) to have the load cleared. This required sending all the paperwork to the broker by fax. This way they could process it ahead of time and have it at the border when we arrived with our properly completed A8A manifest, an eight-copy document, filled out by hand. As required by law, we were both awake when we got to the Pigeon River Customs entry point into Canada, with myself driving. The official on duty was someone I knew from high school. As you can guess, this woman and I did NOT get along during those days. We definitely ran in different circles.

We were cleared through customs but this officer wanted to inspect the load of wet lap. I warned her that she wouldn't like it, but she just shrugged it off, and walked to the back of the trailer, and told me to open the doors. Knowing what's to come, opened the door, and stayed well clear of the opening. With her first breath, she promptly vomited all over her uniform. For reasons unknown to me, (according to her this was somehow my fault), instead of accepting the bill of lading, she decided to climb into the

Wetlap

trailer, with the intent of counting the bales. In my opinion, this was stupidity combined by idiocy, because as soon as she climbed onto the first bale, her feet went forward, and she landed flat on her back on top of the bale. In addition to the smell of wet lap, I can still hear the squishing sound as she landed on the barely solid liquid mess. After that, she was not as interested in an exact piece count. The Customs Agent climbed out of the trailer, told me to close it up and get out of there. Evan, myself, and her co-workers were doing our level best not to bust out in laughter. I, along with at least two of her co-workers had warned her about what she was about to do, but she ignored all warnings, and went ahead anyway. Her next screw up with a load I had was even funnier, no less messy, but not as "odorific".

Evan and I once loaded bulk ping pong balls in Iowa going to a plant in Thunder Bay where they packaged them for retail sale. When they load bulk ping pong balls, they have you back up a ramp, allowing the back of the trailer to be about four feet higher than the front. Then they then just pour them in loose. No piece count, nothing. Just ping pong balls, free to roll with the forces of nature. Once they get as many in as they can, you close the doors, put on a seal with a warning label telling everyone NOT to open the doors. Well, I'm sure you can guess what happened when I got to the Pigeon River Canadian Customs where she was on duty. While most loads have an exact piece count, some loads (woodchips, seeds, potatoes, and so forth). are considered "bulk". They are shipped from the field to the processing plant, then billed by weight. You scale the truck-trailer unit at the shipper before and after loading. The difference is the load weight. For reasons unknown to anyone, she claimed she needed an exact piece count, telling me to open the doors. I called her attention to the way that they were loaded, pointing out the tag on the trailer warning against opening the doors. Her co-workers in the Customs office advised her against opening the doors, but she was adamant. As soon as she opened the doors, you guessed it! Ping pong balls went everywhere, especially since Customs yard there has the front of the truck slightly higher than the back. Took them forever to find as many of the ping pong balls as they could, and load them into dumpsters. I never did see her working that border post, or, for that matter, at any other border post again.

As time rolled on, our run became somewhat predictable. Thunder Bay to the midwestern USA with rolls of paper, reload someplace close by for Toronto, then either food warehouse loads for Thunder Bay, or cores for the local paper mills, take a few days off, and go again. As we were returning to Thunder Bay, we would always stop in near-by Nipigon and call our respective wives to give them our estimated arrival at the yard in enough time for them to come pick us up.

One trip into the city, we decided to run through town (on an official truck route) rather than run the usual highway route. As we passed a local drinking establishment, a long, low, sleek black Cadillac turned onto the road behind us. We noticed, but paid little attention as it didn't really concern us. That is, until he turned into our yard behind us. Odd, considering it was 11:30 p.m. Evan was driving. As soon as he stopped, before starting to back in, I jumped out to meet my wife. Before I got to her, a very intoxicated "gentleman" no more than five feet tall, got in my face (so to speak), babbling on about how one of our drivers in a Peterbilt cabover had harassed one of his dancers. He wanted to know exactly who this individual was. I tried to explain to him that all of our trucks were Internationals, and conventional cabs. The only cabovers we had were worse than garbage. Also, they were Kenworths, and the configuration of our KW's were unmistakable from any other truck on the road. Still, he was yammering and yelling, pointing this way and that, telling us how he knew it was one of our drivers, how he was going to call the police as well as getting the Sicilian Mafia involved, and on, and on. All this time, his driver is behind him, telling him to settle down, he's in the wrong spot, don't do something stupid, and so on. All I wanted to do, was to pack my gear out of the truck, and go home, but this guy just wouldn't let up. After about 25 minutes, he started winding down. I politely explained to him, again, that he's made a mistake as it wasn't one of our trucks. He DEMANDED that I call the owner, manager, or someone in authority with the company. I told him I had no intentions of waking anyone up at midnight for this. He became very serious, lowered his voice, got "nose to nipple" with me, growling through clenched teeth, with a thick Italian accent. "I'll catch the son of a bitch! Remember this face!" I couldn't resist. I just looked down at him and said: "I won't. I see it every time my dog walks away from me". Well, he swung an awesome right hook, that, in his intoxication, threw him off balance, connecting him with nothing more than the pavement. His driver managed to get him back into the Caddy, apologized to us profusely, then left without further incident. To the best of my knowledge, nothing more came of the incident. If he had pressed it, it was his drunken word again that of four sober people, five if you count his driver.

Since Shaw was a very small company, some luxuries were sadly lacking. The owner was the planner and the dispatcher. Everything had to go through him. To be honest, he really was in over his head. He had never driven a truck before, so he really had no idea what truck driving was all about. Nine months into my tenure, things came to a head while Evan and I were on a trip in Toronto. We had arrived the night before, spending the whole day doing city work. Running trailers to deliver, reloading the trailer, dropping it, grab another, deliver it, reload it and drop it. Virtually impossible for anyone to sleep through all this. Finally, around six that evening, he sent us to pick up a load that needed to be in Atlanta, Georgia, for six the next morning. Now, driving 948 miles 12 hours would require an average speed of 75 mph. That's quite a bit over the American speed limit that was, at that time, 55 mph. On top of that, there were traffic concerns to take into account, fuel, eating, and customs delays, not to mention that the truck was mechanically limited to 65 mph. I told him, flat out, that there was no way we could make the delivery on time. He actually said to me; "Why not? It's only six inches (from Toronto to Atlanta) on the map!" That was the proverbial straw that broke the camel's back for me. I told him, in no uncertain terms, what he could do with this load in particular, his job in general, and to get me home ASAP. I'd had enough. We brought home a load for Western Grocers, dropping it in the yard. I packed all my gear, and walked away.

Feeling Chipper
Beer and Trucking Can Mix

After leaving Shaw, my brother-in-law (I'll call him Dave) told me that an owner-operator had a truck at Bulk Systems, hauling wood chips from Upsala to Thunder Bay, twice a day, totalling about 352 miles a day. Dave had really started me along the road to trucking, as he had been driving a few years before I got started, and had taken me on a few day trips when he was hauling road salt in super-B dump trailers.

I went through the whole hiring process, with the company, and the owner of the truck. I completed all the checks. All my paperwork was in order. At least I thought I had everything in order. The new company required a letter from previous employer(s) verifying a minimum of two years driving experience. I only had eight or nine months, and absolutely no experience with super-B trailers. I lied, saying I'd forgotten it at home. I would bring it in the next day. As soon as I got home, I called Dave in a near panic, telling him they wanted a letter that I had no possibility of getting. He chuckled, telling me to come by after supper with a case of beer. I was confused, wondering how getting drunk would help, but whatever. Next step then was a stop at the beer store, then off to his house. When I got there, he already had company. He answered the door, took the case of beer, handing me an envelope. In the envelope, was a letter from his friend, stating I had been driving a pulp truck for him for three years, as well as a glowing letter of recommendation. I never found out who his friend was, but I had my verification letter, and a glowing referral. All it cost me was a case of beer.

The wood chipper in Upsala was just starting production. As the junior truck on the run, we seldom loaded there. When we did, it was one or two load a day. The truck, however, was running twenty-four hours a day, Monday to Friday. The other driver was my wife's ex-husband, who I'll call Frank. Talk about just a little awkward. In the interim, while Upsala was working through it's growing and start up pains, we were loading chips in Thunder Bay then dumping them 68 miles east in Red Rock. We would continue east for another 130 miles to Longlac where we reloaded more chips, delivering them to a paper mill in Thunder Bay. After the run, we would return to the yard, fuel up, switch drivers, then head home for 12 hours while the other driver did his run.

The wood chips we were hauling were very dry. We could load to the trailer capacity without fear of being overweight. When we arrived at the mills, we would scale in loaded, dump, and scale out empty. The difference was the weight of the chips unloaded. At the time, there were three makes of chip trailers being used at Bulk Systems: Knight, Peerless Page, and Ty Crop. The Knight brand were the oldest, heaviest (made out of fiberglass), and most cumbersome to use. To cover the loads, you climbed on top of the chips, and manually pulled the tarps to cover them. Before dumping you reversed the process, otherwise you had to perform a high wire act to remove the tarps before loading them again. Not much fun working 13 ft in the air while walking on a rail about three inches wide. When hooked to the truck, the empty weight was about 50,000 lbs, and our maximum allowable legal weight was 140,000 lbs. These were the trailers we had for the first few months, and they were fine. We never had any weight issues, as we would reach the trailer volume capacity long before we reached the weight limits. I think the heaviest I ever scaled with these trailers fully loaded was 130,000 lbs gross vehicle weight. I only pulled the Peerless Page-brand trailers a few times. I don't recall too much about them.

A few weeks before Upsala came fully on stream, the owner called. Not only were we headed to a different run, but we would be pulling a set of Ty Crop chip trailers. This was a definite upgrade! The tarps on Ty Crop cover from the side, and there is a long handle attached. You can un-tarp them from the ground. They are covered at all times unless being loaded. Once loaded, you walk to the passenger side, take the attached lanyard, and throw it over the trailer. From the driver's side, you pulled the lanyard, and the tarp unrolls across the trailer. You then secure the tarps in place with bungee cords, stow the lanyard, and away you go. It took ten minutes to wind the tarps up to load, with about the same time needed to pull the tarps over and secure them.

On this job, we would be staying in a hotel in nearby Atikokan. Our run started in the small Northwestern Ontario community of Sapawe. We transported the chips another 107 miles to Fort Frances. I was fine with that. Being away from home for a week or two at a time didn't bother me. We headed out to Atikokan. Upon arrival, we checked into the hotel, and Frank went off for his first of two runs, while I settled in to get some sleep. This week was uneventful, save for more wildlife sightings than I can remember.

Fortunately, there were no wildlife collisions for either Frank or myself. Quite a few other trucks weren't as lucky. The highway we were running is part of the Trans-Canada Highway network, but unless you're travelling to or from Fort Frances, Rainy River or Atikokan there is very little traffic along the route. It's a very picturesque drive though the Canadian Shield, dotted along the way with small towns and a few tourist attractions. It is, however, a very desolate highway, with no passing lanes, and an abundance of wildlife.

After a week of running Sapawe to Fort Frances, we were called back to start the Upsala to Thunder Bay run on a part time basis. We would do one Upsala run, then the Thunder Bay - Red Rock - Longlac - Thunder Bay run. The Upsala to Thunder Bay trip was tricky as the chips were green, meaning that they had a high moisture content making them quite heavy. It was a challenge to keep our gross weight legal. To do this, we had to leave about three feet empty on the top of the trailers. More than a couple of times, one of us on this run would get an overweight ticket, either over gross, or over on a set of axles. Luckily, I managed only a single overweight ticket. $66.00 for being 4,400 lbs over on a triaxle, but that was bad enough.

We were paid $125.00 a run to haul wood chips, or 25% of the revenue generated by the load, which ever was higher. Back in the mid-1990s, that was a pretty decent rate, considering the $0.12 cents per mile I made as a student driver at Shaw. Once I finished my Shaw training, I earned $0.20 cents a mile. At the time, I was aware that it was a little below the industry average but considered it part of the price I needed to pay to get the experience. I later learned just how low it actually was.

Any driver with a dedicated run gets to know the route intimately; every rock cut, bump, pavement crack, road sign, twist, and turn. I used my route knowledge as a way to determine my gross weight fairly accurately. There was a particular sign on the highway, and if my gross weight was close to legal, I would pass it at exactly one hour (to the second) from when I turned onto the highway after leaving the chipper. If I was less than an hour, I was underweight. More than an hour, I was a bit overweight. Getting to the paper mill, we had a choice of two routes. One direct, the other about a 20 minute detour. Both routes had an MTO (Ministry of Transportation of Ontario) scale, so either way, there was a scale we had to cross. A little-known fact about these two scales, was that the same crew operated both scales. If one was open, the other was closed. If I was overweight, I'd call the scale on the most direct route, and if someone answered, I pretended I had called a wrong number, and took the detour. That summer, they closed the direct-route scale for repairs and maintenance. I no longer needed to call ahead if I was overweight. Since the MTO scale was closed, no need to load legal.

That Monday, as I drove to Upsala for my first load, I saw that the scale was closed. Heavy equipment had already removed the scale deck, and were now busy breaking the cement approaches. Bonus! I can load these wagons to maximum capacity (25% of load value beats the $125.00 run-rate when you can load heavy). In Upsala I loaded those trailers to the top. I was up there kicking chips into the corners, jumping on them to pack them in as much as possible, forming a nice hump down the middle. I couldn't have gotten any more wood chips in there if my life depended on it. Pulled the tarps over, and they just fit across the trailers. Off I went, headed for the paper mill. It took me an hour and fifteen minutes to reach the sign! I got to the mill, and scaled in at 165,300 lbs! Ouch! 25,300 lbs overweight. To put this into perspective, the truck and trailers empty weighed 44,000 lbs. My wood chip payload was 121,300 lbs. The chips weighed almost three times as much as the truck and trailers. Since there were three trucks on this run, my second load (the fourth load of the day from the chipper) wasn't nearly as heavy. Good thing, because when I got to the mill with this load, the MTO had set up shop at the mill scale. Luckily, none of the chip trucks got tickets, but a few of the pulp wood trucks did. Seems we all had the same idea, but apparently the MTO assumed the same.

When the weather turned cold later that year, a few of the drivers mentioned it was "time to Pam". I had no clue what they were talking about. Dave informed me that because we were hauling green chips in aluminum trailers, we had to spray the inside of the trailers with Pam cooking spray to avoid having the chips stick to the inside during the two-hour drive from the chipper to the mill. Dave and I headed over to a grocer with each of us purchasing a case of Pam. We spent an entire Sunday spraying every inch of the interior on both of his trailers, and both of my trailers. Monday morning, off I went to load, then on to the paper mill, up on the dumper, and everything smoothly slid out just as it should. Head back for the second haul, load up, and head back to the paper mill.

This is where I learned the valuable lesson about "Pam"ing. A driver from a different company, with brand new (less than a week old) aluminum trailers, loading close to Upsala hadn't sprayed the inside of his trailers. I was right behind him in line for the dumper. I saw first-hand, and close up, the value of spraying the interior. He backed himself onto the dumper, followed all the safety rules (dump the air suspension, chain the trailers front and back to the dump platform) opened all the doors (the front trailer dumps through the back trailer), then started raising the dumper. The driver had the unit almost vertical. Only five or six chips tumbled out. The rest were frozen inside the trailer.

The no-Pam-driver now had work to do. Down came the dumper, removed the chains, re-inflated the air bags (lowering the air bags drains all the air from the trailers, and applied the parking brakes as well), started the truck and pulled ahead about three inches. Drained the air again, chained everything back down, and started the dumper. As the dumper rose, the truck slid back the three inches to the backstop, and he hoped that it would jolt things enough to break the chips loose. Nope. No go. The chips refused to leave. He tried four or five times, increasing the distance a little each time. It has quite a bit of momentum, when you have about 132,240 lbs coming to a dead stop, even at a very low speed. Still, no chips came out.

By this time, there was a fairly long lineup of trucks waiting to dump chips. In his frustration (and perhaps humiliation), the driver made a colossal blunder. He got everything back on the ground, pulled it ahead about a foot, drained the air, chained everything down, and up went the dumper at about a sixty-degree inclination, the unit slid to the backstop, coming to a crunching stop. The rear trailer stopped immediately. But the impact was too great for the frame, which buckled. The front trailer slid back about two inches, and the truck about an inch. The frames on both trailers were visibly bent. Still no chips came out. He dragged the trailers off the dumper, and parked them in an area well out of the way. It was about a week before they got a wrecker to come in to remove the trailers. I didn't see it, but apparently, they had a very difficult time disconnecting the trailers from each other. Most likely damaged the fifth wheel, the king pin, or probably both. Either way, it was an expensive lesson, and taught me to pay attention when an experienced driver talks, no matter how silly or outlandish the topic.

One other "game" some drivers like to play, was to open all the doors except the rear most, then "drain and chain", and start the dumper. When it reaches full extension (about ten degrees from vertical) walk to the back door, and give the handle a kick to release the door, and WHOOSH! Both trailers empty in less than a second. As God is my witness, I never partook in this game. Too many things can go wrong if you don't follow procedures exactly. Some guys wouldn't use the chains, some guys wouldn't drain the air, some guys did the backdoor kick. Any of these steps could cause embarrassment, along with potentially life-threatening situations. Forgetting any two created a serious risk of injury or death. Safety rules are in place for a reason. One day, a driver ignored all three. I was there to see it, in all its horror. Thankfully, the only human casualty was a job. Monetarily, it was at least a $750,000 "oops".

Before I continue, I'll explain the air bags. Air ride trailers don't have conventional steel spring suspension, they use heavy duty air bags, one on each side of each axle. The volume of air in each bag is controlled by a levelling valve. As weight is added to the trailer the bags compress. The levelling valve then opens the inlet valve to allow more air into the bags. This brings the suspension up to the proper height. When the weight is reduced the reverse happens. The air bags expand, then the levelling valve opens the exhaust valve allowing the air to escape thus returning the suspension to the proper height. It's a great system, as it keeps everything at the optimum height, especially on the truck. This process maintains the proper angles for the power train, giving the driver and cargo a fairly smooth ride. Steel springs can jolt and jar the driver and the freight around pretty good.

The questionable driver, for reasons I'll never understand, backed onto the dumper, shut down the engine (the only thing he did right this time), opened all the doors except the rear most door, and started the dumper. As it reached the top, he walked out, and kicked open the rear door. WHOOSH! Followed by BANG, CRASH, THUD and WHAM! As all the chips came out, the air bags expanded to the point that a few of them exploded, but not before causing the back trailer to actually jump OVER the back stop, falling into the chip hopper. Had he chained the trailers down, they would have stayed on the dumper, however, with nothing to hold the truck and trailers in place, they toppled off the dumper, onto the ground, coming to rest on their side with the rear trailer still in the dumper. How the driver managed to avoid getting killed is beyond me. The truck, along with both trailers were a total write off. The driver was terminated on the spot. That particular dumper was also damaged beyond repair. It was soon replaced with a much better dumper. To this day, that is one of the scariest events I've ever witnessed in my career.

Super B chip trailers

It was at about this point that Frank quit. He was known for quitting at the first sign of anything not going his way. A simple clerical error on his pay cheque would be enough for him to quit. For a while I was the lone driver on the truck. About a week later, the truck's owner told me he had found another driver to join our team. I'd be training him once he had jumped through all the pre- hiring hoops. The day I started training him (I'll call him John), I knew it wasn't going to be pretty. John was of African-American, and Caribbean decent. He had a chip on his shoulder the size of Texas. If I said: "Look at those black clouds. It's going to rain like crazy up ahead", he'd take that as a racial slur. I have never judged someone on the basis of ethnicity. If I don't like someone it's because of something they personally have done, not because of skin colour. There I was with a new trainee heading to our Upsala location to begin training. John was a good driver, but he had never hauled a long trailer before, let alone a set of super-Bs.

You may have passed a Super-B on the highway. These are the two-trailer units with eight axles often used to haul grain, wood chips, and other bulk loads. They can be backed up, but this can be a tricky maneuver that takes a bit of practice and skill. It took John a while to learn how to back the set onto a dumper. He managed to get it down pretty smooth. By the end of the week, his backing-up skills had improved. I was pretty good at it, but Dave was a pro. He could back those trailers up 300 feet in a dead straight line, as if they were welded together. Occasionally, just to get a reaction from people, Dave would start backing towards the dumper, getting the trailers all twisted, crooked and almost sideways. At the last minute, he'd work his magic, get everything in a dead straight line, then push them onto the dumper.

After about three weeks of running cross-shift with John, the owner called to tell me that the Upsala operation was closing for a week for maintenance. This meant he was bringing us down to run the Sapawe to Fort Frances route. Not my favourite run, but it was his truck, and it was better to be making money than not. That is NOT how John saw it. He was LIVID! Apparently, he tore a strip of the owner a mile wide. The owner called me, asking if I was okay with going to Sapawe. I told him honestly it wasn't my first choice, but if that's what needed to happen, then that's what needed to happen. I wasn't thrilled, but it wasn't the end of the world, either. In the end, I went to Sapawe while John went elsewhere.

After about nine months of running wood chips, things started slowing down. At the time, we had three planners sorting out the runs. When I came in one day to get my schedule, these three planners had me going to three different chipper locations. After listening to them argue for about twenty minutes, I'd had enough. I told them: "I'm going home. When you get this sorted out, call me!" I walked out of the office, driving back to my house. After waiting an hour, I made a call myself. To Shaw. He was ecstatic that I wanted to return. I told him in no uncertain terms that I wasn't going to put up with his stupidity. I wasn't interested in running multiple log books, or taking part in "creative" logging. He assigned me a load with a co-driver on the spot. We were to leave the next morning. About thirty minutes later, one of the wood chip planners called telling me they had sorted it out. I was to head 250 miles northwest to Hudson near Sioux Lookout, Ontario, for a load. I simply told him "Sorry, I've already found a new job." I called my direct boss (the owner of the truck) explaining the situation to him. He was sorry to lose me, but he did understand the frustration. I think he sold the truck not long after I left.

During my time pulling wood chips, they introduced the requirements to wear reflective safety vests. In the beginning, these were little more than plastic straps with reflective material, and a waist strap with a snap closure. Not all that "safe", but the law was the law. We had to wear them, useless and dangerous as they were. One day, while I was outside of the truck closing up all the doors, and getting ready to head to Upsala for my second load, the sounds of the mill were all around me, as they always are. Kind of like white noise. You only really notice it when it's not there. Suddenly I'm airborne, flying backwards. A loader operator cut in just a little too close, and hooked the back of my vest, not only pulling me off my feet, but also dislocating my right shoulder. Once he stopped and we managed to get me unhooked from the loader, I popped my shoulder back into place, finished closing up the trailers and went to the hospital to get everything checked out. All was good. So much for "safety vests". That one damn near killed me.

Back on the Open Road
Good Times and a Good Co-worker

My second go-around with Shaw Trucking was better, but still had its moments. My first co-driver was Blair, who I had met at Bulk Systems while doing the wood chip runs. We had a blast running together. When you are part of a team, if you don't "click" with your co-driver, it can be a long, miserable two or three weeks in the truck. Blair and I clicked. He hated driving days. I was more than happy to drive during daylight hours. This allowed us to run a twelve-on-twelve-off schedule. I was in charge from six in the morning until six at night. He took over at six in the evening, having control through the night until it was my turn again. Not all of the twelve hours was spent driving. In those days, you were allowed a maximum of ten hours driving in the USA before taking the required eight-hour minimum off. In Canada, it was thirteen hours driving before needing eight hours off. The rest of the time could be spent eating in a truck stop, fuelling the truck, loading or unloading, or whatever you want to do, just as long as it was not driving.

As should be obvious, I don't recall every single trip we ran, but certain adventures certainly stand out. In one instance, we had delivered a load of paper to a Kansas City newspaper followed by a trip to a pasta warehouse a few miles east in Liberty, Kansas. Once again this was pre-GPS. I called in for directions. Information in hand, off we went. This facility was in an underground limestone quarry, with tunnels bored into the walls. They tell you which tunnel to use. When you arrive on the site, you turn around, backing your rig down the tunnel. Except they left that part out. We drove straight down the limestone tunnel only to discover that we now had to back out a quarter of a mile, turn around, then back down the long route again. That was tricky as there wasn't room for error in narrow tunnels with very little lighting. We did manage the maneuver, however. We loaded up, heading for Toronto.

In Toronto we delivered the pasta then drove across the city to load cores for the paper mill in Kenora. On these loads, we would simply return to the Thunder Bay yard where a local driver would deliver them to the mill. This driver would then deadhead (run empty) to Winnipeg, returning with a load of lumber. For us, our part of the delivery was over in Thunder Bay. Blair collected his gear and went home while I took care of the "tidying up". This tidying was about as much fun as doing the chores at home. I had to park the trailer, organize the trip paper work, fill out expense forms, then write up the "cry sheet" (noted defects to be corrected before the truck left again). After these tasks were completed, I walked into the building to hand in the paperwork to the office. This time, I was stopped dead in my tracks. There was the owner, beaten up pretty badly, hanging by his belt from a coat hook, five feet in the air. He had obviously been there for a while, as his bladder control had checked out. I got him down at once, asking who had done this to him. He claimed he didn't know. I think he had infuriated one of the other drivers who then retaliated. I also believe he didn't want to identify said assailant, fearing further retribution. To this day, I don't understand why he didn't just undo his belt to let himself down.

Oɴ ᴛᴏ ᴛʜᴇ Bɪɢ Sʜᴏᴡ
Fʀᴏᴍ Rᴏᴏᴋɪᴇ ᴛᴏ Pʀᴏꜰᴇssɪᴏɴᴀʟ.

After about six or seven months, I again had my last with Shaw Transport, I was ready to look for a new job. At the time, I was making $.20 per mile, which was top dollar at Shaw. I went in one day when the boss was away, using his fax machine to send out resumés to every company I could think of. In the end, I chose Winnipeg-based TransX. I worked for the next nineteen and a half years, beginning in May of 1995 and staying with them until December 2014.

I had been with TransX for about four to six weeks, when I found myself in the office getting ready to head out on a trip. I still knew very few people in the company, and even fewer drivers. I was at the planner's desk, getting things sorted out, when a rather short man, dressed in pointed-toe cowboy boots, jeans, a western shirt, along with a rope tie, and the proverbial ten-gallon hat asked me, in a very thick Italian accent, if I had a cigarette. I gave him one, and he stuffed a $5.00 bill in the pack, promptly lighting the cigarette. I sheepishly said something to the effect of: "I don't think you're allowed to smoke in the building." He replied: "I own the place, and I'll smoke in here if I want. And so will you!" I looked at the planner, who was gently but vigorously nodding in agreement. This was my first introduction to the owner.

I had managed to stay a single driver for about two months when Pete, the previously-mentioned friend of mine from Thunder Bay, showed up one morning. I got him a job, but I had to train him. That was the end to running single for a while. The training went well, and we eventually we had a good system down. That, in itself, provided a few good stories.

We were bringing a load of meat out of Texas to Toronto over the Easter weekend. This required an after-hours appointment with the Canadian Food Inspection Agency (CFIA) at the border crossing. We had the appointment all set up for Saturday. When we got there Saturday, the inspector was in a foul mood, even before we presented our paperwork. He grabbed the paperwork, muttering under his breath about missing Easter Mass. To our dismay, the veterinarian at the shipper had neglected one small detail on the meat importation forms. A very small detail. He didn't date his signature. The CFIA inspector blew his top, letting out a string of expletives that I had never heard before, all the while claiming he was missing Easter Mass! He stamped the paperwork "REJECTED", sending us on our way. Neither of us knew what to do, other than call the company, which we did. We were told to go to a meat plant in Detroit, where they could issue new documents. The downside, was that we had to wait until Monday. With nothing left to do, we headed to the closest truck stop, the infamous "Detroiter".

Before long, we learned why this truck stop was infamous. The truck we had was equipped with a 36-inch flat-top sleeper. No storage inside except for the passenger seat and floor. Only one of us could sleep at a time, which made for a long wait. While we were waiting, Pete went inside the building for some reason. I had asked him to remember to lock the door whenever he left the truck. This time he didn't, and I got an unwanted visitor. A "lady of the evening" (or lot lizard – but more on them later!) just opened the door and climbed in. I was definitely NOT interested, yet she was determined not to get

An older style truck. 36 inch flat top sleeper. We ran team in these trucks.

out of the truck. After ten minutes of asking, then demanding, that she leave, I had to physically toss her out. Not too proud of that, but enough was enough.

Eventually we got the paperwork sorted out, and managed to deliver the load. Our Toronto reload was an LTL (a less-than-load, meaning products for more than one customer. More on LTL loads later) headed west. Just outside of Thunder Bay, we got into an argument over something. I don't recall what it was about, but as we had been in the truck together for two weeks, we both had frayed nerves. By this point, it didn't take much to get us at each other's throats. I can't stress enough just how cramped the conditions are in a truck. Anyone who knows me, knows that I'm a Pepsi drinker. To a fault, and to the detriment to anything. I would never ever waste a single drop of Pepsi. Never. Well, whatever we were arguing about, I had reached the breaking point. I grabbed my 20 oz unopened bottle of Pepsi, heaving it out the window. Pete was quite stunned. Possibly he was even scared! Enough of a shake-up, however, that he didn't utter a single word for at least three hours. Far as I know, it's still laying in the ditch near Upsala.

The runs from Toronto, and occasionally Montreal west to Winnipeg along with a rare Calgary, Edmonton, or Vancouver trip were pretty much a routine end-of-a-run at TransX. This meant that they frequently were ripe with stories along with many interesting happenings. The runs west from Winnipeg to Alberta, or south to various points in the United States, were usually a routine start to longer journey. As a general rule, we left Winnipeg, headed south to points anywhere in the United States, then reloaded for Toronto or Montreal. This was generally followed with an LTL back home to Winnipeg. On occasion, you'd get a non-LTL load, but not very often.

We did have one trip from Montreal with a heavy load of 48,000 lbs of Kraft cheese. We were west-bound on a run that proved to be memorable for all the wrong reasons. One of our usual stops along the way was a Shell gas station with a large lot in Clearwater, Ontario, close to the Manitoba border. We would always stop to use the facilities, as well as grabbing a few snacks for the final two-hour run into Winnipeg. On this occasion, we left the stop with me driving, at the company-mandated 55 mph. The trucks were also governed, meaning they could not exceed that speed. In

Manitoba, the first ten or so miles are a two-lane highway, with a provincial speed limit of 62 mph. As a result, we ended up with a fairly good line up of vehicles behind us.

At the Barrens Lake area (close to the community of Falcon Lake, Manitoba), the west-bound highway has a curve in the road that bends to the right. Just before we got there, a car heading east came around the corner, and didn't straighten out as it came out of the corner. I moved as far as possible onto the paved shoulder. I distinctly remember watching the car go past my window, with maybe a foot to spare. I thought: "Damn, I'm glad I missed him!" I looked in the mirror just in time to see him slam into the trailer tires. The impact didn't affect the truck very much, as we weighed about 85,000 lbs at the time. The car, on the other hand was destroyed. The driver's side of his car had directly smashed into the front left axle of the trailer at about a forty-five-degree angle.

The collision was incredible. The impact speed must have been over 125 mph. The car, a 1991 Lincoln Town Car, was absolutely destroyed. The impact split the car's engine block breaking the front axle. Our trailer tires actually rolled up and over the hood for a good three feet before dropping back to the pavement. The car, or what was left of it, was sent spinning back across his lane, ending up against a guard rail that prevented it from falling into the roadside ditch. The damage to the trailer bore testimony to the force of the impact. The outside left front tire was torn off the rim, and the rim was torn off the axle. Ten one-inch studs were simply sheared right off, as if they had been cut with a saw. The rim was thrown about 100 feet. The tire was never found. The rim was bent to the point it looked like Pacman. One of the tire studs hit the windshield of a pickup truck directly behind me, becoming imbedded in the glass. Thankfully, it didn't go all the way through, or it would have killed someone. The impact also bent the front axle back about ten degrees, bent the axle slider assembly, and twisted the subframe to the point that the floor actually split front to back about three inches at its widest. The car and our trailer were both total write-offs. As were my shorts.

I was sure I had killed whoever was in the car. Luckily, there were no serious injuries at all. The car-driver had fallen asleep at the wheel, which probably saved his life. The Royal Canadian Mountain Police (RCMP) and Emergency Medical Services (EMS) were on scene almost as soon as everything stopped moving. Apparently, they were at some nearby function giving a demonstration when they heard the impact. After the police determined there were no fatalities, or even serious injuries, they allowed me to limp the truck to a nearby roadside turnout. Then they could get the highway opened up to the backed-up traffic.

TransX arranged for a tire place to come to where we had hauled the trailer to make the needed repairs. The service truck replaced the hub, tire and rim. Due to the damage on the bent axle, they prepared to follow us for the 95 mile journey to the Winnipeg yard with their service beacons flashing to warn other drivers. There was no way I was going to be driving at highway speeds with the bent axle.

Once we were finished at the scene, and ready to head back on the highway, I told Pete: "Don't even THINK about offering to drive to the yard. If I don't get back behind the wheel and drag this (expletive) to the yard now, I may never get behind the wheel again!". We headed out at a max speed of about 35 mph. Good thing it was now a divided highway, because the trailer was dog-tracking about three feet to the left. Dog tracking means the trailer isn't following directly behind. A three-foot dog track to the right meant that the trailer axles were about three feet to the right of the drive axles on the truck. I was starting to settle down, but I was still a little stressed, when another driver passed me. My "colleague" said something on the CB to the effect of my inability to keep the trailer in my own lane. I don't recall what I said, when I grabbed the CB mic, but I do remember giving said driver a piece of my mind. Later, Pete recalled that I gave the driver verbal instructions of what he could do with his new anatomy after tearing him 15 new ones. We eventually made it to the yard. Neither of us had any luck backing the damaged trailer into the dock. The shunt truck took several tries to get it into place. The car was a write-off, the trailer was a write-off, various pairs of underwear were a write-off, but everyone lived to drive another day, with no more serious injuries than cuts and scrapes from broken glass. I'd call that a good outcome.

Pete and I had some lighter times in the truck as well. There were times when we were both awake. It helps to come up with "games" to pass the time. Since we had been friends for only about ten years, we quickly ran out of things to reminisce about. This meant that we created a few games to help pass the time. One game had us roll down the windows a little more than a sliver, and toss an empty cigarette pack in an attempt to get it out the window. Whoever managed to get the pack out the window won. The loser had to buy the next meal. It wasn't easy, but it would help pass the time. One time when we decided to play, Pete grabbed the empty pack, making his toss. Perfect shot, right out the window. Nothing but net! After a bit of whooping and cheering, he grabbed his cigarette pack, opening it for a celebratory smoke. Nothing. It was empty. He had won by tossing a pack with one cigarette missing out the window!

Another time we played it, I won. Our next stop was in the small British Columbia mountain town of Golden. I was just finishing my driving shift when we decided to stop at the local A & W Restaurant to eat. Neither of us cared for the food at the local truck stop. At that time, I considered it a dump. To this day, it hasn't improved in my opinion. We fuelled up, driving to the A&W. Pete was expecting breakfast. I'd been up driving all night so I'm not looking for bacon and eggs. His meal came to about $4.00. Mine (burgers and fries) came out closer to $20.00. If someone else is paying, I'm eating like a king! It was about that time we set a dollar limit on said winning meals.

In December of 1995, we found ourselves on a trip to Laredo, Texas. We both had time booked off over Christmas making us anxious to get rolling. As I stated, the company speed limit was 55 mph with almost all the trucks were governed at that speed, and we were allowed 4% overspeed. A few were set at 65 mph for specific reasons, one being a team that was on a dedicated Winnipeg to Chicago LTL run. They needed the extra speed to make the time constraints on the route. The truck they started with wasn't spec'd (set up) for that speed, and fuel consumption was too high. As a result, they moved them into a different truck that was spec'd for that speed. For this trip, Pete and I had their old 65 mile per hour truck. All the trucks were equipped with a K-DAC (trucking transportation services) system. When you were driving you had to insert your K-DAC card, then the system recorded your road speed, engine RPM, and braking. When you got back to the yard, you had to plug the K-DAC into a cable to download the data. The process could take up to ten minutes. Of course, this was long before the internet, let alone wireless data.

There we were that December, in Laredo, a Texas-Mexico border town. As we are both Canadian citizens, under US Cabotage Laws, any load we pick up in the United States must be leaving the country (either to Canada or Mexico). Since that meant couldn't deliver interstate loads, we had some time to kill until our Canadian-bound cargo was ready. We decided to join two other TransX drivers (also waiting for Canadian loads) for a walk across the bridge into Nuevo Laredo, Mexico, for the day. We had taken two steps into Mexico, when a boy of fifteen or sixteen ran up to us saying, (in a thick Mexican accent): "Hey Mister, wanna buy my sister? She been virgin three times today!" No takers. What was worse, was she didn't seem to mind his offering her for sale. We wandered around, planning to do some Christmas shopping. One local street vendor offered me a homemade rope hammock for $20. I told him I was interested, but not at that price. We had been told by our terminal manager that haggling over price was not only common, it was expected. In fact, some vendors took it as an insult if you didn't haggle. Not wanting to insult the seller, we haggled for a bit, but couldn't come to an agreement. We continued walking and shopping. All the while, the hammock vendor followed us, talking non-stop as he tried to make a deal. After a couple of hours shopping, he was still following us, offering a new price of $5.00. I told him I'd pay $2.00 not a penny more. The four of us walked into a Nuevo Laredo diner for lunch, before heading back to the United States side of the city. Hammock-dude followed us in, while he kept trying to haggle. Finally, he agreed to $2.00. I paid him as he handed me the hammock. When we got back to the terminal, I mentioned the hammock to the manager. He just laughed. Apparently, some of the vendors consider it bad luck to lose the first sales opportunity of the day. They'll do almost anything to make that first sale. On a side note, if I was to end up in Laredo today, crossing into Mexico wouldn't even cross my mind. Once was enough.

By the time we got back to Laredo, time was getting tight, as we both wanted to be home for Christmas. It was close to noon when we were finally given a load from Laredo to Winnipeg. We picked up the load, scaled it legal, and fuelled up, leaving the Texas border town at six p.m.

on December 22. Pete had just started a relationship with a new girlfriend in Winnipeg, so he was in a hurry to get home to spend Christmas with her. My wife and stepson were already in Thunder Bay meaning I wanted to get to Thunder Bay ASAP. We set it up so that Pete would do the final eight-hour drive into Winnipeg, giving me the break-hours that I needed to "turn & burn" immediately for Thunder Bay. We made it. I was at my parent's house in Thunder Bay 48 hours after we left Laredo. When we eventually downloaded the K-DAC, we were almost fired. 37% overspeed. We ran that trip with our foot to the floor the whole way. We only stopped to fuel, or to switch drivers. While one of us was fuelling, the other was inside using the facilities and grabbing food to go. We hauled ass, but we both made it to where we wanted to be. I was told the only reason we weren't fired was because it was Christmas. TransX was (and still is) dedicated to getting drivers where they want to be for Christmas, even if it means parking the truck to fly the drivers to their destination.

One of TransX's contracts at the time was the Wisconsin Paper Group (WPG). They shipped finished paper products to many points in Canada. Except for rare cases, they were all LTL shipments. During the time I was training Pete, we got one of the worst LTL loads from WPG. This load had 50 shipments (drops) on the trailer. To put this into perspective, each drop requires a minimum of five pages of paperwork: two copies of the bill of lading (BOL), two copies of the Canada Customs Invoice, and one copy of the packing slip. Another copy of the packing slip is attached to the product in the trailer. Of course, some of the drops we had on the trailer had more than the minimum paperwork. As I recall, the paperwork bundle we were given was about four inches thick. Since Pete was still in training, I figured this would be a good chance for him to hone his organization skills, making sure all the paperwork was properly correlated then sent on to the proper customs broker. He had other ideas. He was in the bunk when I got back to the truck. I told him he would be doing the customs paperwork. He agreed. I handed back the paperwork bundle. I heard a few expletives before the entire bundle flew out of the bunk where the elastic broke. About 600 pages of paper fluttered around the truck. It took us about three hours to get everything sorted out and sent to the proper brokers. Even if one broker was handling multiple drops, each customs package had to be sent separately. They could all be sent as a single fax, but the paperwork couldn't be mixed up with another drop's paperwork. I can't even remember what that cost us (we got reimbursed) to fax. That tab must have been at least $100 not counting the time wasted waiting for faxes to be sent. I've had other fifty-plus drop loads since, but thankfully they were all going to a single purchaser, leaving us with just one broker to deal with.

A few months later, Pete & I picked up a load in Lethbridge Alberta, going to a place in Nebraska. After loading, we called in (this was still before satellite communications and cell phones) to give the heads up that we were about to hit the road. I was told that the HR department wanted to talk to Pete. I handed him the phone. While he was chatting, I walked back to the truck to get the customs paperwork started so that we could fax everything off, and be on our way. About five minutes later, Pete stormed out of the building. Considering Pete is the most passive guy I know, this caught my attention. When he threw a right hook into the hood of the truck, he REALLY got my attention! Turns out there was a minor issue with his driver's medical that might disqualify him from driving in the United States. He was definitely NOT happy, but the matter was soon cleared up allowing his driving career to continue. Later on this run, after unloading and reloading, we stopped to fuel in Walcott, Iowa. As usual, we parked after fuelling, going inside to grab food, use the facilities, and call our other-halves. My call went off without a hitch, but Pete couldn't get through. After about ten minutes, I was ready to go, but he kept on trying for about another 45 minutes. After some back-and-forth discussion between the two of us ("I can't get through!" and "Come on, dude, we gotta get moving!") we damn near came to blows in the parking lot. It was about this time we decided it was time to part ways as team drivers. Thankfully, no punches were thrown. I went back to running single. Pete was placed with a mutual friend to run team, along with a bit more training. Pete and I are still best of friends to this day. He actually has reminded me of a few of the stories found herein. There I was, back to running single again. This would bring about a whole new set of adventures.

REEFER MADNESS
HAULING REFRIGERATED FREIGHT

Having parted ways with my friend and trainee, Pete, I was now heading out on my own as a single TransX driver. No partner to share the driving or to keep me entertained (for good or for bad). When I slept, the truck slept. I was looking forward to new adventures!

When I first started at TransX, the company was just beginning to get into refrigerated freight, and they didn't have a lot of refrigerated trailers. The company had ordered a few hundred, but it took time for them to be delivered. They did have a few refrigerated rail containers, so for the first while, we were using those for road loads. Rail containers are usually sent by rail (hence the name). When compared to a refrigerated truck-trailer, they are very heavy. An empty container (can) on a chassis weighs in at between 20,000 and 25,000 lbs compared to a refrigerated trailer (reefer) that can be as light as 14,000 lbs. A huge difference, considering the load limits of the highways.

Refrigerated rail cans, like reefer trailers, are diesel fuelled. The cans TransX had in those days weren't set up to be user-friendly for over-the road-use. They had no fuel pump, and were gravity fed, with the fuel tank on top of the reefer unit. The fill tube was about 13 ft above the ground. Took a bit of nerve and balance to get the fuel hose up that high, then fuelling them without falling off. I think I had two or three loads in these containers. It wasn't fun at all.

The few reefers ("reefer" is trucker slang for the refrigerated trailer) they did have at the time, were, as I recall, older dry trailers that they had mounted reefer units on the front. They did cool the interiors, but without insulation, it was almost a lost cause. I recall one trip with one of these old trailers taking a meat load from Alberta headed to Laredo.

The interior of a properly built reefer is far different from a standard dry box in many ways. First, a dry box has a solid wood floor, front to back, and side to side. A proper reefer uses aluminum for the floor, with one-inch trenches to channel liquids away, and to allow for air circulation. Each corner has a one-inch hole to allow the liquids (mostly water, either from melting ice when the unit defrosts, or from ice used to keep produce fresh) to drain off. For this reason, reefers are seldom used to haul dangerous liquids. A small spill inside the trailer could wreak havoc on the environment. Reefers also have insulation in them to hold the temperature, reduce the workload of the reefer unit, and reduce fuel consumption.

There I was, headed to Laredo, Texas, minding my own business. It was a hot day. This old reefer was running flat out, trying to maintain a temperature of 29 F. When I rolled across the scale just south of Fort Worth, I was told to report inside. I was a bit confused, as I knew my weights and axle spacings were legal. I pulled around behind the scale, parked, then gathered all the paperwork. When I opened the door, I heard some sirens off in the distance, but thought nothing of it. The Department of Transportation (DOT) official was yelling for me to get away from the truck. I hot-footed it to the building where he slammed the door behind me. To say I was confused would be an understatement. He grabbed my bills, inspecting them closely, obviously looking for something. Whatever he was looking for, he didn't find it. Next, he asked what was in the trailer other than meat. I said: "Nothing. Just the meat." He replied: "There had to be something else on the trailer, because meat doesn't burn. You have smoke billowing out the back of the trailer!" I gave him a very confused look. He told me to take a look. Sure enough, what looked like smoke was pouring out the back of the trailer. I again assured him, there was only meat in the trailer, offering to go out to see what was happening. He forbade me to leave the building until the fire department arrived and gave the all clear. The fire trucks were there within minutes. They inspected the rear of the trailer. False alarm (as I knew it was). The door seal at the bottom of both doors was old and damaged, not sealing properly. What he though was smoke, was fog. Cold air from the reefer leaked into the hot and humid Texas air, looking like smoke, even though it wasn't.

From Laredo, I was sent to a small rural town to load peewee watermelons. The fruit description becomes important later in this account. This was one of, if not my first, produce loads, and it was definitely different. The watermelons were still in the field. They had me drive down one of the service roads they have through the huge 150-200 acre field. Watermelons as far as the eye could see. I arrived at the loading place, setting the parking brakes. Because it was brutally hot, somewhere close to 100 F, I left the truck idling. When they load bulk watermelons, they spread hay on the floor, stacking them like footballs about four or five layers high. The loading process began with a crew in the field picking the watermelons, then loading them into a small trailer, followed by one of the field hands bringing them to my truck where another crew stacked them in the trailer. While the crew in the trailer was waiting for the melons to come in from the field, they congregated under the trailer for the shade. I can only imagine how brutally hot it was, as I'm in the truck, stripped down to my boxers with the air conditioning cranked to fifteen and still sweating like a pig on a barbecue. The crew arrived from the field with the last load, but the loading crew was still under the trailer. They appeared to have no plans to come out for a while. I cut them some slack, but after half an hour, it was time to get this show on the road. I got dressed, heading outside to see what the hold-up was. I was met with rapid-fire Spanish. I didn't understand a single word, but the context was easy enough to figure out. They weren't ready to finish yet. I got back in the truck, waited five minutes, then applied the air to the trailer. The air charging the brake chambers makes a very audible noise, as do the push rods and slack adjusters releasing the parking brakes on the trailer. Those workers scrambled out like rats on a sinking ship. They quickly finished loading the truck. When I got out to sign the paperwork, one of the foremen was walking away with two watermelons under his arms. I asked him why they weren't going in the truck.

He replied that they were too small so he was getting rid of them. I said I'd take them, rather than have him just toss them out. He shrugged, and we put them in the bunk for the trip home. I was done loading and on my way to Toronto in no time. When I got home, I unloaded the truck, in addition to my two peewee watermelons, that the shipper said were "too small". Too small? Each weighed in at 42 lbs!

Another experience I had with reefers happened in California a few years later. This one wasn't quite as "enjoyable". I had a load of French fries going to the Sacramento area. Once again, I had made sure my axle weights and axle spacings were legal. As I crossed the scale in Truckee, California, I was once again notified to report in. Following procedure, I drove around the back, parked, collected the paperwork and opened the door. Before I could climb down, a California DOT agent pulled me off the running board, pushing me face down onto the pavement where he then handcuffed me. Bladder control was a real problem. I was dragged into the office, where I was accused of causing a chemical spill on the highway. I was incredulous, protesting my innocence. The officer said he saw the chemical running, not dripping, out of the rear of the trailer. He grabbed the bills, immediately seeing that I had French fries on the trailer. He then demanded to know where the bills for the chemicals were along with the dangerous goods placards that were supposed to be on the trailer. I told him, again, that there were no dangerous goods on the trailer, just 44,000 lbs of French fries, which don't need dangerous goods placards. Just check my weight across the scale, then look at the weight of the French fries. You'll see, there's nothing else on the trailer. Nope, he was convinced there was a liquid chemical leaking in the trailer. Why else would there be liquid pouring out the back of the trailer? I tried to explain that when the reefer defrosts, all the built-up ice melts, running down the channels in the trailer to the drain holes, pouring out. He wasn't hearing any of it. A hazmat team in full gear quickly arrived. They took samples which were tested in the mobile lab they brought. The results came back quickly. Water. Cost me about forty-five minutes of wasted time for an over exuberant DOT officer who was convinced he had a major polluter.

Hanging (also called "swinging") meat loads are not very forgiving, and if you're not paying attention, they'll bite you in the butt big time. For a

Hanging beef load

few months, we were hauling hanging pork from Manitoba to Nogales, AZ, for furtherance into Mexico. The plan was, we would clear the T&E bond in Nogales, then proceed to the freight forwarder and drop the trailer, where a Mexican driver would hook up, and head into Mexico to deliver the load, then reload produce, and bring the (hopefully legally) loaded trailer in about two days. As I had some experience with swinging meat, I had one of the first loads. Upon arrival in Nogales, I went and cleared the bond, and headed to the forwarder. The Mexican driver was already there waiting for me. As I handed him the paperwork, I asked him if he was familiar with swinging loads. He said he had "great experience". I took that to mean he had done swinging loads. Off he went. 200 feet later, as he turned right to head to the border, CRASH! Too fast around the corner, and he was on his side. Well shit! This trailer isn't coming back in two days. I saw him climb out the window, so I knew he was okay, so I took a picture of the wreck with my cell phone, and emailed it to my dispatcher, letting him know I wasn't getting a loaded trailer in a few days. Or even an empty trailer, for that matter. After he let the planner know what had happened, they came up with a plan: Bobtail (driving without a trailer) to Laredo TX, and grab an empty trailer from the drop yard. I asked "Are you freaking serious?" He was. Nogales AZ to Laredo TX is about 950 miles, and running without a trailer is a VERY rough ride. The suspension on a truck is designed to carry a load of about 40,000 lbs. Legally, we can't haul that much, but the system is built with that extra safety margin. Bobtailing, the weight on the drives is about 8,000 lbs. It makes for a very rough ride, and you have to be very gentle with the brakes, or they could easily lock up, because, again, the brakes are designed to have a load on them. Same is the engine brake. Use high setting on the engine brake when bobtailing, and you could easily stall the truck. Yes, I've done this. Not too bad in the summer, but it can send you on a "crash course in skid school" during the winter. So off I went to Laredo to get an empty, and, I assumed, a reload from somewhere in the Laredo area. As a company driver, I was paid by the mile. Empty, loaded, or bobtail. If they told me to drive somewhere, I was paid (at that time) $0.32 per mile. The run to Laredo to get an empty paid me roughly $304.00, and took the better part of two days. The drive from Nogales to Laredo is remarkable for one thing. BORING! The highway runs through desert, and is totally featureless, and almost completely barren of vegetation, wildlife, and civilization. It was a VERY boring drive. I finally arrived at the drop yard, and found an empty reefer that was good to go, so I hooked up, and called dispatch to see where and what they wanted me to load. I was floored when he told me to go back to Nogales, and load tomatoes. Another 950 miles empty (and another $304.00 in my pocket). All in all, the trip from Nogales to Laredo and back took the better part of 3 days, paid me $608.00 (the company made $0.00 during the three days). The tomatoes went to Toronto, and I likely got an LTL back home from there. Future swinging loads to Nogales went to a drop yard, where the forwarding company took care of all the paperwork. We just pulled into the yard, handed the bills to the office, dropped the loaded one, and grabbed a preloaded trailer that was sitting there.

One issue I had with these swinging loads, was the weight. They were all under the maximum GVW (Gross Vehicle Weight), and all the axles were under the allowable maximum, but the manufacturer's plate on the trailer stated a "40,000 lbs maximum suspended load", meaning that the trailer was certified to support no more that 40,000 lbs hanging from the ceiling. All these hanging loads were in the 42,000-44,000 lbs range. Still legal weight-wise, but exceeding the manufacturer's certified weight restrictions. I called the shipper's attention to this, and they just shrugged, and blew it off. That is, until a scale master noticed it. Oh, did that turn ugly! The trailer was immediately put out of service, as the manufacturer's specifications had been exceeded. The trailer wasn't going anywhere until it was inspected, and re-certified as safe for use on the highway. Before that, the load had to be made legal. So it was either send a trailer set up for hanging meat (not all of them are) that was certified to haul that kind of suspended weight, or send two trucks, and two trailers, and have the load split, so that both trailers were under the allowable limit. The number of hanging trailers with an allowable suspended limit over 40,000 lbs that I've ever seen is exactly 0. Not a single one. So, in addition to sending two trucks and two trailers, they also had to send a US Customs official, as the load was travelling under a T&E bond, a USDA meat inspector to ensure all was in order there, a few good men to man handle the load from one trailer to the other two trailers, and a mechanic to come out and inspect the original trailer. All in all, it was a fairly wasted weekend, and cost someone a lot of money. I don't recall ever hauling from that meat plant again. Looking back, I don't think I've heard of any hanging loads since. They're just not profitable, and unless you know what you're doing, they're very unstable, and dangerous. I've seen more than a few hanging loads laying on their sides over the years. The main cause, in every case, is cornering too fast.

THE PUSH FROM WITHIN
PLANNERS, DISPATCHERS, AND THE TRUCK DRIVER

Before we can get on the road and deal with shippers and receivers, we need to visit those that send us out on the road: the planners and dispatchers. The load planners put together the orders from the trucking company's clientele, then schedule the pick-ups and drop offs. They pass the information on to the dispatcher who then makes the final coordination with the truck driver. Often a driver will curse out their dispatcher when the blame for the situation sits with the person who created the original order. In hindsight, this does create some good trucking stories.

One time, I had a load from somewhere in the USA, with a few drops in Ontario, along with two or three in Quebec. I made the Ontario drops, hoping to drop the trailer at the Montreal terminal for local delivery. I had a couple of reasons for wanting to do this. First, I've had issues with the language barrier at a few places in Montreal. I wasn't really looking forward to more of the same. Another reason was dispatch policy regarding terminals. To keep it as fair as possible, trucks are dispatched from the terminals on a FIFO (First In, First Out) basis, with teams getting loaded before solo drivers. Since it was a Friday, I was hoping to drop in Montreal, then get in line for a load out. If I had to deliver the Quebec drops (two in Montreal along with one in Quebec City) it would be Tuesday before I was finished. Everyone who had dropped in Montreal over the weekend would be dispatched out ahead of me. As we're paid by the mile, it wasn't a good weekend financially to make the three drops Monday and Tuesday. Alas, the planner for the Montreal area told me there was nothing in Montreal for the weekend. He wouldn't know until Monday if there was anything on Tuesday, either, but he promised me that if I made the drops in Montreal and Quebec City, he would save me a long-distance paper load from the mill in Trois Rivières, Quebec.

I was instantly suspicious. I've frequently been lied to by planners or dispatchers. But this planner had always been straight with me. He never told me what I wanted to hear. He always gave me the truth as best he could. Of course, if someone gives your planner or dispatcher false information, you can't hold them responsible. I asked him where the paper load was going, and was told "You'll see...". Uh huh. Not thrilled, but what could I do. I made the Quebec deliveries, then headed to the Trois Rivières mill. Checked in, gave the security guard my pick-up number along with the empty trailer number I was dropping. He then gave me the loaded trailer number I was to take. I asked him where it was going. He replied that he had been told not to tell me. Uh oh again. By now, I was certain I was getting shafted with a short load, under 200 miles, or something along those lines. I dropped the empty, found the loaded trailer I was taking, checked the seal number, then scaled it out. Axle and gross weights were fine. I headed back to the guardhouse to collect my bills. The purchaser listed was a company in lower Manhattan. A whopping 450 miles away. I was NOT impressed. My expression must have given me away because the security guard asked why I was suddenly upset with the load. I stayed calm, replying that I was promised a high mileage load, and 450 miles to Manhattan does not qualify as high-mileage. He was even more confused. Then I noticed that while the purchaser was in Lower Manhattan, the consignee was in Reno, Nevada a full 2,822 miles distant! My bad. The planner had kept his word, and my mood improved immensely.

One memorable lie I was handed, happened after my divorce. More on the divorce later. I had met someone online who lived in a different time zone, and we were planning a first meeting. I asked the planner what the chances were to get a load going to a major city close to where she lived, and take my time off there. He said no problem, he'd have a look, and get back to me. A few days later, he said he had a load going almost to the town she lived in. I asked if he was sure, as I was going to call her, and let her know when I'd be there. He said the trailer was being loaded the next day, and would be on the ground in the yard when I got there. He even gave me the trailer number. I called her, and told her I'd be there in three days. When I got to the Toronto yard, I dropped my loaded trailer, and went in to see dispatch. I handed him the bills, and he looked my truck number up in the computer, and told me my Montreal load wasn't ready yet. I told him the planner was holding a Saskatchewan load for me, and I gave him the trailer number. He shook his head, and told me I was planned on a Montreal load. He even checked the trailer number I was given. Said trailer was in Colorado, on it's way to Laredo from Alberta. I was NOT impressed, and never believed a single word he ever said to me again.

At Their Mercy

Shippers, Receivers, and the Truck Driver

As I've mentioned, a truck driver is at the mercy of clients using their services. As we crisscross the continent delivering freight, we encounter all kinds of people, and all kinds of experiences..

One interesting experience occurred after I had delivered a load of paper in Wisconsin. TransX dispatch sent me to a place in Menasha, a small city on the edge of Wisconsin's Lake Winnebago. This was another rush load. I was told the shipper was paying for exclusive use of the trailer, which meant that whatever they load, that's all you get. LTL loads are billed by "cube" and weight. Cube is the volume of the freight, (length multiplied by height, multiplied by width. A 53 foot trailer has a "cube" capacity of just over 4,279 cubic feet plus a maximum payload of between 44,000 and 48,000 lbs, depending on the trailer type. LTL loads usually max out on weight before they "cube" out. Bathroom tissue, facial tissue, and breakfast cereal loads usually cube out. Very light, but they take up a lot of space..

I arrived at the Menasha yard then walked into the shipping office to check in. I gave them the pick-up number, and was told that the load was ready to go. I asked what door I was to back into. Instead of giving me a loading dock location, I was told to "just open the doors" and the load would be brought out. I'm thinking, long tubes of bubble wrap, or foam sheeting, or something along those lines. I walked back to my truck, opening the doors as requested. The shipper was right behind me with a one-foot square box. Just one-foot long, one-foot deep, and one-foot high. He placed it on the floor, duct-taped it in place, then closed and sealed the doors. I signed the paperwork heading out to my destination in Toronto. Apparently, it was a box of replacement batteries that were needed ASAP on an assembly line.

I once was sent to load fruit juice at a place in Spokane, Washington, that turned into a bit of a disaster. I arrived for my assigned appointment time, only to learn that everyone had the same appointment time. The facility operated on a First Come First Serve (FCFS) basis. I had, therefore, to wait my turn. Just before noon, I was finally loaded. I went in to sign the waybills, and get my paperwork. Just as the shipper was about to sign the paperwork, he put down his pen, and said: "Lunch time, come back in an hour", and walked away. I wasn't exactly thrilled, but what could I do? I had to wait another hour for the plant to finish lunch. I went back an hour later. The shipper came back, signed the bills, then handed me the pen. I checked my watch, said: "Coffee time. See you in thirty minutes." I walked back to the truck, reading my book for half an hour. Seeing as they only had a single loading door, they had to wait. I went in, signed the bills, took my copies, continuing out the door. The shipper tossed a string of profanities my way, but I didn't really care. I've been called worse.

Another time that comes to mind was when I was in the southeastern Ontario city of Trenton, picking up a load headed for western Canada. I had a pick-up appointment for four in the afternoon. This particular shipper was fastidious about appointment times. You were on-time, or the transport company was fined for being late to pick up. I arrived half an hour before my appointment time. Right at four o'clock, they backed me into a door. By the time I was loaded with the paperwork in hand, it was midnight. I was NOT happy. I went to the closest truck parking spot, and went to bed. The next morning, I was in line at Tim Horton's to get my morning coffee. As usual, I was wearing a jacket with the TransX logo embroidered on the front and back. A voice behind me asked if I was still a driver at TransX. I was still seething over the previous day's disaster loading, but I kept that in check, replying that I was indeed a driver at

TransX. He smiled, commenting: "We just entered into a contract with TransX to move our products to western Canada and the USA." He identified himself as the plant manager of the place I had loaded at the day before, asking if I had loaded there yet. I calmly, and politely, explained to him the issues I had encountered loading. I told him that there was no way I would be able to make delivery as scheduled due to the eight-hour loading delay. He was stunned, asking for more details. I filled him in with the information I had. By this time, were back in the parking lot drinking our coffee as we chatted. He pulled out his phone, called the Customer Service Representative (CSR) for his contract. In no uncertain terms, he told them that he was sending a cheque for $200 to cover the detention. Half of it was to be paid to me, in addition to what detention fee I was entitled to from the company ($11.00 an hour after the first two hours). As far as I know, there were never any further delays loading at that plant. Myself, I never loaded there again.

TransX had quite a few contracts from all over North America to deliver products to Walmart warehouses in Canada. Say what you want about Walmart, but as a driver, they never "screwed" me over. They always had my back. As long as you had your ducks in a row, Walmart would look after you every time a shipper tried to pull a fast one.

On one occasion, I had a load of salad dressing from a shipper in southern Ontario, heading to the Walmart DC (Distribution Centre) in Calgary. Once I was backed in, they started bringing the pallets of salad dressing out. The pallets were loaded five cases high, five cases long, and five cases deep. 125 cases to a pallet. All Walmart loads, however, need a piece count. This means the truck driver has to count each piece as its loaded on the trailer. The way these pallets were loaded, that was impossible. I mentioned to the loader that this load was going to be SLC (Shipper's Load And Count), or "XXX pallets, STC (Said To Contain) YYY pieces", meaning they were responsible for the piece count. He replied that they don't allow SLC or STC, therefore the driver has to sign for pieces. I told him I wasn't going to sign for pieces I can't see. How do I know what's in the middle? Could be contraband, for all I know. I told him to unwrap the pallets to allow me to see and count what was in the middle. He said no, continuing to load the pallets. I walked outside, placing a call to TransX's

Walmart CSR, explaining the situation. He agreed. If I can't see each case, then it's either SLC or STC. The CSR called the plant. The plant manager repeated that SLC/STC was not allowed therefore the driver had to sign for each case. Even after explaining that I couldn't see each case, SLC/STC was not allowed. Next, the CSR put myself and the plant manager on hold, calling the Walmart Distribution Centre to get their purchaser on the line. Now there was four of us (myself, TransX Walmart CSR, plant manager, and Walmart purchaser) on the conference call. I explained the situation to the Walmart purchaser. The plant manager explained their position. After the purchaser heard both sides of the issue, they told the plant that I was well within my rights to refuse to sign for pieces. The load would have to go SLC/STC. The plant manager steadfastly refused, saying it was against their company policy. The purchaser asked; "Driver, are you still on the line?". I answered that I was. The Walmart representative then clearly stated: "You are free to leave, we don't need their product anymore." The purchaser then terminated the contract with the shipper on the spot.

Some places I've delivered have presented language issues. Most notably, the deep southern states, where Spanish is widely spoken. Laredo, El Paso, Nogales, for example. And in Canada, Quebec. The difference being that most southern states understand English, making an honest attempt to speak it as best they can. Most of the places I've been to in Quebec are the same. They start in French, but if you speak English, they'll switch to English. It's understandable, but the accent and grammar can make it challenging. I'm not disrespecting them by any means, but it can be a language barrier. Nonetheless, sometimes, you meet someone who just has to be an idiot. I loaded frozen fish on Prince Edward Island, destined for a fish packing plant in Montreal. It was to be delivered on the Friday of a long weekend. I called the plant for directions. When the receiver answered the phone, he spoke in French but immediately switched to English when it was apparent my French wasn't good enough. He gave me excellent directions, meaning that I found the plant with no problem at all. When I went to check in, the fun (in his mind) began. Of course, he started in French resulting in me stating that I didn't speak the language. He carried on in French, with a slight grin on his face. I knew he spoke English, because this was the same person I had spoken to on the phone. This "game" went on for about ten or fifteen minutes, until I finally told him: "Look. I know you speak English. Tell me what door you want the trailer in or I'm taking it to the yard. A city driver will deliver it next week.". He kept talking in French. I walked to the truck. Within a few minutes I was heading for the gate. The manager came flying across the lot, arms flailing, yelling for me to stop. I stopped, and he hopped on the running board, talking rapid-fire French. As soon as he learned I did not speak the language, he switched to English. He told me they had been waiting since the day before for this load, giving me permission to back in to any open door. I politely explained to him what had happened. I told him that I'd had enough of the receiver's attitude. I no longer had time to waste. The load was going to the yard. A city driver would deliver it Tuesday or Wednesday. I pulled out the plant and dropped in our yard.

A long-haul trucker takes the loads assigned to him (or her). Here's another story that made me shake my head and wonder about some of the shippers I had to work with. In Montreal, I was given a load of frozen bagels going to Georgia. Now, that was some good miles that could make up for losing three days on the road while I fixed another driver's mess that I was consigned to "save" (a story you'll read about later). This load was on an older trailer, one of the lightest reefers we had at the time. It was 48 long, and weighed about 14,000 lbs empty. The paperwork said there were 46,500 lbs of frozen bagels on board. The truck weighed about 18,000 lbs, meaning that I was pretty close to the maximum of 80,000 lbs, if not slightly over. I scaled the load in the yard, and came up just over 82,000 lbs. No way I could make this legal, not even running on a quarter tank of fuel all the way. Called the CSR, who called the shipper, who said they always send that weight; therefore, the scale must be wrong. I went to a truck stop with a certified scale, scaling it again. Pretty much the same result. I called the CSR again. He said to find a CAT (Certified Automated Truck) scale. CAT scales are the best. Their slogan is: "Weigh What We Say, Or We Pay". Their guarantee says that if you get an overweight ticket after scaling legal on their scale, they will immediately check their scale. If their scale is incorrect, they'll pay your fine. If their scale is correct, they will appear in court (at no cost to you) as an expert witness. The problem was, the closest CAT scale was in New York State. Getting to it meant crossing the border, and if the CAT scale showed the same as the two previous scales, we had a whole new kettle of fish to deal with. Dispatch said to go to the CAT scale..

I headed out for New York State. Crossing the border was no problem. I simply went to the first exit where the CAT scale was located. Sure enough, it was just over 82,000 lbs. Next, I called the CSR, who then called the shipper, who was adamant that the load was legal. I faxed the CSR the scale ticket, who in turned faxed a copy to the shipper. Finally, the shipper got the message. I was told to dispose of so many cases of blueberry bagels, another quantity of apple cinnamon, several cases of poppy seed, and so on until my weights were legal. I told the CSR I wasn't going to crawl through the trailer of frozen bagels, and pick and choose which cases to throw away. I had a better idea. I drove to nearby Scranton, Pennsylvania, as there were no DOT scales between there and the CAT scale, parked at the truck stop, and called the local food bank to see if they'd be interested in four pallets of frozen bagels. They most certainly were, providing me with directions to the food bank. I got there, backed in, and dropped about 3,000 lbs of frozen bagels. They gave me a soft drink, then I continued on my way. The receiver wasn't too happy that his order was short. I explained the whole story, and he asked when the rest of his bagels would arrive. I told him they'd get there whenever the shipper resent them. I have no idea which trucking company usually delivered these loads, but it was the first and last time I'd heard of us delivering them.

Another receiving fiasco I had to deal with involved a load of beef shipped in what's called "combo". These are boxes, the same size as a standard pallet 40 inches by 48 inches, and about 3 feet tall. Pretty much just bulk meat, usually trimmings used to make sausages, hot dogs, and the like. I picked this load up in Toronto, checked the paperwork, then off I went to a plant in New Jersey. With meat loads, the border crossing is always determined by the receiver, depending on which USDA meat inspector they use. As I've mentioned earlier, all meat loads crossing the border need to be inspected. This load was assigned to the USDA house north of Buffalo, New York. This meant that I had to enter the United States at Queenstown, New York. Through customs in a heartbeat, then off to the meat inspector. I handed him the paperwork, which he entered it into the system. It came up as needing an e. coli inspection. Not a big issue, but they have to take a sample from each combo, testing it for e. coli contamination. The process can take three or four days. You're free to leave with your cargo, transiting to your destination, but you can't deliver until the test results come back negative. If you do deliver before the results are confirmed negative, the penalty is the same for not clearing meat inspection before delivering. The penalty is three times the value of the load, and some meat loads are worth over $500,000 US. The fine could be as much as $1,500,000. Ouch! I would have been at the customer's location the next day. This meant that I had to advise them about the e. coli test, notifying them that it would be three days before I got the results back. As the load was "fresh" (maintained at 29 F), I asked them if they wanted me to set the reefer to -10 F to preserve the product. They declined. I informed dispatch of the situation, noting that the receiver had declined lowering the temperature (the CSR also called the receiver to verify they didn't want the temperature adjusted) to preserve freshness. I carried on to the truck stop closest to the customer. Three days later, with the all clear to deliver, I headed in. The receiver opened the trailer to inspect the meat. As I suspected, it had started to go slimy. No longer good for human consumption. On a side note, I heard a few years later the plant had been closed by USDA for repeated non-compliance with food handling regulations. That day, however, I was back on the phone to the CSR for the meat plant. He called the plant, to see what they wanted done with the meat. This started the whole "what could have been done to prevent this claim" rigamarole. Once they were satisfied that I had followed all the prescribed procedures, they said they'd get back to us as soon as possible. Two hours later, I was told to deliver the meat to a pet food plant in Ohio. More than a few wasted miles, as the load had originated in Alberta, then hauled to Toronto, New Jersey, and then on to Ohio.

For a while, TransX hauled dry goods from Proctor & Gamble plants in southern Ontario to Woodland, California, then reloaded diapers from Proctor and Gamble's Modesto, California, plant for a trip north to Vancouver, Edmonton or Calgary. Nice runs, as they were very light loads. The loads to Woodland were maybe 15,000 lbs, while the diapers were about 33,000 lbs.

As a rule of thumb, heading out from southern Ontario to the southwestern USA meant we had two border crossings available for our use, both taking us into the United States through Michigan. One route exited Sarnia, Ontario, crossing the St. Clair River into Port Huron. The other took us a bit further south, through Windsor, over the Detroit River, and into Detroit. Back then, the Detroit crossing was a nightmare. Bad signage meant you could easily become lost in a very bad part of the city. The routes from the border to the Interstates was a hodge-podge of local surface roads with the border in an area that was not particularly safe. It has since improved exponentially. Now, once you are out of the customs facility it takes just a few turns to bring you to the Interstate. If I had a choice, I always crossed at Port Huron, avoiding the Detroit crossing.

Proctor and Gamble, however, always had their own route they wanted us to take. They set up the border crossing for Buffalo, New York if we were south-bound. If we were coming north, they wanted us to cross at Fort Erie, Ontario. Changing the crossing to a more suitable border was usually just a matter of a phone call. One of the loads I got from Modesto was headed for Calgary. As usual, they set me up to clear at Fort Erie, a mere 2,100 miles east of where I actually was! I faxed the broker all the paperwork, indicating that I would be crossing at Coutts, Alberta, about three hours south of Calgary (and in the right location to enter Western Canada). I headed north towards Canada. After a few hours, I stopped to call the broker to confirm all the paperwork was received, legible, and the POE (Point Of Entry) was changed to Coutts. All was in order, except for one thing. Proctor and Gamble was insisting that the load be cleared at Fort Erie. The broker said that they had explained to Proctor and Gamble that crossing at Fort Erie would increase the shipping costs, adding at least a week to the transit time. Apparently, they didn't care. The load was to cross at Fort Erie. I called my dispatcher to let him know the change of plans. He had our CSR (Customer Service Representative) contact Proctor and Gamble to sort it out. Proctor and Gamble was adamant. Fort Erie is the border crossing. Okay, fine by me. More miles mean more pay for me. I ended up dropping the load at the yard in Toronto where they gave it to a team to get it to Calgary. This wasn't the last odd ball routing I had. For the most part, the shippers or receivers had their own reasons for sending us on a wild goose chase across North America.

Here's a good example of how the long-haul trucker just follows the paperwork. I call this the "A" versus "B" adventure. The fun started innocent enough with a run where I pulled a load of paper out of the Kenora, Ontario, paper mill, going to Salida, Colorado. This load was on a 48 foot trailer, which was remarkable, because by this time, almost all van trailers were 53 feet. It was also a very light trailer, allowing them to load more weight in it. As I got close to the receiving customer, I called for more specific directions. Following the guidance list was a set of strict instructions: "Take the left turn as wide as possible, then get into the centre of the alley between the buildings. When you come to the circle, drive to the white line on the building to your left, and stop. Do not proceed any further!" Okaaaaay. I followed the directions, soon discovering why they sent a 48 foot trailer. That last left turn would have been impossible with a 53 foot trailer. I had mere inches to spare with the 48 foot. As I straightened out and drove to the centre of the "road", I saw a loading door directly in front of me. "I have a bad feeling about this..." I pulled up to the line painted on the building, stopping as instructed. The receiver came out, looked at the paperwork and said: "Okay, we'll get you backed in right away, hang tight." I looked in the mirror, no loading dock. The only dock I could see was right in front of me. A few minutes later, the receiver returned, saying: "we'll get you spun around and then you can back in. Don't move." A few seconds later, I realized I was on a 75 foot long turntable! They turned the truck and trailer around 180 degrees. Once turned around, I opened the doors, then backed in. That was the first, and only, time I saw a loading facility like that.

My reload was the spat between company "A" and company "B". I was sent on a two-hour drive east to a company in Pueblo, Colorado, to pick up some machine parts going to Smith Falls, Ontario. At the time, they informed me that I would be reloading at the delivery destination. Bonus! I loaded the parts and then headed off to Smith Falls, which is between Kingston and Ottawa. I crossed the border at Sarnia, and continued east toward the customer. The receiver came outing checked the seal number on the trailer against the seal number on the bills. Everything matched. He broke the seal and took a look inside. Everything was as it was supposed to be. He signed my bills, kept his and gave me my copies. He then closed to doors, applied a new seal, and gave me new paperwork to sign. I signed for the load, then looked to see where it was going. It was heading back to Colorado – Denver this time! I looked at him, commenting; "I just loaded this in Pueblo! He said he was aware of that, but the customer in Denver refused to do business with "that crook" in Pueblo. As a result, he bought his parts from the place in Smith Falls. I just shook my head. Pueblo to Denver is 112 miles. Pueblo to Smith Falls to Denver is 3,535 miles. To avoid "that crook", he paid over 3,000 miles of extra freight costs, at about $5.00 a mile.

Other crazy runs have included hauling frozen chicken from Toronto to Detroit, unload it, where the receiver put new stickers on the boxes (changing "Product of Canada" to "Product of USA"), reloaded the cargo then returned to the exact place where I had picked it up. Another time, I delivered rolls of paper from Kenora to Wisconsin, where they applied new labels with the name of the local mill, reloaded it then took it to Ontario. Then there was the time I loaded powdered ice tea mix in Ontario, took it to Denver where they mixed it with water, labelled it "Product of the USA", sending me back to Ontario with the "new" cargo. There were more loads like that. Why do companies do this? Because they get federal tax breaks by showing a certain percentage of their product being imported and exported. One worth mentioning was a load of mangos from Mexico.

I loaded the mangos in Laredo, Texas, heading for Windsor, Ontario. For reasons I'm not aware of, these mangos were not allowed in the United States. This meant they had to be cross-docked from the Mexican trailer directly onto my trailer. The Mexican trucker wasn't even allowed to open his doors until I was backed in beside him, about six inches apart. Because the load was transiting the United States en route to Canada, it would be travelling on a Transportation and Exportation (T&E) bond. Additionally, because it was food, I was given a specific route to follow. Deviation from this precise path was forbidden, only allowing stops for food, fuel and repairs. Any other reason required written authorization from United States Customs as well as the United States Food and Drug Administration (FDA). The transfer from the Mexican trailer to mine was supervised by officials from US Customs and the FDA. These guys were extremely intense, only blinking one eye at a time. They were serious about these mangos not even touching the ground, never mind one staying in the country. When the loading was complete, I pulled ahead. They closed the doors, sealing them with the cable seals, as well as using anti-tamper tape across any sealed opening in the trailer. They then gave me all the paperwork releasing me to head back to Canada. Since the load was travelling under a T&E bond, I had to cross at Detroit-Windsor, as that's where the bond was sent. I stopped at the US Customs Office in Detroit to have the bond cancelled then carried on to Windsor, where the load was cleared with no problem. I took the load to the warehouse, where it was promptly unloaded. They removed the top off all the boxes, and replaced them with box tops that said "Product of Canada", then reloaded them on my trailer. The receiver then sent me on my way to the new destination – St. Louis, Missouri. Apparently, there was no import regulations on Canadian mangos. To the best of my knowledge, mangos aren't even grown in Canada.

Quite a few of the contracts we serviced, were "drop and hook" loads. This means that you take in an empty trailer, drop it, and grab a preloaded trailer, eliminating the wait time. In some places, the wait time to get loaded is minimal. At other places, especially meat plants, it can take upwards of three days. The biggest problem with drop and hook is that sometimes the trailer can be sitting for a while. I've experienced cases where I picked up a trailer that was sitting for nine months. Nine months of non-activity on a trailer can cause massive headaches, as they need to be safety inspected at least once a year.

On one occasion I went to a shipper in Wisconsin, dropped my empty, then hooked to a preloaded trailer. The first thing I always check is the safety sticker. If that's expired, there is no point even checking anything else, as it has to be safety certified by a licensed mechanic. At best, I could create a list of defects for the mechanic, but the mechanic has to check everything out anyway. In this instance, the safety on the preloaded trailer had expired three weeks previously. I called our shop to have them make the necessary arrangements to get the safety done at a local repair facility. Arrangements were made, and I headed to the repair shop. There were a few minor issues to be corrected, and I was soon on my way. I've been lucky, and only had this particular issue happen twice. The second expired safety was a major head scratcher. I was running the pikes at this particular time, and the trailer in question was a rental we had been using. I was taking it empty as the rear trailer to get it back to the rental company in Calgary. I hooked to the trailer, and started my pre-trip the same way I always do. Checking the safety inspection sticker. Sure enough, it had expired. Not only had it expired, the sticker showed it had expired more than 4 years ago! Impossible! Someone would have noticed it by now... I pulled the inspection certificate that stays with the trailer, and had a look. If the certificate was valid, no big problem. Big problem. The date on the certificate matched the date on the sticker. More than 4 years old. The owner of the trailer had a local yard near the terminal, so they had me drop it there for the inspection. Why we didn't just return the trailer to the local yard was beyond me, but those decisions aren't my call. To this day, it blows my mind how a trailer with an expired safety slipped through the cracks for over 4 years.

However, one of the other drop-and-hook issues I had to deal with was a bit more involved.

I had delivered a load of meat in North Carolina, as I recall. After unloading meat, you have to get the trailer washed out. Meat, especially chicken, as well as hanging beef or pork, makes a huge mess in the trailer. It is up to the driver to get the trailer washed before moving on to the next job, which I then did. In this case, once that task was completed, I was to head to the next job with orders to drop the (now clean) empty unit and grab a preloaded trailer. For the sake of the story, I'll call them "ABC Foods". I checked in with ABC's security, dropped the empty, grabbed the loaded trailer, made sure it was good to go (safety, weights, all that good stuff) and headed on my way. I never gave the empty I dropped another thought. About two months later, one of the planners sent me a message, asking why I had dropped a dirty trailer at ABC Foods. At first, I had no idea what he was talking about, as I hadn't been too ABC Foods in quite a while. You simple can't remember every place you go to. After some back and forth, I then remembered dropping the empty at ABC Foods. I told our planner that I had washed it out. It was clean when I left it, reminding him that I had previously delivered a meat load with that trailer. He did some digging, confirming what I said. He told me that it was now up to ABC to clean the trailer, as there were pea pods all over the floor. We determined that they had used our trailer to move their pea pods from wherever to the plant, then claimed we had dropped a dirty trailer. To the best of my knowledge, we never hauled their loads again. It was the one and only time I was ever there.

One place I delivered to in Philadelphia, cemented my reason of calling for directions. I followed the directions perfectly, and all was well. As I was being unloaded, I heard a metallic screeching noise just down the street. This driver didn't call for directions. He looked at a map, saw he could exit the interstate, turn left and go two blocks to the receiver. Problem was, there is ten-foot bridge between the interstate and the loading dock that wasn't listed on the map, and he hit it.

Another of my regular drops was Agar Supply, in Taunton, Massachusetts. I loved delivering there. Lots of safe overnight parking in their 1,500 foot long, 30 foot wide driveway, accessible at any time night or day. The only stipulation occurs at three in the morning. The receiver sends someone out to the front of the line to start collecting the waybills. If you're not up, dressed, and have the bills ready, they'll pass you by. After they've collected all the bills from everyone who is awake, you'll get a call on the CB where they tell you what door to back into. After about two hours, once the first wave of trucks has completed emptying their loads using the on-site lumpers, they'll call the next wave. Once the first round of trucks who had their bills ready are finished, they'll walk the line for the next series of trucks. You learn very fast to get there early, so you're close to the gate, being sure set an alarm to make sure you're up when they start collecting bills. Otherwise, it can be a long day.

Boston and the surrounding area was, and still is, one of my favourite places to deliver. I used to find myself in the Mass Market quite often. I believe it has changed locations from when I was delivering there. Back then, getting in and out was a massive challenge, due to the (at the time) largest construction project in the world. The Big Dig. The Big Dig involved moving Interstate 93 underground, extending Interstate 90 through to Boston's airport, and building cloverleaf interchanges, all of it under-ground, and in the heart of Boston, while preserving the elevated Interstate

93. Once the Big Dig was completed, the elevated I-93 was dismantled. It was quite an undertaking, with actual construction taking sixteen years, and costing just over $8 billion. As a result of the construction, roads would disappear and reappear at various times, and some would go from one-way west bound to one-way east bound over night. Delivering to the market was a dream. Getting to the market was a nightmare. Sometimes it was a direct route from the interstate to the market, other times it seems like I was detouring through California to get there.

Paper loads, as I've mentioned, were a common way to start a trip. The paper mill was about 120 miles so not too many empty miles. From there, it was always a crap shoot where the paper was going. It could be as close as Minneapolis, (430 miles) or Los Angeles, CA (2100 miles). You just never really knew. Some places we would go to on a fairly regular basis; others were a one off. Occasionally, there would be as many as five loads going to the same place at once. One of these types REALLY stuck out in my memory, for all the wrong reasons. The name of the company escapes me, but the city, and the directions I'll remember for three or four days after my funeral. It was a newsprint warehouse in Pitston, PA, just outside of Wilke-Barre. Getting to the address was a challenge itself, as the area was not designed and built for highway trucks and 53 foot trailers. Upon arrival, I looked at the entrance gate, and the general set up of the yard, and did some quick mental calculations: No way in hell I was getting this truck and trailer in that gate, and even if I did, not a chance of getting backed into the door. So I parked on the road (no shoulder at all) and called them. I explained the situation, and they sent someone out to have a look. The employee and I hummed and hawed for a while, measured this and that, and he finally came to the conclusion that I wasn't going to make it into the yard, not even if I drove past the gate, and backed in. There just wasn't enough room. I ended up dropping the trailer on the road, and they used their shunt truck (a very short, highly maneuverable truck) to get the trailer in through the gate, and backed into a door. Even with the shunt truck (maybe six feet long), he had a real hard time getting that trailer in, and then back out of the yard. And he had two other trailers to put in that day.

One Friday, I had delivered a paper load to Shakopee, MN, and I was patiently waiting a reload at the terminal. About noon, the reload came over my satellite. I was to load frozen bread dough in Chanhassen MN, at 10 pm, going to a suburb of Vancouver, BC for 6 am Monday morning., Roughly 1,800 miles in 2 days. When I arrived at the shipper, I was told I'd have to move a trailer from their loading dock, so I could back in. Not gonna happen. I'm not shunting a customer's trailers around. First and foremost, if anything happens to the trailer, I'm responsible, and secondly, if the next driver notices anything wrong with the trailer I moved, I'm responsible. They found someone to move the trailer, and I got backed in. The load was shipped on the floor. No pallets at all, which means, hand bombing in Vancouver, after having to knock off roughly three days of driving in two days. Not impressed, but seeing as it's now almost midnight, there's no one in authority at the home terminal to make any decisions regarding lumpers in BC to unload the trailer. I finally got away at about 12:30 am Saturday, and made it as far as Fargo, ND, and crashed for the night. When I got up, I let dispatch know what the situation was. I'd have the load there on time, but under no circumstances was I going to hand bomb over 40,000 lbs of frozen bread dough. So they either had to make arrangements to have people there to unload it, or I could drop it in the yard until they could make arrangements to have it unloaded. The company found an employment service to do the unloading, but I was instructed to help. By help, I was told to ensure it was unloaded and stacked properly. I really feel sorry for these people who sign up for temporary employment services. They get minimum wage, and never know what kind of work they'll get from day to day. Most times, it's hard, dirty work that no one else wants to do. Hand bombing definitely falls into that category. It can be back breaking, heavy work. The drive itself was almost a killer. As it was, I ended up starting at two am in Ellensburg WA to make it to Vancouver for six am. Using today's elogs, I'd have very hard pressed to have made it on time.

KEEPING IT LEGAL

RULES, REGULATIONS, AND TRUCK DRIVING

Long-haul drivers have to know more than how to physically drive a truck, how to make sure you're properly loaded and unloaded, and how to find your way from point A to point B. Both the Canadian and American governments have rules and regulations we have to follow. Let's look at a couple we encounter on a daily basis: the log book, and the weigh scales.

I've seen a few drivers get caught using falsified log book, and to me, it never really seemed worth it to run illegal. If you get caught, the fines will exceed any extra money you've made. Why push yourself to the edge of making stupid decisions? I know of one driver (who shall remain nameless) that was stopped at a scale for an American state DOT inspection. He passed with flying colours, only to forget his log book at the scale house. The scale called a state trooper to pick up the log book, chase the driver down, then return his logbook to him. The trooper had a sense of humour, so when he pulled the truck over, he tucked the log book under his jacket, asking the guy for his log book, expecting to see the guy panic a bit. Instead, the driver reached down, handing over a log book. The trooper then produced the one he had forgotten at the scale. The driver was fined for falsifying his log book, then escorted to a safe parking spot where he was placed out of service (parked) for a minimum of eight hours. Driving while being placed out of service is a fine you do NOT want. In most cases, it will cost you your job.

Other than fudging my logs by less than 30 minutes to get to where I needed to be, I almost always ran a legal log book. It wasn't always easy. Sometimes the circumstances I fell into called for a bit of creativity. On one occasion, long in the past, (statute of limitations have long since passed) I left Toronto heading west one with an LTL load. My plan, as usual, was to get to the King City Service Plaza on the northern edge of Toronto to catch some sleep before I got an early morning start. This way I could avoid the Toronto rush hour. As I pulled in, my brother-in-law Dave, who had left the wood chip run to drive for a Thunder Bay-based freight company, was just walking back to his truck. We chatted a few minutes where he said he was going to try to cover a few hours on the road. I wasn't all that tired, so I said I'd run with him for a while. Off we went, chatting about this, that and every other thing we could think of. Before either of us knew it, we were in Thunder Bay. 871 miles. Oops! Under Canadian regulations, you're allowed 13 hours of drive time before taking an 8 hour (at the time) break, either off duty, or in the sleeper. Toronto to Thunder Bay is about 16 hours. Dave went to his yard, while I decided to stop at the Dawson Road truck stop (long since closed) for some rest. As I pulled in, another one of our trucks was fuelling up. I parked, and went over to chat with the driver. He had just started driving in Pass Lake 45 miles behind us. He was headed to Winnipeg as well. I was still pumped, so I decided I'd run with him to Ignace, about 3 hours up the road. Again, chatting about this, that and whatever. Next thing I know, we're in the Winnipeg yard. Toronto to Winnipeg at that time, with a 55 mph governed truck required between 22 and 24 hours of driving. I had just done it basically non-stop. In today's trucking, there's no way you could get away with it. Back then (late 1990's), electronic logs hadn't even been considered yet. Satellite dispatching was still a new thing, and not every truck had them. With the old paper logs, however, you could "creatively" get from point A to point B. Part of the problem was, too many companies would coerce drivers to run creative logs, which caused more than a few bad accidents. When I talked to my dispatcher the next morning, he thanked me, then told me never to do it again. I found out later I had beaten a team truck from Toronto to Winnipeg. I was going home for a few days, but my log book was a day behind me. Only 2 or 3 times did I toss the log book out the window: this Toronto to Winnipeg one-shot run, and another time as a favour.

On the second occasion, a Saturday, I had driven into Winnipeg from Sauk Centre, Minnesota (about a 6 hour drive). I went home for some time off. About four that afternoon I got a call from a "higher up" who shall remain nameless. He said he knew it would be impossible to run this load legal and he wouldn't force me, but could I please take this load that the planner had missed? It had to arrive in Idaho Falls, Idaho, 1,151 miles away by two a.m. Monday. The load had to cross the border at Pembina, North Dakota, as it was the only 24 hour port of entry close to Winnipeg. I had four hours left to drive that day. Ten hours was the maximum driving time in the United States at that time. It's now up to 11 hours. Meeting the client's deadline was, therefore, legally impossible.

Nonetheless, I agreed to make the run, heading to the yard. Before I left, I grabbed a few spare log books for the trip, as my legal log book would be taking a "vacation". I cleared customs, reaching Fargo, North Dakota, at about ten that night. This was the driving limit of my official logbook. I updated it to that point, putting it in a drawer. Won't be needing that for a few days. I went to bed for a couple of hours, waking up at three o'clock Sunday morning feeling refreshed. I pulled out an unused log book, filled in what needed to be filled in, then headed for the highway. Fargo to Idaho Falls is 949 miles. With a top speed of 55 mph, you'll do good to average out at 45 mph, meaning I was looking at about 20 hours of driving, plus about three hours to eat, fuel, and take care of "business". With the time zone change, I had 24 hours to make the delivery. I kept a close watch on the time. When I hit the 10 hour limit, I noted the location, and mileage on a note pad.

I pulled into Billings Montana to fuel, starting another log book, and "back logged" to show that I had arrived in Billings twelve hours earlier, giving me my required minimum ten hours off, and away I went again. Billings to Idaho Falls is 349 miles, but most of it is two lane highway, rather hilly, cutting through a portion of Yellowstone National Park, which has a reduced speed limit. Here the risk of wildlife collisions is pretty high. Driving cautiously meant it took me a good eight hours to get to Idaho Falls. I found the customer, and arrived 1:30 am. The crew showed up, and unloaded me before I drove a few miles to a truck stop to crawl into bed. I woke up about noon, calling my dispatcher, who had no clue what had transpired over the weekend. As I filled him in, I could hear him typing away. He told me they had me on a load of French fries for Toronto, loading at three that afternoon in Nampa, Idaho, 298 miles away, or six hours driving. Before I could say anything, he remarked "Well, THAT ain't gonna happen!" I explained the log book situation. He asked when my official book would catch up with me. I told him it would be about noon Wednesday before it showed up. He told me to make sure I had a good parking spot, then call him on Thursday as I would need my eight hours off once my book "arrived". I ended up loading the fries Thursday afternoon.

Another rules and regulation story began at the scale on a rainy Highway 11, in Cochrane, Ontario. Everyone was being pulled in for a log book inspection. All the truckers knew about it ahead of time, as every driver was talking about it on the CB. There was really no excuse for getting caught. But, inevitably, some people were caught. Some simply weren't listening to the radio, while others hoped to beat the odds that they wouldn't be selected for an inspection. One driver thought he'd get away with it by throwing the incriminating pages out the window so that the inspector couldn't find them. Great plan! But it didn't work. I was going through my log book inspection as he pulled in. I wasn't paying much attention, until I heard the other inspector ask him: "No, your other book." The driver innocently asked: "What other book?". The inspector stepped off the running board, and peeled five or six pages that had gotten stuck on the side of his trailer, pasted there by the rain. He held them up and said; "This book." Busted!

Scales can be fascinating places. I've had a few interesting experiences at them. Once during a Level 1 inspection (the everything gets checked but your prostate type), the inspector was under the trailer inspecting the brakes for wear, and push rod travel. If the travel is too great, it means your brakes are out of adjustment. You'll be just sitting there until you get them adjusted. These days almost all trucks and trailers have automatic slack adjusters. Manual adjusting is basically a thing of the past, but the automatic adjusters can still malfunction. As soon as the inspector wheeled himself under the trailer, he was back out and walking to the cab. He said there was an issue that he wasn't sure what to do about as he couldn't measure the push rod travel. I was as confused as he was, so I got out to have a look. As soon as I saw the brakes, I knew what the issue was. I smiled, Chuckling, I told him this trailer was equipped with disc brakes. There is no way to measure push rod travel, as they don't have push rods. He was uncertain how to inspect them. He called his supervisor, who showed up, had a look, and scratched his head. They even called a local tractor trailer mechanic to come down and help. He looked and he scratched his head. None of them had ever seen disc brakes on a semi. They eventually called the brake manufacturer, who faxed them a technical data sheet on the disc brake system, confirming that all they could really do was to measure the thickness and condition of the discs and the pads. No other measurable parts existed within the system. Why disc brakes haven't caught on in North America is a mystery to me.

For a number of years, I was running exclusively to the eastern seaboard, anywhere from Maine to Washington DC-Virginia areas. Along I-80, just as you enter New Jersey, there is a DOT scale that is seldom open. In the years I ran that way, I only saw it open twice. The first time across was a non-issue. The second time? It got exciting. I was in a line of about ten trucks crossing the scale. I must have hit a piece of metal or something, because as soon as the steering tire hit the scale, it blew. Took the treads right off, destroying the casing. I was down to the rim on the scale. The scale master hit the floor, coming up with his gun drawn. He must have thought he'd been shot at. Once he realized what had actually happened, he calmed down, but the scale was effectively closed for about an hour until a tire shop came out and replaced the tire. All the trucks behind me were happy. I'm sure some were overweight. More on my eastern seaboard years later.

Crossing into Minnesota from Wisconsin on I-94, is the dreaded St Croix scale. This inspectors at this one had a reputation for being sticklers about anything and everything, even though I've never had any problems there. Once, after another Level 1 inspection, we were just doing up all the paperwork, getting everything put back in the binder, when a tanker rolled across the scale about 1,000 lbs overweight. He was given the "report" light. He parked, bringing his paperwork inside. He was informed about the weight issue and was told he would have to get the excess weight removed. He looked at the scale master incredulously, stating: "It's a bulk liquid tanker!" No matter, he was told again to have some of the weight taken off. He walked out shaking his head, I assumed to call his company and make arrangements. I was just getting ready to walk out to my truck, when I heard the tank driver yell: "Let me know when it's (expletive) legal!" He cracked open the valve, dumping peach syrup on the scale. I couldn't believe what I was seeing! I quickly exited the scale, getting back on the highway. I have no idea what happened to the driver, or how big that fine was, but the scale was closed for a few months while they cleaned up the mess. They also decided to repave the approach and exit to the scale while they had it out of the ground. Unfortunately, they made a mistake in the measuring process. When they replaced the scale, it rested on the new concrete approach and exit. Out it came, while they fixed that problem.

Most of the Scale Masters are pretty decent and fair people, but there's always one or two that just seem to make it their mission to split hairs, or trying to pull some unsavoury acts. I've dealt with two. One in British Columbia, and one in Ontario. Sometime in the late 1990s, I was leaving Toronto with a load of LTL, headed for Winnipeg. At this time, I was still running Highway 11 across northern Ontario. The province had started upgrading some scales to what we called "super-coops". There had been a series of accidents caused by wheels coming off trucks at highway speeds with some serious injuries as well as a couple of deaths. The Ontario government decided to crack down on "killer trucks". In reality, it was a few trucks from less than reputable companies causing the incidents, but we were all painted with the same brush.

On the occasion I'm remembering, I approached the northbound North Bay super-coop where I wasn't at all surprised to see the lights flashing, indicating it was open. I knew my weights were legal with all documentation was up to date meaning that both the truck and trailer were fit to be on the road. I do a proper vehicle inspection every morning, so I know the truck and trailer are safe to operate before I start driving. Of course, the truck has the company name prominently displayed, but there's nothing on the sides of the trailer. I crossed the scale, receiving the red "report" light. I parked in the designated area, gathering up all the necessary documents (truck registration, log book, bills of lading). As soon as I exited the truck, the Scale Master was right there.

He said he was going to perform a Level 1 inspection. I shrugged replying "fine," or something to that effect. Before he even looked at the paperwork, he was on his creeper, rolling himself under the trailer to check the brakes, frame, slider assembly, slider locking pins, etc. After a few minutes he came out, announcing that the trailer was being placed out of service for numerous safety violations. According to him, the brakes were worn down too far as well as being seriously out of adjustment, there was too much corrosion on the frame, the air tanks were leaking, the valves to drain the air tanks of moisture were rusted shut, and on and on. The total cost of the fines was somewhere around the $10,000 mark. I knew he was trying to pull a fast one. Unbeknownst to him, I had a major ace in my hand. As he was writing the numerous tickets, I asked him to call his supervisor, because I didn't agree with his determination. Without looking up, he told me the supervisor wasn't necessary. I asked again, and he refused again. I said that if he didn't call the supervisor, I would call him. He refused to give me the number, so I found the number on the wall then made the call, stating I believed I was being wrongly ticketed for non-existent violations. About fifteen minutes later, the supervisor showed up. The Scale Master, immediately and with some anger, stated that he had performed a full Level 1, and found so many violations, that he didn't even bother completing the inspection on the truck, or on myself. The supervisor looked at me, stating that he had to agree with his scale operator. I looked at the pair, replying: "I find it hard to believe you found all this wrong with a brand-new trailer." The Scale Master's face went white. I pointed out the manufacturer's plate showing the manufacture date. The trailer was only three weeks old. All the tickets were nullified. I never saw that scale operator again.

The other Scale Master incident was at the east bound scale in Kamloops, British Columbia. Again, I was given the "report" light. This time I was told that there weren't enough straps on the load of plastic pipe on the trailer. Without getting into too much detail regarding load securement on a flat bed, these pipes were 18 long. The rule is, two straps for the first 10 feet, and one strap for every 10 feet there after. Therefore, a length of 18 feet required a minimum of three straps. I had five straps. He wrote me a ticket for only having two straps (insecure load). I had planned to fight the ticket, but really, what chance did I have? I could get a picture, however all he then had to say was I added the straps, then took the picture. After I was released, I heard talk on the CB that this Scale Master had written a few bogus tickets, including one to a driver who "exceeded 40 mph while crossing the scale". I felt a bit better that I hadn't been singled out, but it still annoyed me quite a bit.

Before the electronic logbook (elog or e-log) came along, some drivers would routinely ignore the Hours-of-Service Regulations (HOS), doing as they pleased while keeping an official, current log available for inspection. As you may imagine, this led to some interesting issues if a driver wasn't careful. While I was never caught with an illegal log, mainly because I chose not to run one (except in very rare cases), I have seen the repercussions from those who decided to ignore the rules. Once, when I was in Bloomington-Normal, Illinois, there was a very disheveled driver moaning and groaning around the parking lot about the scale just outside of town being open. He hadn't touched his log book in 14 days! The law required that your log book was current up to your last change of duty status. I was shocked, to say the least. I can't imagine what kind of condition he was in to be driving, nor could I imagine the company he was working for that would allow (or require) this! I suggested he grab his book, logging enough legal miles with enough time to get himself home, then show off-duty at home. To allow him to carry on he would need to back log from home to Bloomington-Normal. I don't know what he did, as I left on my merry way, having no issues at the scale house when they checked my log book.

My ex-wife used to work in the company's safety department, auditing drivers logs, making sure everyone was running legal. Or rather, logging legal. On one trip she ran with me, they tried getting me to run slightly illegal. We left Winnipeg, headed to the Maritimes (Canada's east coast). I don't recall exactly where, but it was somewhere around Halifax. After delivering, we were sent to Charlottetown, Prince Edward Island, to reload smoked fish for Montreal. The trailer we had (this becomes important later) was a triaxle reefer, with a huge fuel tank. These trailers were originally ordered to be loaded with meat in Alberta, then placed on the train to go to Toronto or Montreal, hence the huge (120 gallon) fuel tanks, and had three axles, to carry maximum weight. The railroads in Canada have since stopped taking road trailers, as they can't stack them two high as they can with rail containers. We headed out to Charlottetown to load the smoked fish. Once we were loaded, dispatch told me the load was to deliver in Montreal the next day (Tuesday) at eight am. I told him there was no way in hell I was going to make Montreal in about 18 hours. I had already driven from Halifax to Charlottetown that day, and in Canada we are allowed 13 hours of driving. The dispatcher told me to tell the shipper we were a team truck (two drivers). I replied: "I can tell him I'm Alexander The Great, this load still isn't going to be there for eight a.m.!" He told me to do the best I could. My wife, the log auditor, was livid, to say the least. Nonetheless, off we went with the impossible-timeframe load. This is what's known in the industry as "70 mile an hour dispatch in a 55 mile an hour truck". Unfortunately, it still happens to this day. We got to the receiver at about two in the afternoon where I was told they only receive PEI smoked fish at eight in the morning on Tuesdays. I replied: "Okay, I guess the terminal will swing the load into a storage reefer, and bring it by in a week." The receiver said they had better not, because if the seal on the trailer was broken, the load will be rejected. That trailer, with its 120-gallon fuel tank had to sit in Montreal, not being used for a whole week. Of course, the dispatcher wasn't too happy with me, but I couldn't have cared less. I'm not tossing the rules out the window because someone tells me I have to. Besides, I had the log auditor with me. She made sure the terminal manger heard about the incident, which, of course, didn't help my working relationship with the dispatcher. Again, I couldn't have cared less.

Many of my "legal" headaches had a California connection. The final California encounter was from a DOT agent splitting hairs. I was at the Mount Shasta scale off Interstate 5 in northern California. Weights and axle spacing were legal, but, again, I got the report light. Parked around the back, collected all the paper work, then walked in. The DOT official asked if I knew why he pulled me in. I said "No, I have no idea. My weights and axle spacings are legal." He confirmed this, and asked me what I was doing when I crossed the scale. I was totally confused, and replied: "About five mph?". He asked me what I had in my hand as I drove over the scale. What? I thought for a minute, and all I could think of was a cigarette. I said: "A cigarette?" Yup. That's it. $320 ticket for smoking in the workplace. Apparently, in California, you can't smoke in the cab of the truck, you can only smoke in the bunk.

The cab is considered your work place, and the bunk (for the purposes of trucking) is considered your "home". As was our practice, I handed the ticket to the HR department when I returned home. Here is where it got interesting. They paid for the ticket which would then be deducted from my pay cheque. Except, this time it was never taken out of my pay. I found out later, through the grapevine, that the company had sent in a cheque to pay the fine. California returned the payment with a letter saying something to the effect of: "We gave the driver the ticket, not the company, therefore it's on the driver, not the company to pay it." To the best of my knowledge, that ticket was never paid. I firmly believe that not all police and DOT officers are corrupt. Far from it. In all my years of driving, I've only come across four or five bad ones. The rest have been true professionals.

Axle spacing is one area where a lot of drivers, especially rookies, get violations. Some places, especially those that have "drop and hook" loading, you need to slide the axles all the way back when you drop them, to reduce "dock walk". Dock walk is an issue that plagues conventionally equipped steel spring trailers. As the loaded forklift enters the trailer, the springs will compress, pushing the rear of the trailer down a small amount, this reduces the weight on the landing gear, which will allow the trailer to creep forward a bit. After seven or eight trips with the forklift, the trailer could have moved forward enough that the loading dock plate is no longer in the trailer. With the axles all the way back, dock walk is almost eliminated. When you pick up a trailer with the axles all the way back, you have to slide them forward to legalize your axle weights and spacing. Depending on the slider mechanism, this can become tricky. And dangerous. I was assisting a fellow driver adjusting his axles on a trailer equipped with an old, almost ancient slider system. Pull the handle, and the locking pins release. Unless there's pressure on any one of the four locking pins. Then, you have to try and position the slider exactly to release the pressure from all four pins, or none of them will release. Future versions had springs, so you could pull the handle, and compress the springs, then gently rock the trailer back and forth, and the pins would release. So I was using my pin puller to reach under the trailer, and pulling on the release handle, while he gently rocked the trailer back and forth. It wasn't going very well, so I really put my back and legs into it. Finally, they released. I landed on my butt, and slid across the snow covered parking lot, and ended up underneath another trailer. The driver I was helping came running to make sure I was okay (I was, and was laughing my ass off). He said he was watching me in the mirror, and one second I was there, the next I was gone. I can only imagine that visual.

One day, about 3 am, I was getting my turnpikes ready to head to Grenfell, and I had to slide the axles. This trailer wasn't equipped with a spring assist slider, and rather than a handle that pulled straight out, it was a lever you had to pull up. So you're trying to lift, but it's not a comfortable position, as the axle release handle is about three ft in front of you, under the trailer. I checked, and it looked like there was no pressure on any of the pins, so I grabbed the handle, and lifted. What came next, felt like a red hot railroad spike being driven into my lower back. I limped back to the truck, hauled myself into the cab, and tried to release the parking brake, to drive to the office. The pain was so bad, with my foot on the brake pedal, I couldn't lean forward to release the parking brake. I managed to get the truck in gear, but shifting wasn't gonna happen. I crept through the yard at idle speed in fourth gear. A toddler just learning to walk could've out paced me. When I got to the office, I left the truck in gear, and shut down the engine. Then I could lean forward to apply the parking brake, then lean back to put the truck in neutral. I went in to report to the night staff, and he called an ambulance to get me to the hospital. As I had suspected, it was a slipped disk in my lower back. They pumped me full of the "good stuff", gave me three prescriptions for powerful pain meds, called my wife, and sent me home. At the time, I drove a GMC Jimmy 4X4. Lots of ground clearance. She drove a Saturn, with next to no ground clearance. My Jimmy was at the yard, so she came with the Saturn. I limped/shuffled to the car, and she expressed concern about me getting in and out of the car. I said getting in would be easy, as I had gravity on my side. Getting out may be a challenge. By the time we got home, the "good stuff" had taken hold. Getting out wasn't too bad, but my driving was over for about six months. If you've never had a slipped disc in your back, do whatever you can to avoid that. The pain is excruciating and debilitating. Getting out of bed in the morning was a 25 minute adventure. I eventually returned to work, but was VERY careful when sliding axles from then on.

Encountering Smokey
Long Haul Drivers and the "Bear"

Most encounters between long haul truckers and law enforcement don't follow the still-popular movie, Smokey and the Bandit. While we frequently encounter police as we do our job, for the most part, we have a good relationship.

In my long list of not-so-happy California encounters, only one involved law enforcement. This, however, sealed the deal. I don't do California anymore, unless I have to transit through the Los Angeles airport. The event I'm going to recount involved a bogus speeding ticket. There I was, cruising along at 55 mph climbing a small hill. Everyone else: trucks, buses, cars, motorcycles were flying past me like I was in reverse. That's when I got pulled over.

The California Highway Patrol officer wrote me up for doing 70 mph in 55 mph. At the time, 55 mph was the truck speed limit on California highways. In California, however, the amount of the fine was not listed on the ticket. They mail the amount of the ticket to you later. I think I know why. The fine – as I later found out - was $271.00! Had the amount been on the ticket, I'm sure some people would pull out a gun and shoot them! As it was then (and still is) our company policy, I turned the ticket in to our safety department. They pay the ticket, then deduct it from your next pay. That way they know the ticket was paid meaning there's no chance it will return to bite them in the butt since all moving violations affect the carrier as well as the driver. As to why I got the ticket, while no one else who was speeding much faster than I did not receive one? Simple. Giving a ticket to a driver with an out-of-state license plate is a good revenue source. It would have cost me far more than $271 to fight it. Even if I did, the chances of winning in court would be slim to none. In today's world, when most trucks are equipped with dash cams, at least you have something to back up your version of events, but there's still no guarantee you'll be successful.

WE GOT A CONVOY
LET THEM TRUCKERS ROLL!

Driving in a convoy is about as old the long-haul trucking trade. Travelling in a group gives the solitary driver some company along with a sense of community as they travel across the continent. In the case of trouble, there's always someone to, hopefully, lend a hand. The idea that truckers do this to save fuel is just a myth. Drafting behind a truck just endangers truckers, as it does civilian drivers who think they are saving gas. This doesn't help their trucks run any better or faster.

In reality, convoys in the past served a real purpose. Before trucks were satellite equipped, and long before cell phones, satellite radio, music streaming services and the like, drivers travelled in convoys so there was some distraction from the boredom, and there was some assistance if something broke down. Back then, if you had a tire go flat, you were the one changing it, and pretty much all road repairs were done by the driver (and the rest of the convoy) on the side of the road. These days, drivers just send a satellite message, or call the repair shop on a cell phone. With all the electronics on trucks these days, most issues are resolved with a computer.

Sometimes I'll join a convoy, but most times I just prefer to travel alone. Of course, there's always a few stories that come out of convoy-travel. The first that comes to mind is about the westbound LTL loads from Toronto and Montreal. They tended to leave at about the same time meaning that it wasn't uncommon to have five or six trucks travelling down Highway 11 all arrive in the North Bay area at about the same time. Some of the drivers would form small convoys, others would prefer to venture on their own. One evening, I left Toronto, once again stopping for the night at the King City Service Plaza to avoid the morning rush. As I was preparing to leave, five or six other company trucks pulled in. I chatted with them for a few minutes, discovering they were just going to use the restrooms, grab coffee, then head for the highway. I decided to run with them, as it helps pass the time when you have someone to talk to. After everyone finished up at the truck stop, we started out. As a rule, when travelling in a convoy, the slowest or heaviest truck leads the way, thereby setting the pace. I was somewhere in back. I didn't stay with this convoy very long. Every place we reached that was big enough to park, they all pulled in for coffee. Not coffee to go. The whole convoy would park, go in, sit down, and drink their coffee, then carry on. I lasted to the second stop, then just carried on alone. I could never understand why drivers would do this. I call them "truck-stop racers". Racing from one truck stop to the next. Waste of time, to my way of thinking.

Doing Some Heavy Lifting

Loading and Unloading

Truck drivers have a vital role in the proper loading and unloading of their trucks. They are responsible for the load on the road. Some loads can easily become unstable, such as timber, pipe, and other materials. Serious incidents have happened when unstable freight has fallen from a flatbed truck, striking the driver. There are records of drivers being fatally injured or having a limb amputated in accidents of these types. It is, therefore, important that a driver be familiar with the load as well as the loading and unloading process even if someone else is doing the actual heavy lifting.

Most times, loading and unloading a trailer is done by fork lift, but not always. In my years, I've been loaded as well as unloaded by hand, pneumatic tube (objects blown into the trailer), fork lift, clamp truck, gravity, and tow truck, amongst others. Scrap metal is usually bulk loaded. To unload, they just slide the axles all the way back, and use a modified truck to hook up to the trailer. Then, using a hydraulic cylinder on the truck, the front of the trailer is raised 15 or 20 feet in the air, where gravity takes over to empty it. In the case of paper rolls, they usually use a clamp truck (similar to a forklift, but with special attachment for handling paper rolls), but again, not always. I've been to places that use an old I-beam, with an electric winch to pick up rolls of newsprint, then they man-handle the rolls, while suspended, back into the building, and lower them into the basement with the winch. Other places just roll them out of the trailer, man-handling them to a storage area. There are three ways to load paper rolls. Shotgun (flat end front to back) suicide position (flat end side to side), and "eye to the sky" (flat end on the floor). Of the three, eye to the sky is the most common, followed by suicide.

One load I had going to Petosky, Michigan from Winnipeg, was eight commercial beer kettles. They were six feet across, and about eight feet tall, including the stand. This was also the only Cash-on-Delivery (C.O.D.) load I ever had. I called the customer for directions, letting him know when I would arrive. Upon arrival, I first made sure to get a certified cheque from the receiver to cover the cost of the delivery from Winnipeg to Petosky. Once the cheque was safely put away, he had me move into position on the street, then open the doors. Okay, now what? There was no way you could unload the kettles by hand. This was an interesting off-load to watch. The brewery used a tow truck along with a fabric strap to pull the kettles, one at a time, to the rear of the trailer. Next, they wrapped the strap through the kettle legs, picking it up. The tow truck driver then drove ahead very slowly, backed onto the sidewalk, extended the boom though a hole they had made into the brewery by removing a floor to ceiling window. Each kettle was lowered into the basement, where eight guys muscled them into position. The whole process took all day. To this day, I have never again been unloaded by a tow truck.

These days, I'm pulling flat decks, and I've seen some even more unusual, and unexpected unload methods. As with all aspects of trucking, we're pretty much at the mercy of others to get us good, honest, accurate information. And when that fails, it can either be a disaster, compete mayhem, or side splitting hilarity.

There are a few loads that travel by deck that I try to avoid. Structural steel being top of the list. They're not too bad to secure, but almost all of them require tarpping, which is where the "fun" begins. All sharp corners needs to have carpeting, or a similar material taped over them, so they won't cut through the tarps. This endeavour alone can take upwards of six hours, while you crawl around on hands and knees 10 to 13 feet off the ground. Yes, the law says that's a major no-no, but some shippers just don't seem to care, and some trucking companies don't either. Thankfully, the company I work for DOES care, and they'll work with the shipper to get everything done legally and safely. Once all the sharp corners are covered, you can start strapping the load down. I won't go into strapping specifics, as that could take another book altogether. Then you get to tarp. If you're extremely lucky, they have a tarp station. You roll the tarps out beside the trailer, attach the tarps to a crane, which lifts them up, spreads them across the trailer, and down the other side. Then you just have to tuck the excess tarp underneath, and secure the tarp with bungee cords. To tarp a full trailer load this way takes between an hour and an hour and a half if you're doing it by yourself. Of course, having someone help cuts the time more than in half.

Recently, I had a structural steel load going to a very small town in Idaho. I called for directions, as the address was an open field (according to Google Maps). The directions I got were "The intersection of this highway, and that highway". Okay, job site delivery (not uncommon with deck loads). So I headed off towards the intersection I was given. Upon arrival, I saw there was a temporary driveway through a ditch. Just gravel dumped to level the ditch, but it was at the exact intersection I was given. Rather than pull right in, I waited until someone showed up to confirm I was at the correct place. As I said, there was a driveway, but nothing else I could see from the road, save for a huge pile of rocks and dirt. A gentleman showed up about five minutes later, looked at my paperwork, and confirmed I was in the right place. He told me to pull in, make a big U-Turn around the pile of rubble, and I could begin untarping, as the crew would be arriving soon, and they'd help with the untarping and unstrapping. I maneuvered into the proper position, and began removing the bungee cords. About ten minutes later, I had ten or twelve gentlemen helping remove bungee cords, and helping me pull the tarps off, and get then folded and rolled up. While one group was folding and rolling tarps, another was going around removing, and rolling up the straps, and another couple of gents were collecting and securing all my bungee cords. To do it all by myself would have taken two or three hours. This time, it was all done (straps off, rolled up and put away, bungees off, tied in bunches of 25, and put away, all three tarps off, folded, rolled and put away) in about 20 minutes. I profusely thanked the crew for their help, but instead of starting to work at the job site, they all walked to the road and drove off. Turns out, my helpers weren't the crew working the site. They were just Joe Average local citizens who were driving by, and decided to stop and help! When I learned this, I just stood there for a few moments, too stunned to actually believe what I was hearing. Recalling the story now, it still brings a smile to my face, and a sense of disbelief that that had actually happened.

ROAD SIDE ASSISTANCE
TOWS, BREAKDOWNS, AND MECHANICAL ADVENTURES

Long-haul truckers (and their trucks) spend the majority of the time on the road. Even though the trucks are regularly maintained along with a general respect for the challenges of the road, things happen. When we need a bit of help, it's not the average tow truck and AAA/CAA to the rescue. Heavy-duty towing involves tow trucks about as a big as the trucks we drive. Many freight companies have roadside assistance partnerships with services capable of helping out heavy duty trucks and trailers. For the long-haul driver, some knowledge of how their unit operates is essential. We're not always in a place for outside help to easily reach us. The creativity of the trucking community is often visible when these adventures happen.

One time, I saw a truck that needed a tow truck. Circumstance, however, meant they needed to be towed in a rather unconventional means. For a while, we had a contract to haul garage doors from a plant in Mount Hope, Ohio, to various points in western Canada. Mount Hope was (and likely still is) an Amish colony. The only electrical power in the colony is at the manufacturing plant. No other building uses power. Even the truck scale at the plant is manual. As the trailers are all loaded by hand, it's pretty much an all-day affair to get the job done, so you'd best bring a good book to keep you busy. If you want, you can go into the colony to the small cafe they have, getting yourself some real, good homemade food. Everything they serve comes from within the colony. Eggs, bacon, bread, butter, peanut butter, jams, jellies, and everything is cooked on an old-style wood stove. It was pretty cool. The food tasted better than most other places I've eaten at.

My second or third time at the Amish colony, another driver with a big Kenworth was having an issue with his truck. For whatever reason, it wouldn't go into gear. He and I tried everything we could think of, but it would not go into gear. The closet repair shop was about 15 miles away, but it may as well have been 15 light years away. He was about to ask at the plant to use the phone to arrange a tow truck, when one of the locals came by to offer any assistance. Of course, he knew less about the truck than we did, but he did offer to help get the truck to the repair shop. The driver and I shared a look of "and just how are you going to help get this truck to the shop?" The driver agreed to let him help. The Amish gentleman left, returning about five minutes later. He wasn't alone, however. He had brought a team of six Clydesdale horses! The horses were hitched to the truck. The truck driver climbed up to the cab, and off they went. I don't know how it all played out as I was loaded and had headed out before either of them returned to the colony.

The company I worked for kept trucks for three years before turning them in. This helped reduce the risk of breakdowns during pick-ups and deliveries, helped preserve the company's reputation, as well as helping to attract and retain drivers. Who wants to drive a ten-year-old truck when you can get into one that is less than three years old? One lovely spring day, I was moved from my "old" truck, into a brand-spanking new one. I spent the better part of the morning packing, moving, unpacking, and setting up my new digs. Once I had everything sorted out, I hooked up to the trailer I was taking, fuelled everything up, and scaled it out. All was in order. I went in to grab the paperwork. Walking back to the truck, I passed another driver storming into the building, obviously upset about something. As he passed, he said: "Sorry, man. I scratched your new truck a little". My shoulders dropped as I heaved a huge sigh. Brand new truck, not even 60 miles on the odometer, and already a scratch on the bumper. I walked outside. There was my "scratched truck". The front left bumper was torn off, the driver's side mirror was torn off, and the hood was laying on the ground in three pieces. If that's "scratched", I would hate to see what he called damaged! All in all, it took three days to repair the truck. I ended up with an extended, albeit brief, holiday.

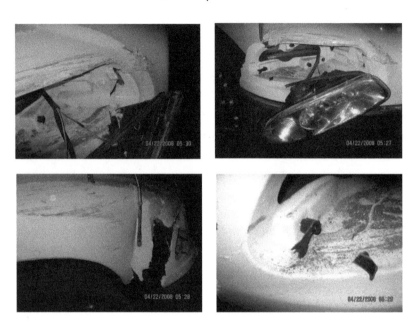

The results of the hit and run I had in San Antonio TX

This wasn't the only time I ended up with a damaged truck from someone else not paying attention. I parked for the night in San Antonio, Texas, then went for a shower along with a bite to eat. When I came out, the front end of the truck was in pieces. Someone had backed into it, taking off right away. There were no witnesses. I had a real streak of bad luck with this truck. With this incident, they decided to fly me to an available truck in Vancouver British Columbia instead of waiting in San Antonio for three weeks until the repairs were done.

I've had quite a few trucks in my years… Macks, Freightliners, Kenworths, Peterbilts, and Western Stars. All but one was conventional rigs. The one COE (Cab Over Engine) I drove was such a piece of garbage, that, to put it politely, I wouldn't take it to a shit fight, even if I had first throw. It was a tandem drive, tandem steering axle monstrosity, with a ten-foot cargo box between the sleeper and the 5th wheel. It was powered by a 444 HP Cummins engine, (known back then as a "triple four come apart" for their inherent unreliability) into an 18-speed transmission. It was used mainly for local deliveries in the Thunder Bay area. Some of the younger drivers loved it because the engine was ungoverned, and they could race along at over 80 mph. I was assigned the truck one evening to fill in for a driver who had booked the night off. I drove it around the yard, called the owner and told him flat out I wasn't driving that hunk of garbage. Fire me if you want, but I refuse to drive it.

For three years, I was delighted to be partnered with a Freightliner, long my favourite truck. Eventually, the time came when I had to bid farewell to my ten-wheeled buddy. The company leased the trucks for three years, or about 470,000 miles. My truck was now scheduled to be returned. At this time, the company was ordering a mix of trucks, as they had had a run of bad Mack trucks, which had been a mainstay of the fleet. When the run of bad Macks started, the owner had told the shop to try other trucks to see which ones were the best. As a result, we had a few Macks left, some Freightliners, and Volvos. Just before my Freightliner was retired, Mack had called, saying they had fixed all the issues. They were prepared to send us ten trucks, free of charge, to prove it. From what I heard, there was more to this story, but I can't prove the allegation, so I won't go into it. Anyway, I was told my truck was being "killed" and I was moving into a brand-new truck. I asked what kind of truck, as there was a mix of brand-new Mack and Freightliners in the yard. I was told it was a Mack. At the time (March 2008), we had started running turnpike doubles between Winnipeg and Calgary, using specially ordered Peterbilt day cabs (no sleeper berth) trucks. These trucks were equipped with 600 HP Cummins ISX engines, and 18 speed transmissions. These trucks were built to work!

Way back in 1996, I had taken the course to operate turnpike doubles, but the plan to use them never really materialized, as the restrictions on turnpike doubles at the time made them almost unfeasible. By 2008, the restrictions were being lifted. Their feasibility was at the point that it could become profitable. When I was told I was getting a Mack, I told them I'd drive it until I went on holidays (I was going to Australia in November). When I returned, I wanted onto the turnpikes.

I reluctantly moved everything into the Mack. I was in that truck from March until November. Eight months. Eight very long months. In that time, it was towed at least 24 times. Twice before I even left the city. On the first occurrence, I hooked up to a trailer, pulled to the fuel pumps to fill the tanks, and the passenger side tank fell off. Towed to the dealer for repairs. Second time, four days later, I hooked up, fuelled up (tank stayed in place), and off I went. Made it about a half-mile this time. The thing was vibrating and shaking so bad, I couldn't even light a cigarette! Back to the shop. After about 20 minutes, they found a defective tire. The two steer tires were supposed to be identical in size, but the circumference of the left steering tire was a half inch greater than the right steering tire. That was an easy fix and in half an hour, I was off again. Three miles later, the dashboard lit up with warning lights and error codes, including the dreaded red stop sign, meaning the engine will shut down in 30 seconds. I pulled onto the paved shoulder, then contacted the shop. They sent a wrecker out to get me. Dispatch sent another truck to recover the load. To say I wasn't impressed is an understatement.

Once again, I was towed back to the dealer. They hooked up the computer to see what the issue was. The active error codes filled the screen. I didn't (and still don't) know what any of them meant, other than that this wasn't going to be a quick fix. This repair took three weeks. From what I was told, they "forgot" to install a head gasket when they built the engine. As a result, the truck required an "in-frame rebuild". In other words, they rebuilt the entire engine. New cylinder head, pistons, rings, injectors, gaskets, the whole nine yards.

The next trip in this (I'm sure) cursed truck resulted nine hours down the road. The low voltage light came on. Huh? How can the batteries be going dead when I'm driving? Called the shop, then limped it into the nearest Mack dealership. Dead alternator was the issue. They replaced the alternator then tested the electrical system. Defective batteries. The batteries wouldn't take, nor hold a charge. Wonderful. The fix was done and I was back on the road three hours later headed for Calgary. From there, I took an empty 40 miles south to High River, then grabbed a load of meat going to Dallas, Texas. Then the fun began!

Just south of Casper, Wyoming, the dreaded "Check Engine" light came on. The computer started derating the engine. Engine derate reduces the power available, in turn reducing the maximum speed. I pulled on to the highway shoulder – again. Called the shop. They sent a wrecker to haul me back to the Mack dealer in Casper. I should say that when a truck is towed from the front for any great distance, the drive shaft is removed to prevent damage to the drive-line. So before towing the truck, the tow truck operator removed the drive shaft, strapping it down behind the bunk using bungee cords. Since it was well outside normal business hours, I slept in the truck at the dealership with the trailer attached. In the morning, I lowered the landing gear on the trailer, disconnecting the airlines, so the shop could pull the truck into the building to start working on it.

The mechanic came out, telling me to bring the truck into the shop. I told him the wrecker driver had removed the drive shaft, securing it behind the bunk with bungee cords, so I wasn't driving it anywhere. He walked back to the shop returning with a socket to reattach the drive shaft so I could drive into the shop. Alas, no drive shaft. And no bungee cords in evidence. I made a quick call to the towing company where the driver confirmed that he had secured the drive shaft to the truck behind the bunk. Well, it wasn't there. The tow company said they'd send the driver out. While we waited, the mechanic hooked the truck up to the computer to see what the error codes meant, and why the engine had derated. Once he matched the error codes to the manual (the error codes come up as numeric, which you then cross reference with the manual, to get the meaning in plain English) his head rocked back, and a very puzzled look came over his face. The ECU (Engine Control Unit) had lost contact with the number eight fuel injector. This is extremely puzzling for two reasons: First off, the truck only has seven fuel injectors. One for each cylinder, and one for the DPF (Diesel Particulate Filter). The DPF is an emissions control device, which traps minute particles of unburned fuel and exhaust particles. Once it reaches a specific level, the particles are reignited at a very high temperature, somewhere around 1,200 F, reducing the particles to ash, then expelling them through the exhaust system. Secondly, the ECU wasn't even programmed to look for eight injectors. How can it lose contact with something it's not programmed to look for? I'm not a mechanic by any stretch of the imagination, and even I had this issue solved already. It's a defective ECU. Of course, no one believed me. By now, the tow truck driver showed up, and, as we had already determined, the drive shaft was nowhere to be seen. He pulled the truck out from under the trailer, backed it into the shop, and re-traced the trip from the night before in hopes of locating the missing drive shaft. No such luck, that drive shaft was gone, and lost forever. Since the shop didn't know exactly what the issue with the truck was, I was off to a hotel courtesy of Mack as this was a warranty issue.

I have no idea what all they tried, but it was a week before the truck was ready to go. When I picked it up, I asked what the issue had been. The response? They had to replace the defective ECU. The exact issue I had diagnosed a week earlier. I just looked at them with a raised eyebrow and a crooked smile, collected the keys, and I was on my way. During the week, of course, they had someone drop an empty trailer, and had them recover the Dallas load. For the life of me, I can't recall where they sent me after getting that lemon fixed yet again.

Just as gasoline in your car can crystallize in the winter, diesel fuel can gel up in the winter, especially if you run the less expensive summer fuel (#2 diesel). Winter fuel (#1 diesel), is less likely to gel, but it will under certain circumstances. Only once have I experienced winter fuel gelling up, and it was caused by a mechanic's brain fart. I was headed home to Winnipeg one frosty day, and all of a sudden, the truck started vibrating, and losing both power and speed. I pulled onto the shoulder, just as the truck shut down. I called the shop, as it was obvious I wasn't going anywhere, and they send a service truck out. First thing he did, was remove the fuel filters. Sure enough, they were clogged with gelled fuel. This confused me for two reasons: First, I had filled up with winter fuel. Secondly, the truck I was driving had heated fuel tanks. The tanks aren't actually heated. The engine draws excess fuel from the tanks. What it doesn't use is heated by the engine, then returned to the tanks. As you drive, the fuel in both tanks is eventually heated to prevent fuel gelling. As I had filled up with winter fuel, and had driven about six and a half hours, no way the fuel should have gelled. The mechanic replaced the filters, thinking they were the issue, and off I went. Not even a mile later, I was back on the shoulder. He spun off the filters, and again, gelled fuel. This time I was towed to a repair facility, where new filters were installed, and the fuel tanks drained, and refilled with fresh winter diesel, and a sufficient quantity of a high grade fuel condition was added to each tank. Again, off I went. Not even a mile later, I'm on the shoulder again. Now it's getting seriously annoying. Towed back to the shop, new filters installed, but before I left, the mechanic crawled under to inspect every part of the fuel system. After about five minutes, the culprit was identified. Somewhere in the past, the fuel system had been repaired. A fitting was removed, and replaced with a brass fitting. Brass, as you may know, is very susceptible to temperature changes. With the winter fuel, and heated tanks, it didn't affect the fuel flow enough to cause a problem. This particular day though, it was just too cold, and the fitting was just cold enough to negate the heated tanks, and winter fuel, and it gelled up the filters. A quick change of the fitting, and I was off again, with no more fuel issues.

One hot day in July, I was puttering around in the yard waiting for my trailer to be repaired, when one of the managers asked me to jump in a recently killed truck, and head to the reefer line up ASAP. Trucks that have ended their service life (close to the lease limits on age and/or mileage) are "killed". So I jumped into one, and headed to the reefer line up. As I rounded the corner, what I saw was both scary as hell, and funny as hell. The shunt truck had been moving a trailer load of meat from the shop, and was returning it to the line up, when the fifth wheel on the shunt truck let go. The trailer, a triaxle, was loaded to the max, probably having about 50,000-52,000 lbs of meat inside. When the fifth wheel let go, the trailer fell off.

I'll stop here to flesh out shunt trucks and their fifth wheels work. A shunt truck, sometimes called a yard jockey, is a short truck, usually about ten feet long, with a remotely controlled fifth wheel lock, and the fifth wheel can be raised and lowered by either air or hydraulic pressure, meaning the driver doesn't have to keep climbing in and out of the truck to crank the landing gear up and down. He just backs under, the fifth wheel automatically locks around the king pin, and he pressurizes the fifth wheel lift system, which raises the landing gear off the ground. He then connects a supply air line to release the brakes, and off he goes. When he gets the trailer where it needs to be, he removes the airline, releasing the air from the brakes, releases the fifth wheel pressure, flips the control to open the jaws on the fifth wheel, and drives away.

This time, something in the fifth wheel broke, and the trailer, with 50,000 + lbs came crashing to the ground from a height of about three feet. The sudden lose of weigh on the back of the shunt truck, sent the fifth wheel lift plate up with enough force to flip the shunt truck on it's nose. I personally would have found this hard to believe, but there was the shunt truck, windshield to the ground. The trailer, however, was in far worse shape. As it fell to the ground, the landing gear folded as if it was made out of cardboard, and was crumpled up under the trailer. Thankfully, it hadn't been pushed through the floor of the trailer. Next to hit the ground, was the fuel tank, and it faired even worse. With the fuel tank split wide open, the reefer died almost instantly. So they called the closest heavy wrecker to lift the front of the trailer, and I backed the kill truck under, hooked up the air lines, and took it to the shop, so they could get the wrecked fuel tank replaced, filled with fuel, and get the reefer going before the meat got too warm. A properly insulated reefer will hold a temperature for four to six hours, but the floor in this trailer may have been damaged. Turned out, after they got the reefer running again, and surveyed the damage, the trailer was written off. In all my years, I've only seen three or four fifth wheels fail, and I've only had one fail on me. Like axle slider assemblies, they seldom fail, BUT... Unscrupulous drivers can cause them to fail, so I make it a habit to check everything when the truck has been out of my sight, even for a few minutes. Take your eyes off it for two minutes, and some prankster (or worse) can ruin your whole day, or even your week. This habit was drilled into me by an incident I saw, but was not directly involved in, as I was delayed a few hours while they cleaned up the mess.

A couple of drivers got into a pissing match over something at a truck stop, and one of them walked away, and went inside the building. I was fuelling at the time, and I have no idea what the argument was about, and really didn't care. After fuelling, I went it to use the facilities, and have a bite to eat. After about half an hour, I was back in the truck, and headed down the road. I made it about three miles, and came to a stop. Accident up ahead was the word on the radio. After about 90 minutes, traffic started moving again, but very slowly. When I got to the scene of the accident, I noticed it was one of the drivers who had been in the pissing match at the truck stop. What had happened was, the other driver in the pissing match, had unlocked his axle slider. When he used the broker brake (the dash valve that applies the trailer brakes. Brokers use it to reduce wear and tear on the truck brakes. Brokers have to pay for truck brakes, but not the trailer brakes), the axles stopped, but because the locks were released, the trailer slid along the rails, and the weight and momentum broke the stop pins, and the axles came right out from under the trailer, and were laying upside down on the highway about 15 feet behind the trailer. The trailer was, of course, loaded with perishables, and said trailer was damaged beyond repairs. The ICC bar (the bumper you see on the backs of trailer. It's known unofficially by drivers as "Datsun stopper") was pushed up, which bent the back of the trailer up, and made the trailer look somewhat like a mirror imaged check mark. Ever since then, when I return to the truck, I always double check the fifth wheel and axle sliders are properly locked. Only once did I find the axle slider not locked. The driver who brought the trailer in from the Alberta meat plant had slid the axles to make the weights legal, then forgot to lock the slider in place. Good thing he didn't use the broker brake, or he'd have been in the same boat.

When it comes to repairs, who actually does the repairs can be a grey area. If you're in the yard, obviously it's the local shop that affects the repairs. If you're a few hundred miles from the company repair facilities, obviously an outside repair facility makes the repairs. But where exactly is the dividing line? Is it the perimeter fence around the yard? Is there a 20 mile radius around the yard? And how "strict" are the boundaries? I found out one day as I was coming to the yard with a heavily loaded triaxle trailer. I was maxed out on weight, just over 102,000 lbs, when I heard a "PISHHHHH" and came to a screeching halt. I knew exactly what it was. A broken airline on the trailer. Not quite. One of the brake chambers had broken right where the airline connects to it. This depressurized the entire trailer braking system, and all six parking brakes came on. No way I was going to move the trailer until it was fixed. I called the shop, and explained the situation, and told them I was 100 feet from the gate leading to the yard. I could look out the window of the truck, and see him through his office window talking to me on the phone. But, company policy was, if you're not in the yard, they have to arrange for an outside vendor to make the repairs. I told him, if he looked out his window, he'd see me on the road. He looked, smiled and waved, and said again, he'd have to arrange an outside vendor, unless I could drag it through the gate. Nope, wasn't gonna happen, and I wasn't interested in waiting for an outside vender to come fix it. It took about an hour for the repair truck to arrive, and even he mentioned that it was a colossal waste of time and money, when one of our mechanics could have walked out with the part, and tools, and made the repair in about ten minutes.

One other failure I witnessed could have had catastrophic effects, but luck was with someone this day.

I was headed east through Chicago, on my way to Ontario. I had already gone through downtown, and I was close to the Pershing Ave exit, in the middle lane, to avoid as much of the exiting and entering traffic. A city truck with a set of "A"-trains (two 28 ft trailers connected with a single axle converter dolly) exited at Pershing Ave. Well, part of him exited. The truck and front trailer took the ramp. The converter and back trailer continued down the highway, and eventually ended up in the ditch. Of course, this caused a massive traffic backup, as no one knew where the runaway trailer and dolly were going to go. In reality, they shouldn't have gone more than a few feet. When the air lines separated, all the parking brakes on the trailer should have come on instantly, and stopped everything in it's tracks. Had the driver done proper pretrip inspection, he would have known there was an issue with the parking brakes on that trailer, and (hopefully) have left it behind for repairs. The parking brake system is almost fool proof, so I'm pretty sure he just hooked up, and headed out. As long as the truck is supplying sufficient pressure to the system (at least 60 PSI), the spring brakes are released. If the pressure drops, as it does when the air lines are disconnected, the springs will apply more than enough pressure to keep the tires from turning. Unfortunately, this didn't happen this time. There are a number of reason why they wouldn't have come on, but failure to inspect and test the brakes is almost guaranteed.

Malfunctioning brake pots, while not an every day occurrence, do happen from time to time. Usually, the malfunction is the parking spring breaking, which is usually noted by an audible air leak from the brake pot that can't be visually located. The spring breaks, and punctures the internal diaphragm, creating a leak that's impossible to locate. On occasion, something thrown up from the road can damage brake pot to the point of failure by cracking the brake pot, or damaging the air line(s). If the brake pot is damaged, it needs replacing. There is no repairing them. Once on the road, I had a brake pot badly damaged, and needed to be replaced. The problem was, the trailer was equipped with disc brakes. Replacement parts at that time were very hard to find, and there simply wasn't a replacement part within 200 miles. With an older drum brake pot, it would've been a simple fix. Use the caging bolt (used to manually release the parking brake spring), seal off the air line, and carry on to the closest repair facility. With disc brakes, there is no way to manually release the brakes. At least neither the mechanic who showed up, nor I knew of any way to release the parking brake spring. He finally had had enough messing around, and clamped off the airline, and removed the brake pot. I have no idea what I had hit, but the hole in the pot was almost big enough to put my hand through it.

DRIVING WITH MOTHER NATURE.

ON THE ROAD NO MATTER THE WEATHER!

When thinking about safety in trucking and the logistics of delivering loads across the continent we have to consider the role played by the weather. Weather can be as hazardous to the trucker as any other potential dangers that are encountered. Weather alert technology has come a long way since I started long-haul trucking. These days routes can be monitored and alerts can go out early enough to allow shipments to be re-routed. Not only is time saved, but so is potential damage to trucks and loads, as well as the lives of drivers. I have been on the road long enough, and far enough, to have had several "adventures" of the weather kind, thanks to Mother Nature.

Somewhere in early 1997, when I was still training my friend Pete, we were given a load headed to the United States, crossing at Pembina, North Dakota, due south of Winnipeg. It was snowing, but not THAT bad, although the winds were fairly strong. We got to the US Customs entry, parked the truck, and went in. The customs booth we visited that trip has since been demolished and rebuilt. After customs cleared the load, I was informed that the Interstate 29 was closed because of the weather. I almost told the agent off. When the highway is closed, travel is illegal. I mentioned that I guess we would have to stay right where we were. The customs agent said we couldn't stay there, we had to vacate the premises. I said that it would be illegal for us to leave as the highway was closed. I also told him that had he informed me the interstate was closed BEFORE he cleared the load, we could have returned to Canada, taken the load back to the yard, and taken a load that stayed in Canada. After a few minutes of back and forth, his supervisor came out to see what was going on. When he learned what had happened, he told his subordinate that the only way we could leave the border was if he supplied us a police escort to the closest suitable facilities, which were two miles away at the Gastrak Truck Stop in Pembina. We ended up with the escort, along with a few other trucks in the same situation. All other trucks were sent back to Canada. As I recall, I never saw that customs official at the border again.

Gastrak was long been popular as a regular stop for all cross-border traffic, not just trucks. Fuel is cheaper there than in Canada. If you're north-bound, it's a good spot to stop to make sure all your paperwork and receipts are in order for Canada Customs. It's also the last place to make any snack or duty-free purchases before heading into Canada. When the roads close though, their parking lots fill up fast. We managed to get a place to park, although it was not an official or marked spot. Gastrak has a "normal" capacity of about fifty trucks. By the time everything was said and done during this winter storm, there were three times that number. Every available inch of pavement had a vehicle of some sort on it. Even the fuel pumps had vehicles parked in front them. The storm that had caused the road closure bore down on the area like nothing I have ever seen, before or since. The winds were gusting to 50 mph, and the bottom fell out of the thermometer. At one point, I remembering hearing on the radio that the temperature was now -70 F, but when its that cold, the numbers don't really matter. It's just freezing!! It was very cold, resulting in some trucks starting to "gel up". When diesel fuel gets to a certain temperature, dissolved wax particles start to solidify, plugging the fuel filters. Winter fuel has additives to retard the wax from solidifying, but this product is not widely available in the United States, save for some of the more northern states. If someone fuelled up in Iowa or Nebraska, chances are winter fuel wasn't available.

Most truck stops sell fuel conditioner, to retard fuel gelling, but it can be expensive. We fuelled in Winnipeg, so we had good winter fuel.

We were stuck there for three long, boring days before the highway opened up. It took the North Dakota Department of Transportation (NDDOT) another three or four days to clear the cars and trucks that littered the ditches. I only heard of one serious accident, although I didn't witness it. It apparently resulted in a massive crack down by USA Department of Transportation regarding logbook violations. The story I heard, remembering that I didn't see the accident or the aftermath, was that a truck decided to risk running the closed highway. In the severe adverse conditions, he didn't see a state trooper stopped to help a stranded motorist, and killed the trooper. The investigation apparently also revealed he was running over his legally allowed time. For all intents and purposes, if this is what truly happened, his driving career was finished.

All Gastrak had for food at the time was soup, chili, and hotdogs, plus convenience store snacks. In those days, they also closed the soup and chili service from eleven at night until six in the morning. During this storm, however, everything stayed open. For the most part, it was because the staff, too, couldn't get home. The only way anyone could get around was by snowmobile. The parking lot was tightly packed, so this meant that if someone needed fuel, it was all-hands-on-deck. We'd use five-gallon jerry cans, creating a bucket brigade to get the fuel from the pumps to the trucks and trailers. Drivers with double bunks (sleepers with two beds) were offering the second bed to stranded families. More than a few drivers doubled up to give a family of four a double bunk truck to keep everyone together. One driver brought his TV/ VCR combo into the truck stop along with a collection of VHS tapes to help pass the time. The collection was heavily laden with martial arts movies. Not my cup of tea. I stayed in the truck for the most part, playing cards with Pete.

When we finally got moving, the Interstate was in decent shape. We made good time driving the 150 miles to Fargo, North Dakota. They had started clearing the parking lot at the Petro Stopping Centre, which was (and still is) one of my favourite places to stop. The scene was like nothing you can even imagine. As bad as it was in Pembina, Fargo had it worse. The lot was a complete mess, even three days after the storm ended.

Fargo ND three days after the 1997 "Blizzard of the Century"

The yellow indicates the area flooded by the 1997
"Flood Of The Century

This was just one of eight blizzards the Fargo area experienced that winter. Whereas the average snowfall for that part of North Dakota is 50 inches the winter of 1996 – 1997 ended up with a whopping 117 inches! That's juts shy of 10 feet! Of course, after the "Blizzard of the Century," comes the "Flood of the Century." This one was a doozy. By April of 1997, all that snow was melting into the Red River. Unlike most major river systems in North American, the Red River begins in the United States (at the southern edge of North Dakota/Minnesota), flowing north into Canada and eventually into Lake Winnipeg. All the snow that had piled up during that winter melted and eventually ran into the Red River. I was fortunate to be on the road away from the area when the flood began. For April and May, the Red River spilled its banks reaching more than three miles inland. Grand Forks was completely inundated (along with the highway). Manitoba was luckier. The Red River Floodway, built after the 1950 flood, was designed to divert 60,000 cubic feet per second of water around the eastern side of Winnipeg. During the 1997 flood it diverted 63,000 cubic feet per second. For reference, Niagara Falls' average flow rate is 83,000 cubic feet per second. The Red River Floodway kept all that flood water off of the Trans-Canada Highway (which crosses over the floodway), keeping us long-haulers in business until the southern highway opened once more.

One winter, I was headed west from Trois-Rivières in Quebec to Reno, Nevada. I had crossed over into the United States, taking me to I-80 just west of Cheyenne, Wyoming, when I encountered some bad road conditions. This area is famous for rapidly changing weather conditions. Travelling between Cheyenne and Rawlins, Wyoming, can be a crap shoot at the best of times. I checked the weather before leaving Cheyenne. Favourable road conditions were reported. Time to hit the road! Cheyenne to Rawlins is 147 miles, but it can be a gruelling drive when the weather turns ugly. This time, it turned VERY ugly. The first 50 miles to Laramie was awesome. Bone dry roads with temperatures just above freezing. I was making good time. About five miles west of Laramie, everything went to hell in a hand basket.

Dark, low, clouds came in, and the snow started. The snow soon changed over to rain, which is NOT a good sign when the temperature is close to freezing. The conditions that create freezing rain are responsible for quickly turning the road surface into a skating rink. Rule of thumb when driving in these conditions is to keep an eye on your mirror. Trucker's wisdom is to be followed: if you see spray, then you're okay. If there is no spray, you'd better pray, meaning if there is spray coming off your tires, the road is just wet. If there's no spray, then the surface is covered in ice, and you're on borrowed time. Another trick, is to run your hand over the leading edge of your outside mirror. If it has ice on it, chances are the bridges are covered in ice as well.

On a small aside, I'm sure you've seen the signs saying something to the effect of "bridges may ice before the road". Ever wonder why? The reason is, the road can absorb whatever heat the ground is storing, and the wind can only affect the road surface. On bridges, the wind can cool both the surface, and underneath the bridge, lowering the surface temperature faster, so the road surface could be as much as 4 degrees warmer the surface of the bridge. I kept a close eye on my mirrors, as the temperature was right at the freezing point just as the sun was setting. I knew from experience that driving conditions were going to get very bad, very soon. I slowed right down, looking for a rest area, truck stop, or any place with enough room to get off the highway. Of course, no such luck.

I'm very confident in my driving skills and abilities. It's the others on the road that you have to watch out for. Before long, I was down to about 10 mph, and just white-knuckling it. I had the CB on, getting updates on the road ahead from drivers heading the other way. I knew it wasn't getting better anytime soon, so I just kept plodding along, nice and slow. Of course, there were cars, pick-up trucks, SUVs, and the odd semi just flying by at dry-highway speeds, oblivious to the road conditions. Joe Average in his car or pick up, I can almost understand, but the semi drivers? In the industry, we have a few names for these types of drivers: "Steering wheel holders" and "Billy Big-rigger" are the two most common (and least offensive). About three miles ahead of me, another truck was doing about the same speed as I was. We kept in touch via the CB discussing the road conditions ahead. I kept him apprised of what was coming up behind us. At one exit, on the eastbound side, there was a pretty bad accident. We were calling all the east-bound trucks to warn them about it. Not all of the east-bounders, however, were listening to their radios. Inevitably, a few added their mass to the carnage, along with quite a few of the cars and pickups.

As we slowly progressed westward, the driver in front of me suddenly yelled over the CB: "OH SHIT!" I was checking my mirror at the time, and snapped my head forward to see a Jeep four-wheel drive spinning around in the eastbound lanes. As the Jeep spun, it came through the median, heading towards the west bound lanes. This is was going to be close! I had to rapidly sort out my options. What do I do? If I step on the throttle to get out of his way, I'll spin out, possibly jack-knifing into the ditch. If I hit the brakes, the truck brakes will likely lock, causing the trailer to push the truck out of the way, and I'll still be jack-knifed into the ditch. Damned if I do; damned if I don't. Only thing I could do was to just maintain control, keeping the truck straight and slow, hoping to all-that's-holy that the out-of-control Jeep didn't hit me or the truck ahead, cause a huge wreck, and probably killing the Jeep-driver in the process. Thankfully, the Jeep passed between us spinning all the way, before ending up on its side in the ditch. Apparently, the driver wasn't injured, as a truck behind me said they were out and walking around. Pretty sure they needed a change of underwear, though..

*Left: Snow coverage at the summit of Donner's Pass. **Right:** Donner's Pass. Note the red fire hydrant for scale of the snow depth.*

Mother Nature wasn't finished with me on this trip. The day I delivered in Reno, the weather reports for the Sierra Nevada Mountain range called for inclement weather. Four storms were lined up to come ashore and hammer the area. I knew what was coming. Even before I delivered, I told the planner and dispatcher that if they needed me in Modesto, California, for a Proctor & Gamble load, they needed to tell me now. I needed enough time to get over Donner's Pass before the highway was closed. They told me to hang tight in Reno until they heard back from Proctor & Gamble. I was quite frank, telling them straight out: "If I wait, I may not be able to GET to Modesto." Dispatch replied that I was to wait. Wait I did. Finally, three hours later, I got the message: "RUSH load from Modesto! Get there ASAP!" Of course, by this time, that wasn't even an option. I told dispatch that I couldn't, as the roads were now closed. He told me to get tire chains, and get moving. I responded: "No. Chains won't help. The road is CLOSED! I'm not getting over the mountain with anything short of a snow mobile." His answer? "Can you get around the closure?" I gave him my best advice: "Sure. It's a four day detour up to Washington State. If I can cross the mountains (providing Snoqualmie Pass doesn't close), I can then head back down to California." Well, that idea didn't go over very well. I reminded him that he had been warned about the possibility of a highway closure, but he ignored me. It turned out to be a LONG wait at the truck stop in Reno. It was three days before they finally opened the highway and I could get through.

On another trip, I continued my relationship with Mother Nature. This long winter delay happened in Boston Bar, British Columbia. Boston Bar is a very small community with under 1,000 residents. I was headed west on the Trans-Canada Highway, towards Vancouver. As you come into Kamloops, there are signs giving the current road conditions along the various routes from Kamloops to Vancouver. The two most common routes are Highway 1, the Trans Canada Highway – also referred to as the Fraser Canyon route, and Highway 5, known as the Coquihalla, or more commonly called "The Coq". In those days, The Coq was a toll highway. We were encouraged to "run the canyon" which was non-tolled, but very twisty, and not divided. The canyon also lacked passing lanes. It is scenic, however, following the Fraser River for the most part. This trip, I had no choice. The Coq was closed, which meant that I had to run the canyon. As I pulled into Boston Bar, I saw a few trucks at a complete standstill on the highway. Over the CB, they were saying an avalanche had completely buried the road under about 20 feet of snow, ice, mud, and other assorted debris. Well, there were two choices at this point. Wait for the highway to be cleaned up, or turn around, driving the two-and-a-half-hour route back the 131 miles to Kamloops we had just completed. In Kamloops we could to wait for the first of the two closed highways to reopen. Before anyone had the chance to ponder the options... RUMBLE, RUMBLE, CRASH! Another avalanche just east of Boston Bar. So much for that, or any idea!

We were stuck between two avalanches. As I recall, it was three nights and two days before the road towards Vancouver was finally opened. The people of Boston Bar were all great folks. They made sure no one went hungry and everyone had a place to sleep. The long-haul truckers were fine in their trucks as far as sleeping accommodations. Most of us had enough food and water to get us through, too. The families in their cars and mini-vans weren't as well prepared. The community was a great help to them. It was, however, a long, boring wait, all thanks to Mother Nature.

Another storm I was caught in, caused a small truck stop and gas station in Northwestern Ontario to close as the result of bad management and judgement.

I was heading west on Highway 11 when we heard that the road ahead was closed even before we could reach Nipigon (where Highway 11 and 17 join). I pulled into this truck stop, just east of Beardmore. The place had parking for about ten or fifteen trucks, along with a small restaurant. It wasn't a 24/7 truck stop; however, they did have parking space for the big rigs. Since the road was closed ahead, the lot filled up quickly. At ten o'clock that night, their normal closing time, they sent everyone out of the cafe, locked the doors, and left. Now when the highways are closed, it's not just the long-haul truckers that have to get off the road. In this case, there were a few families with kids, with no warm, safe, place to go. The closest hotels and motels were fifty miles west in Nipigon as the village of Beardmore didn't really have public accommodations. With the road shut down they, like us, were stranded. All of the drivers who had a spare bunk soon worked out a plan giving everyone had a bed. As long-haulers, we were experienced with sorting out sleeping space when the weather closed us in. Without any hesitancy we stepped up to care for the car-driving public. Some drivers doubled up with another driver. This way, they could let a family all sleep in the same truck. The general consensus of all the stranded drivers and families was that they would never stop at this place again. Within six months, the place was closed. It has since reopened as a machinery place, but no road services. I was stunned that a place that depended on the travelling public for their income would toss people out into the elements during such miserable weather, but they did, and it cost them dearly.

One year, about a week before Christmas, I was in the Winnipeg yard looking for some local work. It was not long enough to take a serious load, but too long to just sit at home, so I was looking for something that I could knock off in four or five days. The shop, of all places, had the perfect solution: They had a couple for brand new city trucks to be delivered to the Toronto terminal, and therefore, had a few kill trucks to be returned from the Toronto terminal. A perfect four day round trip, and seeing as I was to be in Thunder Bay for Christmas, it would work out almost perfect, so I jumped at it. Packed a few changes of clothes, and other items I'd need, grabbed a loaded triaxle meat load (this becomes somewhat important later) and headed off to Toronto. As I've mentioned before, there are two routes between North Western Ontario, and the Greater Toronto Area: Highway 11 (via Cochrane, ON) and Highway 17 (via Sault Ste Marie). Up until Jan 6, 2000, I almost always took Highway 11. On that fateful day, I lost two friends and co-workers in a horrendous head on collision between two tractor trailers. One of the drivers had been a student of mine a few months previously, and it was determined that he was driving. I struggled for a few months, wondering if I had somehow helped cause the collision by forgetting to teach him something, or did I over emphasis something that spooked him, etc. It turns out the other driver was 100% at fault, but it still haunted me for a few months. So on this trip, I took Highway 17. It's shorter, but a more demanding drive, as it follows the shores of Lake Superior (a VERY beautiful drive), but it has numerous hills, curves, and is susceptible to "lake effect snow". So off I went, with a day cab, and a heavy triaxle. As soon as I passed the split for highways 11 and 17 just north of Nipigon, I realized the error of my ways. The day cabs were not equipped with a lot of horsepower, so it was a long, slow pull up all those hills, and descending the hills was a bit of a challenge as well, as the day cabs were not equipped with engine brakes either. I was a bit of a white knuckle drive to Toronto. On the upside, I was put up in hotels every night. I made it to Toronto without any incident, and dropped the trailer and truck at the yard, and went it to see what they had for me to return to Winnipeg, after my Christmas in Thunder Bay. I already had the truck number, but the trailer number hadn't been determined before I left Winnipeg. Alas, there was no trailer. I was to bobtail back. As I've said, bobtailing isn't fun, and for braking action, especially in the winter, and you have to be extra cautious. Hammer the brakes for any reason, and you could be in a tail spin. Traction to get going, and when climbing a hill is iffy at best, due to no weight on the drive axles. I checked the weather forecast, and it seemed to be okay along highway 17, so off I went. All was great, until I got to the top of Lake Superior, and started heading south towards Thunder Bay. There are two stretches on highway 17 that are famous for lake effect snow. Sault Ste Marie to Wawa, and Terrace Bay to Nipigon. Of course, all of the biggest hills are in these stretches. Murphy's Law hit me between Terrace Bay and Thunder Bay. The show started just as I left Terrace Bay, light and fluffy at first, but it quickly changed to heavy, and wet snow. The speed limit along this stretch is 55 mph, but before long, traffic was down to about half that, as road conditions slowly deteriorated, and visibility dropped to a few hundred feet. Between Terrace Bay and Thunder Bay (specifically between Schreiber and Nipigon, a distance of about 55 miles), there are two fairly serious hills. Rossport and Caver's. The road descends into Rossport, then climbs out of Rossport. The climb out is about a 7% grade (for every 100 feet you travel horizontally, you climb seven feet). After cresting the hill, you descend down into the Pays Plat First Nation. As with all small communities, the speed limit drops to 45 mph. Just outside of the community, the speed limit increases to 55 mph, but by that time, you've already started climbing Caver's. Back then, Caver's didn't have a passing lane, and it was about an 8% or 9% climb. It was a long, slow pull when you were loaded. This evening, it was a very white knuckle drive. As I left Pays Plat, there were a few police cars with lights flashing at the bottom of the hill. As I approached, they just waved me on through, so I continued up the hill. When I got to a somewhat level spot on the hill, I backed right off the throttle, and engaged the power dividers (which basically locks both side of both drive axles, basically turning the truck into an eight wheel drive to improve traction, and reduce a spin out). I ended up moving a bit to the right, to put some tires in the snow that hadn't been compacted. After what seems like forever, I made it over the top. Now the fun REALLY began... I had to descend the hill. The gradient is not as steep, but it is longer, open to the lake, so the prevailing wind adds a few degrees of difficulty, and there are three or four turns, just to add some interest. Near the bottom of the hill, the gradient does increase to about 9%, but only for about 100 feet. I white knuckled it all the way down, doing maybe 20-25 mph, and managed not to lose traction, bounce off the rock cut on the right, or drop off the cliff on the left, or skid off into a ditch. At the bottom of the hill, there were more police cars, and this time they requested me to stop. I stopped, and the officers asked me what the conditions were going over the hill. I told him how treacherous it was, and he got on his radio, I assume talking to the police on the east side of the hill, confirming that the highway was now closed. I managed to get into Thunder Bay without further incident, but that was some of the worst snow I've ever driven in.

I've heard more than a few stories were someone blames the road and weather conditions for an accident. I know I'll catch some flack for this, but. Road conditions do NOT cause accidents. They might be a contributing factor, but the road conditions themselves do not cause accidents. What DOES cause accidents, is almost always, human error. If a rock falls off a mountain, and crushes your car, that's an accident. Almost everything else is human error in disguise. And yes, I'm guilty of such errors myself, and I've come across more collisions than I could possibly relate here, but there are seven that really stand out. One I already related earlier (driver asleep at the wheel). Of the four I'm about to share, two were 100% my fault, no ifs, ands or buts about it.

One January, I was delivering a load to a customer in the Minneapolis area, and due to the way the yard was set up, I had to blind side back in. In retrospect, I should have gotten out to check, double check, and triple check clearances, but I didn't. Alas, I backed into a parked city truck belonging to the company I was delivering to. My fault, 100%. I pulled ahead, took pictures of all the damages, including unit numbers and licence plates before backing in and unloading. As they were unloading the truck, I filled out the company accident report, and filed it away with the one-use cameras we used to document incidents. The next time I was in the yard, I turned in the report and the camera, and pretty much forgot about it. The company's safety bonus program runs from January 1, to December 31, with the annual Driver Safety Awards Dinner being held on the Saturday of the May long weekend. The list of recipients is released in February or March, so any errors can be corrected in time.

A collision doesn't necessarily disqualify a driver, as there can be some very minor bumps, and the monetary cut-off limit for damages was (and may still be) $2,500. Every incident is reviewed by the company's internal Accident review Committee (ARC), and the outcome is communicated to the driver in question. I heard absolutely nothing regarding the incident. When the list came out in March of the next year, my name wasn't on the list. Having forgotten about the incident, I asked why I wasn't on the list. I was reminded about the incident, and pointed out that I'd heard nothing regarding the incident from the ARC. Since the damage was very minor, I was certain it was under the $2,500 limit, so I asked what the repair bill was. The director of safety (no longer with the company) checked the files, and told me it was $2,500. This sounded a bit suspicious, and I questioned the amount being the exact amount that would disqualify me. He then told me that it was an estimate, as the other company had never submitted a bill. I told him that the truck had already been repaired, and if they hadn't submitted a bill by now (15 months after the incident) and had already made repairs, then they weren't likely to submit a bill, therefore, the cost of the incident was $0, and I should be invited to the awards dinner. He replied that they had up to two years to submit a bill. Again, if they haven't already, they won't be submitting a bill. Then, he made a decision that everyone in ear shot couldn't believe. He asked one of the office staff to call the other company, and ask if they were planning to submit a bill for the repairs. Everyone who heard that, was stunned, and more than a few told him it was a stupid idea. Call someone out of the blue and say: "Hey, we damaged something of yours, and even though you've already repaired it, and didn't send us a bill, would you like some money?" Who in their right mind would say: "No, We're good, thanks." Of course, they sent in the bill for the repairs. The bill was under the $2,500, but by the time it was all sorted out, the awards dinner was over. The whole handling of the situation left a rather bitter taste in my mouth, and as a matter of principle, I seldom ever attended the awards dinner after that.

One wintery day in 2012 (if memory serves) I was running a set of turn-pikes to Grenfell SK, to switch with another driver. The roads weren't all that bad, but I was apparently driving too fast for conditions. Just past the junction in Whitewood, SK, as I rounded a left hand bend in the road, and noticed a car in the median ditch. I backed my foot off the throttle, and the engine brake automatically engaged. I should've turned it off earlier, when the road conditions started to deteriorate, but I didn't. I was loaded very light that day, and when they engine brake came on, the drive tires broke traction. The engine brake uses the compression stroke of the engine to slow the drive line, causing the drive tires to slow

My worst wreck. Thankfully, no one was injured. Note the car in the ditch, visible under the rear trailer

down. With good traction, this will help slow down the entire vehicle. As the drive tires slowed down on the slippery road surface, they broke traction and the trailers basically pushed the truck out of the way. Before I knew it, I was all twisted up in the median. I managed to avoid hitting the car that was already in the ditch, but that was pure luck. I had nothing to do with that. Fortunately, I walked away from the mess, but the truck, both trailers and the converter weren't so lucky. Some minor damage to the two trailers, and some torn off airlines, but the truck was a write-off. And the way the safety department handled this incident was, I believe, the beginning of the end of my almost 20 year career at TransX. As I've said, Saskatchewan has always had very strict regulations for lcv operations. 0 tolerance for just about any violations. So in order to retain the company's lcv operating authority in Saskatchewan, they have to come down on violators like a ton of bricks. This, I completely understand. So the company's decision was that I be suspended for three days. It sucks, but whatever. What sucked even worse, was the way I was informed of the decision. The director of safety, after the ARC meeting decided I was to be suspended. Apparently he told someone else, who told someone else, who told someone else to tell me I was suspended. The way I finally go the message was pure luck. I returned from my run that day, just after regular business hours, and asked the planner what trailers I had the next day. He gave me a very curious look, and asked: "Haven't you spoken to so and so yet?" "No," I said, "I haven't spoken to anyone, what's up?". He said he didn't know if it was his place to say, and he called one of the supervisors. He didn't get an answer, and he was visibly uncomfortable, and unsure what to do. I asked him again, and he told me I'd been suspended for three days. The suspension didn't bother me anywhere near as much as the fact that no one thought it was important enough to let me know I'd been suspended. As my run usually left the yard at 4am, I was usually in the yard before 2am to allow myself enough time to get everything legal, and hooked up so I could leave on time. Had I not bumped into the planner, I would have found out when I got to work at 2am, and then I would REALLY have been pissed off. I got ahold of the director of safety the next day, and tore a strip off him. He said he had told (fictitious names used here) Frank, who had told Joe, who had told Peter, who had told Ernie to tell me I was suspended. I simply reminded him that, since YOU made the decision, it's YOUR responsibility to deliver the message. Passing the buck is too often a dodge to avoid responsibility. As I said, that was the beginning of the end of my time at TransX.

A particularly bad accident I came upon that was blamed on poor weather conditions was in Whitewood, SK. As far as I know, there were no serious injuries, but I'm betting clean underwear were required all around. This intersection, where a two lane road intersects a four lane divided highway, with a speed limit of 62 mph. The speed limit has since been reduced to 50 mph. This day, it was very foggy. Visibility was down to about half a mile, and most traffic was driving well below the posted speed, some with 4-way flashers activated. One truck was coming off the side road, and attempted to turn left to head west. To do this, he had to cross the east bound lanes. Carnage ensued, and it was a right royal mess. As he was making his way across the eastbound lanes, he was hit in the rear axles by a truck travelling east at highway speed. The impact send the truck and trailer spinning , but before they came to a stop, two more tractor trailer units, and a 5-ton refrigerated truck joined the carnage. The damage was incredible, and how no one was severely injured or killed is still a mystery to me. As I was switching in Grenfell at the time, I wasn't too far behind it. Whitewood to Grenfell is a 30 minute drive. All was fine when I went through west bound to Grenfell, but the road was closed when I came back east bound about an hour and fifteen minutes later. Of all the incidents I've seen in my years out here, this was the worst.

Carnage in Whitewood, SK.

One of the first bad accidents I saw, and one that sticks with me to this day, was when I was hauling the wood chips in North Western Ontario. I was doing the night runs, and I was headed to Upsala empty at about 6pm. There are two fairly good uphills between Kaministiquia, (pronounced "Ka-ma-NIST-i-kwa") and Shabaqua (pronounced "SHA-ba-kwa"). Between the two hills is a relatively flat stretch of highway. As I crested the first hill, I was greeted by flashing emergency lights, and 4-way flashers. I came to a stop, and climbed out to see what the issue was. As soon as my feet hit the ground, I was on my butt. The road was coated in black ice. Of all the road conditions, black ice is by far, the most dangerous, It's nearly invisible, and it can take you by total surprise. The road can look perfectly dry, yet be covered with black ice. Black ice, while hard to see, can be predicted and anticipated. When they roads are wet, or precipitation is falling, and the temperature is close to the freezing point, say one or two degrees above or below freezing, conditions are perfect for black ice. Another good indication that black ice forming? Freezing rain. My best advice if you come across these conditions? Get off the road, and park. At this point, I was still a fairly inexperienced driver, but I learned right quick. As I got to the front of the line, there was a tractor trailer that had jack knifed on the icy road. He slid into oncoming traffic, and the drive tires, and the front of the trailer had ridden up and over the huge snowplow on an MTO (Ministry of Transportation Ontario) snow plow and sanding truck, and were sitting on the hood and cab of the plow truck. I stayed quite a ways back, as I didn't want to see too much, but I overheard on of the attending paramedics say: "As soon as we get that truck off him, he's gonna bleed to death." I just turned and walked back to my truck and waited. I wanted no part of witnessing what was inevitably going to happen.

Here in Canada, we get winter for about six months every year, yet for some reason, people seem to forget how to drive in the wintery weather. That, and the fact that some people take great pleasure is fish tailing in the snow, sliding this way and that, under dubious levels of control, really astounds me. These two, one of each, learned their respective lessons the hard way.

I was fuelling at the truck stop just west of Winnipeg one day, and it was snowing lightly. Those big, fluffy, heavy wet snow flakes. Some guy comes whipping in off the highway, way too fast, and he cranks the wheel left, and hits the brakes. Of course, the steering tires didn't respond at all, and he runs into the back of my second trailer, damaging the ICC bar/Datsun stopper. Damage to his pickup is minimal, as is the trailer damage (visually speaking), but unseen damage could be quite extensive. I called my company's accident department, and they wanted the police to attend, just in case the damage was more than it seemed, and to have a police report in case this guy tried the "I was injured" routine. I told the other driver it would be a while, as I was instructed to wait for the police to attend. He said he wasn't waiting, as he was already late for work, and he reminded me that it was illegal not to exchange insurance information. I reminded him, that since the police had been called, if he left, he could be facing a change of hit & run. As it turned out, the damage to the trailer was more than met the eyes. I think the repair bill was $11,000 or something. Well, not only was he late for work, but he was charged with dangerous driving and leaving the scene of an accident. Since he was driving a company vehicle, I'm sure his employer had a few words for him as well.

I was headed west towards Calgary, after delivering in Swift Current, one wintery day, and I was about 10 miles west of town when the roads turned iffy, at best. Being empty, I slowed right down, turned on the 4-ways, and just plodded along, trying to stay out of the ditch. A few minutes later, what do I see in my mirror? Yup, Billy Bigrigger is gonna show me how it's done. I'm doing about 45 mph, and he's running flat out, hell bent for leather. On goes his left signal, and he moves over into the left lane. Except, he didn't STAY in the left lane. His momentum, and the slippery road surface put him right into the ditch, and I had a front row seat to watch him prove how foolish he was. He did manage to keep it on it's wheels, though. Me, I just kept on plodding along. I may have been a little later than planned getting to Calgary, but I managed it without a tow truck.

On the Wild Side
Encounters with the Natural World

Animal incidents, as you'd probably expect, are quite common when you drive for a living. Thankfully, I've only had a couple serious animal collisions, with just one encounter that could have been quite serious, but actually turned into a good laugh. As I recall, it was late summer, early autumn, and I was headed to Vancouver, going over the Coq. It was about three in the morning as I went through the toll plaza, when "nature called". There were no facilities around, but they had a wide, paved shoulder with a few overhead lights that was called a "rest area" for trucks to pull over and stretch, sleep, or what have you. I stopped at the far end, jumped out and walked to the passenger side to "take care of business". Half way through, I noticed a rather strong, pungent odour, along with some rustling, growling sounds. I looked around. Nothing. I looked up. Standing on the top of the rock cut, about 10 ft above my head was a grizzly bear, looking down at me. I swear, he looked as big as a house! As soon as it registered what I was seeing, I dropped, rolled under the trailer to the driver's side, climbed back in the truck, and started grabbing gears as quickly as I could. After a few minutes, my heart returned to somewhere close to its natural place in my chest. I then realized that the nature-call had still been in progress when I was rolled under the trailer. Sweat pants off, and out the window they went. This created a new problem. My duffel bag with all my clean clothes was in a compartment not accessible from inside the truck. Thankfully, it was late enough at night that my one adventure at streaking wasn't noticed by anyone.

One of the more serious animal encounters was on December 29th in 1996. It was six in the morning, 11 miles east of English River, Ontario on the Trans-Canada Highway. I'll remember this for the rest of my life. I was westward-bound, heading home, after spending the night in Thunder Bay. The truck at the time was governed at 55 mph, and I was trucking along with my foot planted to the floor. Since leaving Thunder Bay about two and a half hours earlier, I had seen more than a few moose. Seeing moose isn't all that common, but it does happen. This morning, I had seen about 20 of them in the ditches. In the winter, moose, deer, and other animals will come to the highways to lick the road salt off the roads. Another time, in another part of Ontario, I was woken up when the truck started rocking. Turned out a large bull moose was licking the salt off the truck. This time, however, I'm cruising along, minding my own business, when I saw three moose standing in the ditch. Seeing one moose is unusual, seeing three in the same place is almost unheard of. I immediately slowed down, as they can be unpredictable, and if spooked for any reason, you have no idea what they'll do. They got spooked. Two headed into the bush. The largest one (of course) headed to the road. I slowed down even more. As soon as he got to the pavement, he made a U-turn, heading back to the bush. He went about five feet before making another U-turn, bolting back into the road. I nailed him full broadside, grill to ribs, at about 45 mph. This sent him sliding on his right side across the highway right into the opposite ditch. When we hit, all I could see through the windshield was dark brown fur. I pulled over to check the damage as well as to make sure he was far enough off the road to ensure that someone coming the other way would not hit the carcass. Even with the full broadside, the damage to the truck wasn't too bad. Broken grill, some truck body damage with pieces of fur stuck in it, along with a bit of moose-blood. The truck was still drivable. The moose, however, wasn't as lucky. He was dead. I'm not a veterinarian by any stretch, but it looked like the impact broke all the ribs on that side of his body, which probably caused some serious internal injuries. Judging by the size of him, I'd estimate he weighed in at about 2,000-2,500 lbs. This was the worst moose encounter I had, but far from the only one.

In another case, I had one of the creatures irritated with where I chose to park. This time I was on Highway 17, just east of Marathon, Ontario. On the side of the highway, there is what appears to be an old chair lift, with a parking lot. It's a great place to park any time of the year, but in the spring, summer and autumn, it's a total delight. This spot is at the top of one of the majestic northwestern Ontario hills. The view over Lake Superior is breathtaking. The sounds of the waves rolling in will lull an insomniac to sleep in seconds. Add in the aroma of the natural boreal forest, and it becomes a wonderful place to stop for a few hours, or even the night. There I was, that night, sound asleep. No engine running, no auxiliary power unit (APU) running, and the vents wide open to catch the Great Lake's breeze. A lovely warm summer night, with just the crickets and Lake Superior's waves making nighttime music. Suddenly, I was jolted awake by the truck rocking from side to side. I lay there wondering what had woken me up. Did I imagine something? Was it a dream? Did someone back into me? Was the wind picking up? Where exactly was I? As I lay trying to figure out what was going on, the truck rocked again. Okay, not a dream, and I'm not imagining this. Where am I? Perhaps someone had backed into me? It does happen in truck stops, seldom causing damage, but both drivers can feel the bump. I thought for a minute, remembering that I was in the Marathon rest area. Being backed into, therefore, wasn't likely. No evidence of the wind picking up. What in the devil was going on? THUMP! The truck rocked again. Okay, definitely NOT imagining this. I got up, put on some clothes, not sure what was outside the truck. I opened the curtains, trying to see what was going on. Total blackness. Pitch black. I turned on the work lights (which shine backwards down the side of the trailer), and lo and behold, there's a moose, head down, head butting the trailer, trying to push it out of the way. It took him about another five minutes of head-ramming before he gave up, and wandered away.

I did have another moose collision, kind of, in Northern Ontario. Again, late at night, but this time I was closer to Nipigon, near the top of a rather long, hard climb known as Cavers Hill. This spot has since been reworked with a passing lane, which has made the hill a lot safer. People used to take some crazy chances passing the big rigs as they slowly climbed the steep almost-mountain-like hill. I've seen more than a few near head-on collisions. In this case, I had just crested the hill, starting to pick up speed again. Suddenly, I thought I saw something out the corner of my eye. One of those quick "somethings" we've all experienced. I dismissed it, since nothing else untoward happened, carrying on to Nipigon, where I would fuel up. As I was fuelling, I walked around the truck, checking tires and lights, and in general, inspecting the truck and trailer. Down the passenger side of the trailer, as well as along the front of the placard holder, there was a small piece of what looked like bloody leather. From there to the front of the trailer, I saw what looked like a smear in the dark brown dirt on the trailer. The only thing I could think of was that the "something" I thought I saw was my lights reflecting off of the eye of a moose. The big animal must have been standing on the dark shoulder of the highway, blending in perfectly with the surroundings. When it heard me coming, it must have turned his head towards the sound. This resulted in the large protruding moose nose to make contact with the side of trailer. The sharp edge of the placard holder trimmed a piece off its nose, leaving a trail along the trailer side.

As you may have noticed, Northern Ontario is prime source for wildlife. You're not wrong. Seldom do I have a run through Northern Ontario where I don't see wildlife. Moose, deer, bears, hawks, eagles, owls, skunks, porcupines, turtles, beavers, and countless small animals, like chipmunks, squirrels, otters, and such are all over the place. Except for otters, I've hit them all. Deer most often. Like moose, when they get spooked, it's anyone's guess where they'll run. Of these, moose and bear pose the biggest danger. Moose due to their size, and bears because while they're really small compared to a truck, they are solid mass. With a truck, you don't hit a bear and push him out of the way. You'll knock him over, then the truck will just roll over top of him, putting your truck in a precariously uneven situation. Due to the bear's mass, there's a good chance you may end up on your side, with a very upset, injured bear nearby. The one time I did hit a bear, I was lucky enough that the truck was equipped with a "moose bumper". I'm sure you've seen them. Aluminum, tubular bumpers that sit close to the ground. The frame spreads around the grill to protect the grill in case of wildlife strikes. Trust me, they work. I hit the bear on Highway 11/17 by Red Rock, Ontario. The moose-bumper prevented the animal from getting under the truck, just rolling it off into the ditch. I don't know if the impact killed the bear or not. I wasn't about to get out and check. If I had, and it was only injured, this book may never have been written.

In my early days of team driving, my co-driver Evan and I had an interesting wildlife experience. The run from Duluth, Minnesota, to Thunder Bay takes you along Minnesota Highway 61 which is a two-lane road to the Canada/USA border. It's about 150 miles of awesome scenery following the shore of Lake Superior. Over the years, erosion of the hilly lakeside has caused some concerns for the roadbed resulting in various changes to the highway. Most notably, two tunnels were punched through the semi-mountainous rocky landscape. One of the tunnels is fairly short, the other longer tunnel has an "S" bend in it, meaning that you can't see one end from the other. There we were, trucking along at about 60 mph, no sweat. Very little traffic, until we get about half way through the longer tunnel. Right there, in the middle of the road were about a dozen deer. I had about three seconds to decide what to do. In the end, there was really nothing I COULD do, except brace for the impact. Surprisingly, nothing happened. They all managed to scramble out of the way. After this, I probably should have bought a lottery ticket.

Not all wildlife encounters involve creatures on four legs. One February, I was on a westbound-run towards Thunder Bay on the northern route of Highway 11. Around five in the morning, I was cruising along the section of highway between Hearst and Longlac in Northwestern Ontario. It was a fairly mild mid-winter night with a completely overcast sky (which helps hold in the heat), and no moon. Dawn was still several hours away meaning that I was in the midst of total night-blackness with just my headlights cutting a path through the darkness. Without any warning, there was a SMASH! I was instantly covered in broken glass all the while getting slapped in the face by something big. It was both soft and hard at the same time, confusing me even more. I managed to get the truck stopped without hitting the ditch, a feat in itself considering the shoulder along that stretch of the highway is little more than about 18 inches of snow-covered dirt. I turned on the interior light. There in the passenger seat was an owl! The huge feathered-creature had come through the passenger-side windshield, leaving a rather large hole in the glass. Now the bird was trying to fly away! I got out, left my door open, opened the passenger door, just waiting for the owl to find a way out. Eventually the shook-up bird simply flew off, a good end to its encounter with my truck. I, however, had another challenge. Now I had to find something to plug the hole in the windshield until I could get to Thunder Bay to get it replaced. I ended up driving the rest of the route to the city with a pillow stuffed in the hole. I had to put on every sweater I had, plus a winter jacket, wool hat and gloves while cranking the heat up to maximum for the remaining three-hour drive to Thunder Bay. Bird strikes, while rare, aren't unheard of. Larger birds, while hit less often, obviously do more damage. In addition to the owl, I've hit one or two Canada Geese. These beasts are slow on take off, and climb even slower. The fact that you can see them from a greater distance, allows you more time to slow, and maneuver to try and avoid a bird strike, but it also means they can't get up and out of the way as quickly, either. During the early spring and summer is when they can be the biggest threat. When their chicks hatch, they don't fly. They walk. Slowly. And they don't obey pedestrian crosswalks. Drivers try their best to avoid hitting them, but it's not always possible. When the chicks grow stronger, and they do start to fly, they can become a real hazard. Fortunately, I've never had one come through the windshield. Anyone who has experienced a Canada Goose can attest that they aren't exactly friendly. Twice, I've narrowly avoided having one hit the windshield, and had them bounce off the air dam just above the windshield. One of them survived to the best of my knowledge. The other one I saw land with a thud on the road behind me. Felt sorry for it, but that's life. Smaller birds are another story. Usually, they're quicker to react, and get out of the way, but one summer a few years back, I was hitting five or six a day, every day, for three weeks. I was running a dedicated run from Winnipeg to International Falls, MN, crossing at Warrod, MN, and running MN 11 to International Falls. I'd drop and empty trailer at the paper mill, and pick up a preloaded trailer that another driver had brought from Minneapolis. I'd then cross back into Canada at Fort Frances, ON, and return to Winnipeg, then head out again the next day. The drive along MN 11 is beautiful. Lovely scenery, and a few towns along the way to break up the monotony. In late August/ early September, I noticed I was running into a LOT of very small birds, many of which were actually stuck head first in the screen grill of the truck. This went on for about three week, and it was very puzzling. Until I had to take my dog to the vet. I asked him if he had any ideas what was causing this "mass bird suicide". Due to the weather that year, there was an abundance of fresh fruits in the area. Raspberries, strawberries, and more importantly, apples and crab apples. As the season drew to a close, the fruit ripens, and fall to the ground, starts to rot and ferment, to spread the seeds, and perpetuate the cycle of life. This is where the birds entered the picture. They were eating the fermented fruit, and getting drunk, which causes erratic behaviour in all creatures, great and small. So they may or may not have even known there was a truck in the immediate area, and SPLAT! Bye bye birdie.

As my driving adventures take me all over North America, I've had a few run-ins with wildlife indigenous to those regions. On a trip along US 191 through Yellowstone National Park, I came across a heard of buffalo sunning themselves on the road. Nothing to do, but wait. I set the brakes, just enjoying the view of these giant beauties doing what they do best. Of course, it wasn't long before a few cars were lined up behind me. They couldn't see what was going in front of me. One curious guy appeared to think I was "just another dumb trucker stopping to look at something". He got out of his car, walking up to my window and telling me to get moving. I just pointed at the dozen or so buffalo laying all over the road. He looked, saw them there, then walked up to the closest one, kicking it in the ribs! I was expecting carnage on an epic scale. But the buffalo just turned its head, and looked at him for a minute, then turned back and put his head down again. The smart-ass guy kicked him again. This time the buffalo climbed to its feet, turned full on, snorting at the irritation. Here comes the carnage! Thankfully, no. The somewhat-wiser guy just high tailed it back to his car, quickly jumping in. The buffalo then resumed its on-road sunbathing. About an hour later, the herd finally shuffled off the road, letting the traffic through Yellowstone start moving once more.

Texas has some awesome wild life. Like armadillos. I've been told that they have very poor eye sight, but are easily startled. Evidently, when they are startled, they jump. It's been said that more vehicles have been hit by armadillos, than armadillos have been hit by vehicles. My one experience with an armadillo was about 20 miles north of the Mexican border, near Laredo. He was on the shoulder of the highway. I assume I startled him, as he jumped, bolting across the road in front of me. Next thing I felt was a series of THUMPS. He was wedged between the tires on the trailer. Didn't even have to get out to check, I knew what it was.

I parked on the shoulder, got out, grabbing my crowbar from behind the cab, hoping I could pry him out. As luck would have it, he was in a good position. I didn't have to move the truck at all to get at him. Crowbar in hand, I started trying to pry him out. It took about 15 minutes to get the armadillo free. To my surprise, the little guy wasn't dead. I got it back on its stubby little feet, watching as it scampered off into the scrub brush. Tough little critters those armadillos. They're not the only tough animals I've encountered.

Just outside of Dryden, Ontario, I was running with a friend back home to Winnipeg. We were chatting about this, that, and the other thing on the CB. I saw something on the road. I swerved to get around it, when my friend, in mid-sentence, just started laughing his fool-head off. It took a few minutes before he could regain his composure enough to speak coherently again. He finally said; "That poor turtle spent four hours getting half way across the road, then you come along, clip his shell and send him back to the middle of the lake!". I guess I didn't swerve far enough, catching the edge of the shell with the trailer tires. Apparently, it looked just like when you squeeze a pumpkin seed between your fingers. The poor turtle was launched across the shoulder of the road right back into the lake. Sorry dude, that wasn't my intention.

For a few months, we were hauling meat loads from Alberta to various points in Florida, then reloading house plants in Loxahatchee, Florida, for Walmart Canada. I had one of the first loads going to Florida, but it was a load of paper in a reefer trailer. Since reefers are heavier than dry vans, I had to be aware of my axle and gross weights. Paper loads are usually 46,000 to 47,000 lbs. Dry vans can carry that weight, while staying under the 80,000 lbs legal limit. Reefer loads are usually 42,000 to 43,000 lbs keeping the total weight under the 80,000 lbs limit. I had to run all the way from Toronto to just outside Miami with no more than a half tank of fuel, to keep the gross weight legal. Diesel fuel weighs about seven lbs per gallon. Running on half-tanks reduces your gross weight by about 1,400 lbs, depending on the capacity of your fuel tanks. As soon as I passed the last scale, I pulled in, fuelling to capacity. I delivered the paper, then headed to Loxahatchee, north of Miami up near Palm Beach. I called for directions (again, pre-GPS days), following them to the letter. On the dirt road into the farm where they grew the plants, again, nature called. I remembered the shipper advising against getting out of the truck along the dirt road, because alligators lived in the neighbourhood. I just stood on the top step of the running board, with about 10 feet of dirt road between me and the water filled ditch, figuring I was plenty safe. That gator came out of the ditch like a rocket, grabbing the bottom step of the running board, about 18 inches below me. Scared the living daylights out of me. He had bitten into the running board before I had even registered what was happening. Bathroom break was over right quick. I got to the shipper's location, bedding down for the night. They had an electrified fence around the perimeter to keep the alligators out, along with a cattle guard across the driveway to prevent them from entering that way. A cattle guard is a series of steel tubes running perpendicular to the road. When cattle, or other wild life try to cross it, their feet fall through the openings and they get stuck. I spent that night hoping it worked on alligators, too.

Anyone who has driven in the greater Toronto Area, is more than well aware of the exit from the east bound 401 to the northbound 400. The ramps from the collector and express lanes merge, then turn sharply to the left, and climb a rather short, but steep uphill. The curve has a posted maximum speed of 25 mph, but due to the hill, some drivers tend to push the limit somewhat. This is NEVER a good idea. One evening, as I was preparing to take this exit, I found it closed. The reason? A cattle truck had taken the ramp too fast, and flipped over on it's side. Cattle were everywhere. Some injured, and spooked, some just grazing away on the grass beside the highway.

10-4 Good Buddy
My Colleagues - the Good, the Bad, and the Ugly

In North America, about 90% of all consumer products are delivered by truck. Add to that all the bits and pieces that are needed to manufacture more consumer goods, industrial operations, and numerous other projects. For many years now there has been a trucker shortage. For some reason, long-haul driving does not appeal to younger workers looking for employment. In recent years, there has been a major shift on who the long-haulers are. One study in 2016 found that almost half are new Canadians coming from South Asia and other overseas locations. That is very different from when I started trucking. The 1991 Canadian Census reported that only 8% of truckers were immigrants. Another interesting dynamic of the trade are women drivers. Less than 8% of long-haul truckers are women, and the vast majority of women are part of a husband-wife team. Long-haul driving can be challenging. As the title suggests, long distances are involved. To meet this definition of a trucker, you need to travel at least 100 miles from your home terminal, often crossing international borders, and being on the road for long periods of time.

Most drivers you'll encounter are decent, honest folks, more than willing to help, but not all of them. Some will even lie to hand off a bad situation to another driver. One such incident happened to me. If I ever find said driver again, it won't be pretty. I was sound asleep in Montreal at the terminal. I had a reload the next morning that that would bring me home for my days off. About 2:30 a.m. my phone woke me up. It was the night dispatcher in Winnipeg, telling me a driver was just south of the border with a "hot load" of frozen chicken that had to be delivered at six a.m. but he was having electrical issues with his truck. Could I go and recover the load? Being the nice guy I am, I readily agreed, asking dispatch to send the details to my satellite. I got dressed, grabbed a coffee, and off I went to Champlain, in upstate New York, about 46 miles south of Montreal. When I met the guy at the truck stop, he was already unhooked from the trailer, with the paperwork in a bag, tied to the trailer. I hooked up, checking the paperwork to be sure all was in order. It wasn't. As I mentioned earlier, meat loads crossing the border have to be done perfectly. Any errors can create a disaster. This one was missing the original meat certificate. A photocopy, or even a certified fax copy isn't good enough. It must be the original. By the time I realized the original was missing, the other driver miraculously had his electrical gremlins solved, and was on his way to Montreal. There I was, two miles from the border at three in the morning, with a load that will be rejected unless I can sort the mess out. I called dispatch to tell them what was going on, emphasizing that I needed the original meat certificate, or this load will be rejected. Of course, at that time of the day, there was no one around who could help sort the problem out. As there was nothing I could do at this point, I went back to bed. At least there was now a record of the time this mess started. The next morning, I called the CSR for the load, putting him to work to get this mess cleaned up. He called the shipper, who said they never send the original, always a photocopy, and they've never had an issue. Next, I went to Canada Customs, handed the officer the paperwork, telling him the story I had been told by the shipper.

The customs agent chuckled, telling me to park in the lot, then come in to the building. Of course, the load isn't going to be cleared without the original certificate. They didn't flat out reject the load, which was surprising, but they did tell me I'd have to get an original certificate for the load to continue into Canada. I called the CSR back, explaining the situation. Once again, he got the shipper on the line, and, once again, explained the situation. The shipper had no idea what to do, as the original was in their office someplace.

All meat certificates have a serial number on them, which must correspond to the serial numbers on the boxes with the meat. For example, if all the boxes in the trailer have number "1234" on them, then the meat certificate needs the "1234" on it as well. The shipper prints the stickers that are placed on the boxes, matching them to the certificate they'll be using. To issue a replacement certificate, they would have to use a supplemental certificate, which has the "issued in lieu of certificate 1234", then send along the original version of the replacement to accompany the load. Since the load originated in Mississippi, it was going to be the next day before they could courier the original to me at the Canadian border crossing (where I was still awaiting entry into Canada). I had no option but to sit there until the certificate arrived. And trust me, there's NOTHING to do at Customs. The law says they have to provide you access to food, water and toilet facilities. A bathroom, vending machines and a water fountain fit those requirements. At 10 the next morning, FedEx arrived with a package for me. I opened it up, immediately seeing that they had, again, screwed up by sending a photocopy. I went to explain the situation to Customs. They were sympathetic, but not impressed. Once more, I called the CSR to tell him what happened. Once more, he called the shipper, giving them an earful. They promised to fix it as soon as possible. The next morning, (day two) FedEx showed up again. Opened it up, there's the original! It even said: "Issued in lieu of 1234". Bonus! Except, the inspecting veterinarian hadn't signed the form. Back to Customs I went. Now they're most definitely not impressed. Before I could call the CSR, Customs called the shipper, explaining in no uncertain terms what was required, and if they got it wrong this time, the load would be rejected, with monetary penalties assessed. Next morning (day three – I should have been home by now) FedEx showed up once more. Open the package, all is in order, except the pre-clearance required by CFIA hasn't been received yet. This is a minor issue, happening fairly often. An hour later, the pre-clearances were received, and I was cleared by customs to carry on and deliver the load. I didn't deliver it, I just dropped it in the yard. I was completely done with this load, I just wanted it off my truck. Whether it was ever delivered or not, I don't know.

Some of the other drivers I've met on the road leave me scratching my head, wondering how they manage to get through the day without suffocating.

Of course, when I meet such people, I just have to have fun with them, or else I just stare in utter disbelief at what comes out of their mouths. Case in point: A driver I met in Laredo Texas. It was the height of summer, and it was HOT! I was at the truck stop, and the truck was idling away with A/C on, so that I wouldn't melt in the truck. This was back in the days before the anti-idling laws, long before Auxiliary Power Units (APUs) were available. I climbed out of the truck, finding two drivers beside the truck, trying to figure out why there was a plug-in under the door. Rather than explain it was for the block heater, to help ensure the truck will start in the winter, I just went off the cuff, telling them that Canadian trucks are all electric. This is how we charge them up. A full charge will give us three to four weeks of running. They bought it, hook, line, and sinker. The whole time, the truck was idling away, making all the expected noises.

Another driver in Laredo once asked me where he could get winter fuel, as he was going "up north". Winter fuel (commonly known as #1 diesel) is needed in northern climates during the winter months to prevent fuel from gelling. It is more refined, with additives to prevent gelling, which clogs fuel lines, and plugs fuel filters. As it was mid-summer, I gave him a strange look, asking "just how far north are you going?" Unless he was headed to Alaska, winter fuel wasn't needed. Even if he was, he wouldn't need it for a few days, if he even needed it at all. He said he was headed up north to Dallas. Texas. 380 miles north of Laredo. No need for winter fuel, even in February, and I told him that. The look he gave me told me he wasn't sure whether to believe me, or not.

One driver I used to work with, was a bit of an ego-driven sort, that I really had no use for. I'm sure you know the type: ten-gallon hat, cowboy boots, tight jeans, cowboy shirt, rope tie, and a belt buckle that looks like a melted down Cadillac. In 2001, TransX started testing trucks with higher horsepower, to see what the fuel economy would be, as opposed to the old trucks. The older trucks were equipped with 350 hp engines, and a ten-speed transmission. Ten of the newer trucks were equipped with 460 hp engines, and 13 speed transmissions. I was one of the drivers selected to test the 460 hp trucks. I got the second one in line, but because I lived near the home terminal, I was the first to drive one. About this time, TransX also took delivery of a few trucks another company had ordered, but had gone out of business. These trucks were a variation of the old ones TransX had, but with double bunks, and the "maxi-cruise" engine, which could be programmed for anywhere from 350 hp to 380 hp. This particular driver, let's call him Cowboy, decided to lease one of the maxi-cruise trucks from TransX. He had them turn the horsepower up to 380. As luck would have it, one day Cowboy and I both picked up paper loads from the old Kenora paper mill, going to the US, crossing at International Falls, Minnesota. The highway from Kenora to International Falls is a twisting, winding, hilly road, with a single passing lane along its 96 mile length. The whole way down this highway, Cowboy was "maxi-cruise this, and maxi-cruise that, blah blah blah." All the trucks were governed at 65 mph, so his "higher horsepower" wasn't readily apparent. Since he was ahead of me, the only hope I had of getting away from him was to stop and wait until he was out of CB range. As we approached the passing lane, he said: "Now watch what a REAL truck can do!" As he started up the passing lane, I dropped a gear, and planted my foot to the floor. Before he knew what was happening, I was beside him, and still passing him. Before the passing lane ended, he was behind me. The next thing I heard from Cowboy was: "WTF?!?!? How the hell did you do that?" I just replied "460 beats 380 every day of the week." Never heard another word from him. Not that day, and not a single word since. Not that I miss it, either.

In trucking, some loads are carried by more than one truck, as the loads to New York were. One truck brought the load from the Alberta meat plant to Winnipeg, then I took it from Winnipeg to New York. You are, however, at the mercy of the previous driver's integrity regarding pre-trip inspections. The trailer I received should be in good running order as it had already been inspected by the first driver and had travelled 700-odd miles to get to me in Winnipeg. On one occasion, the lack of the previous driver's inspection resulted in an incredibly huge and expensive ordeal. During the pre-trip inspection, we are required (by law) to inspect and report the condition of various aspects and items on the truck and trailer, all related to safcty. One of the items to be inspected is the frame and support cross members on the trailer. The cross members run under the floor, from side to side, providing support, so the floor doesn't buckle and collapse. Cross members are spaced about 8 inches apart running the full length of the trailer, with more cross members closer to the king pin, and above the axles. This is an easy check so I expected the previous driver to have completed the process.

Now, for New York runs, I'd leave Friday at six a.m. in order to reach Pembina, North Dakota for an eight-a.m. meat inspection. The pre-trip check shouldn't take long as I was taking a load that had already been on the road before I arrived at the yard. This particular Friday, I hooked up, then started the supposedly-no-problem check. Instead, I found five or six badly damaged cross members. This condition was not something that had occurred during the 700-mile trip between Alberta and Winnipeg. It should have been caught by the original driver.

I contacted the shop, who were just getting their day started. They notified me that it would take at least two hours before they could even get the trailer in the shop to start the repairs. This would inevitably make me late for the meat inspector, possibly delaying the meat inspection until Monday, then delaying the delivery in New York. I let dispatch know what was going on, complete with pictures. With input from the shop, it was decided to get across the border, clear customs and meat inspection, then get the repairs done. By the time everything was done in Pembina, I had wasted five hours. I had some serious driving to do to get back on schedule, all because someone didn't do their job. Unfortunately, this problem always has been, and always will be, an ongoing problem in the industry.

Hey, Teach!
There are No Stupid Questions... Are There?

In the late 1990's, TransX started a program for new drivers. They even briefly operated a driving school, but it didn't last very long. Some of the students stayed at TransX, entering the long-haul training program. The program had three stages of trainees. Level One were drivers with less than three months experience. Basically, these drivers had just passed their road tests. Level Two, was for drivers who had between three months and one-year worth of experience. Level Three was one to two years' experience. For a while I was a Level One instructor, which basically meant while they drove, I sat in the passenger seat giving instruction, helping to mould them into a safe, professional driver. It wasn't always easy, nor was it always fun, but it was rewarding. And it paid pretty good, as well. I was paid my regular rate, plus an extra five cents a mile. We were supposed to be given loads with "soft" ETA's (no rush loads), and no "hard" loads.

My first student, Dave, was a nice enough guy, about as green a driver as there ever could be. The first load we were given was a set of super-B's going from Winnipeg to Vancouver. Talk about going to the wolves straight out of the gate! We were loaded pretty heavy, as well - almost 130,000 lbs. Due to the weight, we went the easier route: via Edmonton and the Fraser Canyon. He did pretty good, except for the last hill coming into Hope,

British Columbia, which is a 10% grade. He blew the shifting, causing us to come to a dead stop. Unfortunately, his confidence also came to a dead stop. I got us up the hill. He declined to drive the rest of the way to Vancouver. He tried again on the trip back to Calgary, doing much better, as we had a much lighter load. In order not to scare him too much, I drove through Kicking Horse Pass. He was still shaking, even though he was in the jump seat. Kicking Horse Pass can be very intimidating, even in the summer. It has a speed limit of 25 mph, consists of a series of near-hairpin turns, with a road that looks like they just carved a notch in the side of the mountain and paved it. Doing 25 mph in a semi is not a good idea. Top speed in those corners would be about 15 mph if that. Back in those days, the highway ran through a short valley, then climbed "10-Mile Hill", which was a winding, two-lane hill, with a 10% grade. It's now a four-lane divided highway, and the gradient of the hill is much gentler, but still a pretty good pull.

We delivered in Calgary that evening. The next morning, we were given a reload back to Winnipeg. Off we went, and waited. We arrived for our 10 am appointment, then assigned a door to back into. Dave backed in with a little difficulty, but not too much. Then the bottom fell out. We were finally loaded at 6 pm! I was NOT impressed. Actually, I was seething. I told Dave I'd drive back, as this had suddenly become a rush load. Had they loaded us on time, we'd have been fine. I don't remember the details, but it was a JIT (Just In Time) load, that had to arrive be in Winnipeg for 8 am the next day, or the production line would come to a stop until the freight arrived. We left at about 6:15 p.m. after fuelling up. That is the one and only time I have ever driven 13 hours non-stop. Not even bathroom stops. We arrived in Winnipeg at 7:15 a.m. where our city driver was waiting to deliver the load. Dave and I packed our gear to go home for our days off. I never saw, or heard from, him again. I guess he'd had enough.

My next student was the son of one of our seasoned drivers. A nice guy, and eager to learn. We'll name him Sonny. Any menial jobs to be done, he was on top of it. We took on an LTL load for Regina. Sonny's first action was to pull out the map, and plan the route (easy route, one highway, just over 300 miles). Again, this was pre-GPS/Google Maps days. When we got into Regina, I directed him to the terminal. We arrived, dropped the trailer, and were given an empty reefer to take to nearby National Meats in Moose Jaw, Saskatchewan. We'd drop the empty one, and hook onto a load to Chicago. I told Sonny flat out, that there was no way he would be driving in Chicago. He was fine with that. We headed for Moose Jaw, dropped the empty unit, and hooked to the loaded trailer.

Our new cargo turned out to be a load of swinging beef going to the south side of Chicago. Wonderful! Not a nice area of Chicago. Add to that, swinging beef in the trailer. One of, if not the hardest loads to drive. Swinging meat has a high centre of gravity. As the name implies, it swings in the trailer as you move. Turn right, the load, and your centre of gravity moves to the left. Turn left, it swings right. Hit the brakes, it moves forward; accelerate, it moves back. And it can be very unforgiving. I looked at Sonny, then told him to enjoy the scenery. No way he was going to be doing any of the driving. Back on the road, we crossed the border at Portal, North Dakota. US customs decided they wanted to check the interior of the truck, as well as search our duffel bags. I thought, "Dude, you wanna rummage through my dirty shorts, have at it!" I didn't say it, but I thought it. The agent was rummaging though, coming upon an old plastic powdered lemonade container that I used for laundry detergent. He opened it, asking me what the powder was. I told him laundry soap. It was the white granular type that had some blue crystals mixed in (I don't remember the brand). He looked at it again, giving me the raised eyebrow, suspicious look. Whatever. I know what it is. He asked me again, and I told him again, "laundry soap". He took a whiff; again, the raised eyebrow look. He asked a third time, and for a third time I replied "laundry soap." Then he decided to taste it. He immediately spit it out, put the lid back on, then told us to get the hell out of there. We quickly left, heading for the USDA meat house, had the load inspected, passed, and off we went to Chicago.

At the drop off, Sonny wanted to back the trailer in. I let him, warning him that with swinging loads, you have to be perfectly positioned to the door, as the roof rails in the trailer need to line up within 1/8 of an inch of the rails in the building, or they can't unload. You can't, however, see either the rails in the building, or the trailer while you're backing in. Fortunately, this place sent a helper out with a two-way radio to assist drivers backing in.

After delivering the load of swinging meat, we were given a load of LTL from the Chicago yard to the Toronto yard. LTL loads are never ready before 6 p.m., usually they're not ready until 10 p.m. This meant we had time to wash the trailer out as swinging meat loads make a mess of the trailer's interior. We dropped the clean unit at the Chicago yard, then we sacked out for a while. About 10 pm, our LTL was ready to go. We headed to the truck stop in Lake Station, Indiana, where I showed Sonny how to set up a customs clearance. He caught on quick, and set up all the other clearances, sorting paperwork out by drops, and faxed everything off to the proper customs brokers. These days, setting up customs clearances is much easier, and less time consuming. Back then, it was at least two hours for the brokers to process the paperwork and submit it to customs. We continued on our way to customs. We stopped about half way there, calling all the brokers to see if everything was okay, or if there were any issues. No issues at all. We carried on, and breezed through customs.

About an hour out of Toronto, we received a dispatch request for another load, this one was a load of paper sitting in the Toronto yard, going to Cranston, Rhode Island. I checked the map to see exactly where it was, in relation to New York City. At that time, I wanted nothing to do with New York City (this would change later on). Cranston is more than 300 miles away, meaning I could comfortably accept the load. We dropped the LTL in the yard, and hooked to the paper load, which was in a reefer. I was a bit confused, as paper doesn't need to be temperature controlled, but whatever. I guess the only trailer they had available was a reefer. Our gross weight was a little high, maybe 2,000 lbs over, but that easily fixed by running half-tanks of fuel. At Customs we were confirmed good to cross, and off we went. We easily found the place, and delivered the load.

It was at this time that I found out why we had a reefer. We were to load prepared salads at Blue Ridge Farms in Brooklyn, New York. I almost came unglued. I called the planner, telling him what he could do with said load. I had to remind him that since I had a Level One student driver with me no big city loads and unloads were allowed. In reply I got the standard "we need this load covered, and there's no one else in the area". Yeah right! They knew what they were doing. Why else would the paper have been loaded in a reefer? Being the nice guy that I am, I begrudgingly took the load, telling Sonny, my trainee, that he couldn't drive until we were out of the city. I called the shipper for directions, which I got, along with a warning that it's "a bitch of a place to get in and out of. You'll see when you get here."

When we arrived, I learned what the term "understatement" really meant! It was an older facility, built when 40 ft trailers were the longest available. Sonny and I arrived with a 53 ft trailer! The road they are on is a six-lane divided street with a low bridge just beyond their entrance meaning that there was only one way in, and out. Getting in was hell. In my 26 years of driving truck, it is still the worst place I've ever had to back into. As you drive up, they are on the right-hand side of the street, but there's not enough room to pull into the lot or to turn around to back in. You have to start on the street, blindside reverse into the yard, 180 degrees around the fence posts, then swing the trailer 90 degrees to the left to line up with the docks. Imagine backing in a backwards question mark. It wasn't a lot of fun, especially since they only ship between ten p.m. and four am. The shipping times were necessary as every truck backing in holds up traffic for at least 10 minutes. We got loaded, and were ready to leave. We had two choices. Drive against traffic (head east in the west bound lanes) to the next intersection, then move over onto the right side of the street, or drive over the median to get to our side of the street. Turning right was out of the question, due to the 10 ft bridge, which we couldn't fit under. I waited for the lights to stop oncoming traffic, and drove on the wrong side of the street to the lights, then moved to our side of the road. We got back onto the Interstate, drove to the first service plaza, and that was it. We were told the load had to deliver at noon the next day in Toronto, but I couldn't have cared less. I was still pissed off at the trickery that had been pulled, along with being pretty stressed out from driving through Brooklyn. I pulled the plug, and we sacked out for the night. They could reschedule the delivery.

Sonny and I dropped the salad load in Toronto, then headed home with LTL for Calgary. As my family lives in Thunder Bay, I always plan the trips through Ontario to allow me to stop for at least a meal or two. I usually spend the night, having both supper and breakfast with my family before carrying on. When we were getting ready to leave Thunder Bay at about four the next morning, I decided to drive to Winnipeg. It's about an eight-hour drive, and not challenging at all, so I figured Sonny would like the break, which he did, of course. But I think I spooked him a little. I was driving what I considered normal, but when we stopped for lunch in Dryden, a driver that had been following us started talking to us at the truck stop. He had deduced that one of us was in training, and that the trainee was riding shot gun at the time. My trainee asked how he knew that. He said he figured it out by the number of cigarette-butts he saw flying out the passenger window (I don't, and never have condoned littering, especially cigarette butts. I always have, and always will use an ashtray). Trainee Sonny admitted to being a bit nervous about the speed I was driving, which, I'll admit, was above the speed limit.

All I really recall about the rest of Sonny's time with me was our last trip from Toronto to Winnipeg. Part of Level One training included how to handle dangerous goods loads. Since we hadn't had any dangerous goods loads at all, while we were still in Toronto, I told Sonny that we would simulate some danger goods being on the trailer for the trip to Winnipeg. As it turned out, the load we were given back to Winnipeg was full of dangerous goods. It had everything except radioactive and explosive. We spent about two hours preparing as I had him go through the entire LTL shipment to make sure all was legal, and the proper placards were on the trailer. Hauling dangerous goods can be tricky. Some dangerous goods can't travel together, while some can't be in the same trailer as non-dangerous goods. For example, you don't want rat poison on the same trailer as food products. Some dangerous goods can't travel with other dangerous goods in the same class. You don't want dynamite on the same trailer with blasting caps. Unless you want to spread the truck, trailer, cargo and yourself across a wide stretch of the countryside. But it has been done. One company went bankrupt when a part load of dynamite went off, as the trailer also contained blasting caps. That load left a nice divot in the road about 20 ft by 20 ft and 6 ft deep. I have picked up illegal loads with dangerous goods. Rat poison loaded with food products. Those go right back to the dock to be corrected. I don't take chances with loads like that. If you ever got caught at a scale, you will find yourself in a world of hurt. The cost to get it fixed at the scale is staggering. It has to be corrected before you can even leave the scale.

For a time, I was asked to take out Level Three trainees. Level Three is running full-team miles, as the students are supposedly fully trained, just needing some road experience. I had three such trainees, two of which nearly killed me, the third severely tried my patience.

The first one didn't last two days. We had a load to Vancouver, and we were going to switch drivers in Golden British Columbia, just west of Kicking Horse Pass. I told him: "If you feel drowsy, tired, or whatever, wake me up. Even if you just need to know the correct time, WAKE ME UP! I'd rather be woken up for something stupid than to die because you didn't want to disturb me!" I've never really been one to sleep very well when someone else is driving, and this one cemented it for me. We were coming down Ten-Mile Hill, with me already awake and dressed. I climbed out of the bunk and into the jump seat. I looked over, and this guy was pretty much asleep at the wheel. I yelled at him to wake up, pulling the trailer brake since the speed was getting a little excessive. He jolted awake, saying: "I'm not sleeping!" I asked him where we were. He had no clue. He'd definitely been asleep. When we got to Golden, he parked, then I went in calling our dispatch, who put me through to the director of safety. I told the director of safety what had happened, telling him: "Only one of us is taking this truck to Vancouver. Me or him. Your call." The director asked to speak to the trainee. After the call, he got up to go to the washroom. After I'd finished eating, he hadn't yet returned. When I got back to the truck, all his gear was gone. How he got home, I do not know.

The second Level Three trainee I had was marginally better. We had a meat load going to Vancouver, with a firm delivery appointment. Before I crawled into the bunk, I gave him the same spiel about waking me up if needed. He didn't. He got tired, pulling over for a nap. Six hours later, I woke up, realizing what had happened. There was no way we were going to make delivery on time. I called dispatch, telling them what had happened, noting that we were now on our way, giving them an ETA. They called the receiver, rebooking the appointment for our new ETA. As we drove, I chewed his butt pretty good. He was supposed to be trained, meaning he should know better than to risk missing an appointment without a good reason. He apologized continuously, saying that he would handle the unloading while I caught up on some sleep. I basically told him: "You got

THAT right!" We arrived in time, where I backed into the dock, gave him the bills and said: "Don't bother me until the trailer is empty!" I crawled back into bed. The load was boxed beef. 500+ boxes, all on the floor. It took him three hours to stack them all onto pallets. I'm betting he never made that mistake again.

On the trip back to Winnipeg, I was driving when we were shut down in Brooks, Alberta when the Trans-Canada highway was closed. A winter storm had dumped a fair bit of snow making travel impossible. I left him a note on the steering wheel that the road was closed, then I crawled into the bunk. About five hours later I woke up when the truck moved. I crawled out to see what happened. We were now in Swift Current, Saskatchewan, 200 miles east of where I went to sleep! He was just parking the truck. He said he woke up, figured that everything looked good, so he started driving. He was amazed that there was no traffic at all on the highway. I told him there is seldom traffic when the highway is closed. He shrugged saying: "It wasn't that bad". After that, I pocketed the keys. When we got back to Winnipeg, he was out of the truck. I think he stayed with the company for a while, but I was done with him.

The final Level Three trainee I had wasn't really a trainee. He had plenty of driving experience, but he needed training on cross-border shipments. Should be easy enough, but he REALLY pushed my buttons. We were taking a load of French fries from Portage La Prairie, Manitoba, to Laredo, Texas, for furtherance into Mexico, meaning that this load was travelling on a T&E bond. We were scheduled to leave Saturday, so I told him I'd go get the load Friday, then get everything set up so we could leave at eight a.m. Saturday. He was okay with that. I picked up the load, scaled it, adjusted the weights, and got everything ready to go, except for filling out the customs paper work. I got to the yard at about 7:30 Saturday morning, and waited for him to arrive. And waited. And waited. And waited some more. At 10 am, I called him to see what was going on. He had just had breakfast, and was going to take a shower. Not off to a great start. He showed up at 11:30, eating a McDonald's breakfast, and informed me (the trainer), that we would be doing four-hour shifts. Four hours driving, four hours in the bunk all the way to Texas. I always preferred a 10 on, 10 off rotation. Less stopping, more driving. He got all bent out of shape. I (being the nice teacher) agreed. I showed him how to fill out the customs paper work, then off we went. Minimal delays at the border. When we were done, he jumped in the bunk saying he'd be up in two and a half hours to switch. We stopped in Fargo (four hours south of Winnipeg) to fuel and switch. He grabbed his duffel bag, heading into the truck stop for a shower. I scratched my head, heading for bed. He finally got back to the truck and started driving. Four hours later, we stopped in Sioux Falls, South Dakota, to switch again. Where he had another shower. This "four-hour shower" routine continued all the way to Laredo.

After dropping the trailer at the freight forwarder, we headed to a hotel, as we had a two-day layover. At the hotel, we met another team who was also being laid over. Together, we grabbed a taxi, crossing into Mexico for a while. When we got back to the hotel, showers (this time) were definitely in order. We then walked to the restaurant next door for supper, then back to the room, where he had another shower. I just fell on the bed, channel surfing before calling it a night. The next morning when I woke up, he was in the shower again. When he came out, he asked if I was going to shower. I told him I didn't need one, all I'd done was channel surf. He gave me a bit of a dirty look, but didn't say anything.

When we got our reload for Toronto, he crawled in the bunk, saying: "See you in four hours". Not likely. I put the truck in gear, and off I went. I woke him up in Oklahoma City to switch. Again, he had a shower (I have no idea where he kept finding all these clean clothes to put on), saying he'd wake me in four hours. I told him: "Nope, I've done my 10 hours, I need at least eight off before I can drive again," closing the curtains. He wasn't happy when I got up to switch again, He told me that he was setting his alarm for four hours. I told him not to bother, as he now needed eight hours off before he could drive again.

At customs, he made a major mistake. There used to be a Canada Customs agent in Sarnia, with a HUGE chip on her shoulder. She was never in a good mood, and was actually downright nasty. She didn't ask you any questions, she snarled them in your direction. We happened to end up at her booth. As soon as I saw it was her, I told him "Don't get an attitude. Answer her questions honestly, and politely. Don't say, or do ANYTHING to annoy her. She's already in a bad mood, and I don't want to be here any longer than I have to." We got to the booth, where I handed her the paperwork. She snatched it from me, closing the window. I saw her stamp the paperwork (meaning the load is cleared into Canada). She opened the window, but didn't hand me the paperwork. "How long have you been out of the country?" she snapped. I answered politely and correctly. "Anything to declare?" I told her what I was bringing back (I was under the personal exemption limit). She said: "Lemme talk to him." I leaned forward. Same questions, until she asked what he had to declare. He replied "None of your f%^king business!". I sat up, threw my head back, sighed, looked at her and said: "Where do you want me to park?". She gave me one hell of a dirty look, pointing forcefully to the parking lot. She went through the truck and trailer with a fine-tooth comb. We were there for about three hours as she searched everything. After we were finally released, I chewed his ass all the way to Toronto. He seemed totally unfazed. He tried pulling the four on/four off on the trip from Toronto to Winnipeg, but after his four on, I had full driving hours available. We switched in North Bay, where I promptly drove straight through to Ignace. He had the last six hours to finish the drive back to Winnipeg. When safety asked me how it had gone, I gave them the whole story with all the details. Far as I know, they sent him out as a single driver. I can't see anyone putting up with his "rules" for any length of time.

On Today's Menu

Feeding the Long-Haul Trucker

When you are driving the long-haul, your life takes place in your truck. It's where you work, sleep, relax, and eat. Eating in restaurants can become expensive so most drivers look at other options, too. In Canada there are very few all-purpose truck-stops along the 3600 mile Trans-Canada Highway from the east coast to the west. Truckers, though, get to know where to stop when the belly rumbles. Many of our trucks are outfitted with a small fridge and microwave, meaning that we can take care of our meals. Some drivers fill Tupperware containers with their favourite home-cooked meals while others shop-and-eat as they run. Food adventures are always part of the long-haul trucker's life.

When I first started driving, trucks weren't equipped with fridges, and there were no power inverters, so it was truck stop menus all the way. The upside was, I could try various local cuisine, some of which were awesome, some I simply couldn't finish for one reason or another. I came to enjoy biscuits and gravy, a popular breakfast food in the southern states, and I once tried grits. Grits are, to me, like watery, runny oatmeal. Not my thing at all. I also developed a taste for hot, fresh cornbread.

Back in the day, most truck stop chains had their own branded restaurants, with reserved seating for truckers. All tables had phones, so you could call shippers, receivers and dispatchers. The truck stops also had phone rooms, for the same reasons. Most of these phone rooms are still available, but seldom, if ever used, now that satellite communications, cell phones, and even phone apps are available. My current company even has an app we can use to send paperwork in to payroll, and send in customs documents. Of the previous "big three" truck stops (Flying J, Travel Centres of America and Petro Stopping Centres), the number of sit down restaurants has dropped considerably. The growing popularity of trucks equipped with APUs means that the trucks can now accommodate fridges, microwaves, hot plates, toasters and toaster oven (to name a few), and the rising costs of restaurant eating (both financial and health costs) have reduced the number of sit down restaurants in truck stops. And what sit down restaurants do still exist, the quality and menu selections have taken a serious hit. Now, with most of the sit down restaurants gone, the truck stop offerings are fast food places. Not bad once in a while, but definitely NOT healthy, nor inexpensive. In the late 1990's, you could easily spend $40.00 a day just eating. Before the power converters, all you had for electrical power in the truck was 12 volts outlets. Basically, cigarette lighters, so all appliances were of the 12 volt variety. Boiling water in a 12 volt kettle to make a cup of tea takes about 20 minutes, For a fridge, you needed a 12 volt cooler. Hot food? Good luck! I had a 12 volt lunchbox oven (more of a slow cooker), but to heat even a can of soup would take upwards of 90 minutes. So you had a choice: Eat in truck stops, or deal with slow reheating of canned goods, or you could live off sandwiches if you had a 12 volt cooler. Somewhere along the line, a company came up with a great idea, but it never really took off. They were called "Heater Meals". They were similar to a TV dinner, but to heat them up, you added water to a pad containing a material that generated heat when wet. You would add the water, and place the tray on the pad, and wait five minutes. They were great, but the variety was limited, and they didn't always work, so you would have to improvise. Turn the defroster on high, and crank the heat. It would take about half an hour just to heat it enough that it was tolerable. Another trick drivers have used to heat left overs, is to wedge it into the engine someplace while driving. Since the engine operates at just below 212 F (the boiling point of water), it's a great way to heat up left overs. Just be sure it's well wrapped in tin foil, or other heat resistant material.

For a while, I used a small, single burner butane powered stove. One of my first adventures was to make spaghetti. I boiled the water, and cooked the noodles. That's when I realized I hadn't exactly thought this idea through. How am I going to drain the noodles, and into what am I going to drain the water? I ended up draining them into the parking lot. I mostly used it to heat up canned pasta, or to make small meals, like chicken fried rice, where there was no need to drain away unwanted liquids. My current truck has a small fridge, a microwave, a toaster, a coffee maker, a kettle and a toaster oven. On my days off, I do some serious cooking, package it all up, load up the fridge with eight or ten meals, and microwave them as need be. My usual fair is a cup of tea and instant hot oatmeal, or toast for breakfast, a sandwich or hot dogs (done in the microwave) for lunch, and a prepared meal for supper. As an evening snack while enjoying Netflix, or Apple TV, I'll microwave some popcorn.

For a while, we were running loads of beef liver from a meat plant in Alberta to Pascagoula, Mississippi, on the Gulf Coast, for furtherance by ship to Russia. There were five or six of us just running from Alberta to Mississippi with 42,000 lbs of livers. We'd run various loads back to Canada, then turn and head back to Mississippi. In Mississippi, we had to clear the T&E bond, then go to a warehouse at the port, where the livers were unloaded from our 53 ft trailers. Here they were reloaded into 40 ft shipping containers (sea-cans). Sea-cans are designed and built to fit into the cargo hold of a ship. The reefer version of the units are electrically powered, drawing power from the ship's electrical system. This run pattern went on for about three months, ending around Christmas. On the last rounder, I had my 16 year old stepson along for the ride. After delivering the last load, dispatch told us we were free to pick a nearby place to sit over Christmas.

We contemplated a beach on the Florida panhandle, or maybe New Orleans. In the end, we chose New Orleans. On the way there, we stopped at a small mom & pop truck stop in Escatawpa, Mississippi for dinner. One of the appetizers they had were "firecrackers". These looked and tasted like egg rolls, coming with a steaming bowl of dipping sauce. When the waitress put them on the table, she instructed us: "Be careful, they're hot." The steam coming off both the food and the bowl of dipping sauce laid proof to that! I tried one, sans sauce. Yup, it was hot. And tasted awesome. I tried a bit of the sauce on a finger. Hot, but a rather pleasant flavour. We dove right in. After about ten minutes, we realized the "they're hot" warning didn't refer to the temperature! My mouth felt like I had been eating lava! I'm not one for spicy food at the best of times, meaning that now I was really in a world of hurt. My stepson, on the other hand, had been known to eat Jalapenos raw and not break a sweat. Even he was feeling the adverse effects, it would be a few days before the effects wore off, and, unfortunately, a pre-cursor to more discomfort on my part.

We, along with another truck, parked at a small truck stop, heading to downtown New Orleans to play tourist, which is something truck drivers don't often get to do. We were walking down Bourbon Street where all the sidewalk scammers were out. One tried to clean my stepson's brand new Airwalk shoes but we put a quick end to that. Next, he said: "Tell me where you're from, and I can tell you how many letters are in your last name." I've been around long enough to hear quite a few scam lines, including this one. The answer is always "12 letters. Y-O-U-R L-A-S-T N-A-M-E". We didn't fall for it.

One surprise that awaited us happened around about eight in the evening. Bourbon Street was closed to vehicular traffic with posts placed in the road. All the bars along the street opened their doors, and you could buy drinks to go. There we were, my 16 year-old stepson, my fellow-driver, and myself, walking down Bourbon Street, enjoying our "beverages" while checking out all the fabulous Dixieland jazz emanating from the various clubs. Life couldn't get much better. Of course, the other driver who was with us was busy trying to find "company" for the evening, becoming quite intoxicated in the process. All in all, we were there for three days over Christmas. This was my stepson's first trip to the deep south and his first experience with waitresses calling him "Hon", "sweetie", and the like. He was getting a bit of an ego, until he learned that was just the way they talked.

Back at the truck stop, we went to the deli to get a snack, and another cultural difference hit him. He asked for a "Pogo". The cashier looked at him like he was crazy. He pointed to it. She said: (in a thick southern accent) "Oh, y'all wanna corn dog"? He was like: "Yeah, whatever you call it."

Our reload destination from Mississippi was at Pace Salsa in San Antonio, Texas, going to Toronto. We pulled in, backed up, and I went inside to talk to the shipper. I asked if they had any damaged, or mislabeled jars we could have, since most places just toss such items away anyway. He walked to a pallet, grabbed a case, said: "oops!", dropping it to the floor. SMASH! He picked through the wreckage, signed the labels of three undamaged jars, handing them to me. After loading the trailer, I signed the bills, grabbed the jars, and headed back to the truck. We stopped at the first truck stop to scale the load, as well as grabbing some tortilla chips for our snack. Weights were all good. Back on the road we went. I had one chip, dipped in the salsa, and that was it. I checked the label on the jar. "Pace Chunky Salsa Extra Hot". I couldn't eat it at all. Instant heartburn. Stepson, on the other hand, practically inhaled it. At the next stop, I found a jar of mild, which I enjoyed very much, thank you.

As time marched on, more and more amenities became available to drivers. Trucks started to be equipped with APUs (auxiliary power units) to provide heat and air conditioning without idling the truck. One of the extras the APUs provided was 120V AC power, capable of running microwaves, toaster ovens, small refrigerators, and the like. Before this, though, a few companies started selling 12V DC appliances.

One of the products available to purchase for our trucks, was a 12V oven, called the "lunch box oven". It actually reaches 300 F. In reality, it was mainly a food-warmer, good for reheating the leftovers I brought from home and kept cold in my 12V cooler. It wasn't perfect, but it sure helped save money rather than eating in truck stops all the time. Plus, it was healthier that truck stop food.

Lunchbox Oven

After a few months of using the lunch box oven to heat leftovers, and canned foods, I noticed a cook book for the lunch box oven at a truck stop. I bought it looking forward to a change to truck-stop diet. Inside were a nice selection of recipes, using the lunch box oven as a slow cooker. What a great idea! I found a recipe I wanted to try, made note of the ingredients, then stopped at the first Walmart Supercentre I saw. $20 later, I had all I needed to make slow cooker chicken stew. The recipe took 10 hours, so I waited until the next morning. I prepped everything, put it all in the oven bag, put the bag in the oven, and decided the best spot to place it, to keep it from falling off anything, was on the floor between the seats. Can't fall from there, so I plugged it in, and started my day driving. Four hours into my day, I learned the error of my ways. I could start to smell it cooking, and it smelled fabulous. Problem was, I had to endure the wonderful aroma for another six hours before I could even think about tasting it! Yes, it was a real treat when I got around to eating, but it was pure torture being able to smell it, but not eat it. To give you an idea how torturous it was, sit in a closet with your slow cooker making stew for ten hours, with your only escape is to when you need to use the washroom.

A few times I took my then (now ex) wife with me on the road. She had a few eye-opening "dining" experiences. Just outside Kansas City, she decided to have a cinnamon bun for breakfast. The waitress asked if she wanted half a bun, or a whole bun. She said she wanted a whole bun. I said: "Trust me, you want half a bun". No, she said she wanted a whole bun. She got a whole bun. All fourteen inches of it. Most of it came back to the truck for the day.

On another trip with me to Prince Edward Island on Canada's east coast, we and I we stopped at a road side vendor, buying some Prince Edward Island potatoes. PEI is famous for their potatoes. She decided to use my lunch box oven to bake said potatoes. I told her would take far more than the usual hour to bake them, but she wanted to bake them. We arrived at the shipper, and while they were loading the trailer, she got the potatoes ready, and plugged in the oven. They took a LOT longer than in our home oven, but they were worth the wait!

Left: Not an easy place to back into. ***Right:*** Normal congestion at the Westchester Exit from the Sheridan Expressway in The Bronx

Left: Very tight loading dock in Queens, NY. **Right:** He has a 48 ft trailer, and a city truck. I was about 20 feet longer trying to back in.

My first trip into New York City to Hunts Point Meat Market brought not only new experiences driving in the Big Apple, it provided me with excellent food memories. Not 20 minutes after I had parked my truck in the Market's secure lot for off-loading the next day, there was a Chinese gentleman knocking on the truck door. As the meat market is a secured facility, (at that time it cost $25.00 to enter), I was mildly surprised that someone not from the facility would be allowed in. They did have a security guard patrolling the market, who was big enough to give a gorilla pause, carrying what looked like a bazooka with a pistol grip. This gentleman, however, ran a Chinese restaurant a few blocks from the market. Several times a day, he would come through the staging area to hand the drivers a menu. You circled the items you wanted, and off he'd go, returning about 30 minutes later with your order. The prices were more than reasonable. I ordered a dozen deep fried wontons, a small order of chicken fried rice and a soft drink. The price was something like $5.00. The food, though, was enough to last two days. The small order of chicken fried rice would fill a dinner plate. On later trips to Hunts Point, I found the Sicilian style pizzeria. That was a bonus!

WHAT IS THIS?

LONG-HAUL LOADS THAT HAD ME SHAKING MY HEAD

While most of my long-haul loads were nothing too wild or crazy, every once in a while, I had a load that made me shake me head. The shipper, planner, dispatcher, and receiver all treated it as business-as-usual. They, however, did not have to drive these strange cargoes across the continent. Take a look at some of the loads I hauled.

This story has a bit of start before we get to the cargo. Let's start with the initial run that eventually brought the load onto my truck. After being on the wrong end of a hit-and-run, my truck was out of commission for three weeks for repairs. There was no way my Winnipeg head office was going to put me up in a hotel in San Antonio, Texas, for three weeks. The revised plan was to fly me from San Antonio to Vancouver. When I arrived back in Canada, I was to pick up a special-use truck (one set up for running the west coast, with all its peculiarities for weights and axles), then take a load to Calgary bringing another load back to Vancouver. After that, I would take a Boeing load to Seattle. Next, I was scheduled to pick up a Seattle-load coming back to Vancouver, then a flight home to Winnipeg from Vancouver. As this was all before the 9-11 terrorist attack, everything went smoothly with the flights from Texas to British Columbia. I was soon back on the ground and on my way with the specialized truck. It was a flat top sleeper (no standing up) with high horsepower. As far as I could tell, there was no speed governor. It had an airlift axle, which was always up unless it was needed to carry extra weight. The trips to Calgary and back, along with the trip to Seattle were uneventful, save for my having fun with a fast, powerful truck. The load from Seattle back to Vancouver was another story.

The Seattle to Vancouver consignment was a full load of hickory smoked bacon, except for one box. That one box, caused a world of delays, and in my opinion, was one of the worst varieties of bacon imaginable. To this day, I haven't seen it for sale in any store. Apple Cinnamon Bacon. I picked up the load, verified all the paperwork was in order, and off I went. Canada Customs had a few issues with that one box. Since it wasn't being "sold" per se, it wasn't subject to the same duties and taxes as the rest of the load, according to the broker. Canada Customs disagreed. The broker and Customs got into a heated discussion as to what the duties and taxes on the box should be. The broker said it was a sample, for in-house evaluation, not available for sale to the public, therefore, an in-company sample transfer. Customs pointed out that it was packaged as a product for sale, which it was. The broker stated that under federal import legislation, all food products crossing the border must be packaged this way, whether for sale or as samples. This carried on for about three hours, while I just sat there, caught in the middle of hair-splitting contest. The load was finally cleared, allowing me to proceed to the receiver, who wasn't impressed that the load was late. I explained to him what the issue was. He was unaware of the sample box being on the trailer. He took one look at the box, saw what it was, declaring there was no way he was going to try it. As I said, I've never seen this "flavour" for sale in any grocery store.

That wasn't the only unusual cargo I carried. One February, in Edmonton, I had an LTL load headed for Winnipeg. It wasn't a full trailer, therefore they had me stop in Saskatoon, Saskatchewan, to load three pallets of "rush" freight to deliver 160 miles south Regina, on the way to Winnipeg. Not ideal, as it would add a few hours to my trip home, but whatever. It would be an extra $40 ($20 to load, and $20 to unload) in my wallet. I pulled into the shipper in Saskatoon, heading inside to check in with the shipping department. When I gave them the pick-up number, they gave me a door to back into. I was quickly loaded, and on my way. When I got to the receiver in Regina the next day, they were mildly surprised at the "rush" freight. They were expecting weather stripping. What they got, was screen doors. Not a high priority load in the dead of winter.

Another one of those "what were they thinking" loads was a load of plumbing fixtures I picked up in Kansas, going to a hardware store in Calgary. I tried calling the receiver, but couldn't find a phone number anywhere. I called my dispatcher to see if he had the number in the computer, or maybe the planner or a salesperson had a contact number. I mean, someone had to have ordered these fixtures. Nope. Never did find a phone number. Instead, I called the Calgary terminal to see if they could tell me how to get to this place. They had never heard of the place, but they knew where the address was, and gave me directions. Turned out, the address was in a newer industrial park in the north east side of the city. A very new industrial park. The fixtures I had on my truck were not stock for the store, they were the fixtures to be used in the store's construction! They didn't even have the loading dock built yet. Back to the yard the load went until they were ready for the fixtures.

Back in the 1990s, loads that couldn't be cleared at customs were sent to the closest customs-bonded warehouse. If the carrier was a "post audit" carrier, they were allowed to handle the freight, then send it to a customs-bonded warehouse closest to the delivery address. For example: if you were an ordinary long-haul trucker coming into Winnipeg with a Vancouver-destined load that needed to go into customs bond, you had to take it to a bonded warehouse in Winnipeg. If you were a "Post Audit Carrier" you could take it to a bond warehouse in Vancouver, have the bond cleared, then deliver the load.

As it happened, one August, I had to place a load of chocolates in customs bond in Calgary. I got the bond paperwork taken care of, drove to Calgary, fuelled up the reefer, and dropped the trailer at the bond warehouse. When I turned in the paperwork to the official, I told him someone might have to come by to take the trailer to fill up the reefer fuel tank, or they may send in a mobile fuel truck. I left, making sure to inform my company that the reefer tank was full when I dropped it, but if the load wasn't cleared in a couple of days, the tank would need filling again. They acknowledged this, telling me there was a trailer at the bond warehouse that had finally been cleared. I was to take the load, deliver it, get the trailer washed out, then take it to one of the meat plants we serviced in the Calgary area. After that, I didn't give the chocolate load much thought. I was off onto other loads.

A month or so later, I was in Calgary. I was sent to the bond shed to grab a trailer, deliver it, get it washed out, and take it to a meat plant. Off I went, checked in to the bonding location where the official handed me the paperwork. It was a load of chocolate going to a grocery warehouse. I found the trailer, backed under it, then got out to hook up air lines and light cord, and do a pre-trip inspection. First thing I noticed was the "error" light flashing on the reefer. Similar to the "check engine" on your car, this blinking light could mean almost anything. I scrolled though the screens until I got to the error messages. "Engine Stopped, Reason Unknown", "Low Battery Voltage", "Box Temperature Out of Range". Not good. First things first. Clear the codes, then try to start the reefer. No such luck. The battery didn't have the juice to turn the starter. Check the fuel tank. Dry as a bone. A load of chocolate, in an aluminum trailer in September. This could get messy. And it DID get messy. I soon realized that this was the trailer I had dropped there about a month ago. The trailer had a twenty-gallon fuel tank. At best, it lasted four days before running dry. This meant that the load of chocolate sat inside a metal trailer, in the sun for more than three weeks. I called dispatch to tell them what was going on. They had me take the trailer to the terminal, where they could open it up to check the condition of the load before deciding what to do. I already knew what the decision was going to be. When they opened the trailer at the terminal, there was melted chocolate everywhere, about three feet deep in the trailer, mixed with waxed cardboard from the boxes, shrink-wrap that had held the boxes together on the pallets, all mixed in and over the pallets. The load was destroyed. I just dropped it in the wash bay. They could clean it out before sending it to the meat plant.

Somewhere along the line, I had a reefer load going to Atlanta. I was parked for the night at a truck stop, minding my own business, when there was a knock on the door. Turned out it was another driver from the company and he was in a bind. He had a frozen load (-10 F) and his reefer had quit. He had no idea what to do. I got dressed, then climbed out of the truck to see what the issue was. First thing I checked was the fuel tank. It was empty. I asked him when he had last filled the trailer tank, getting a blank look in return. He was under the impression that the reefer drew its fuel from the truck's fuel supply. I told him to go fill the trailer's tank. When he came back, I'd show him how to get it going again. He was back in about 15 minutes, very eager to get the reefer started again. That eagerness evaporated when he found out what he had to do. To restart a reefer that has run dry of fuel, you have two options. First, you open the bleed valve to allow air to be "pumped" out, then, using a modified fuel cap, hook an airline to the fuel cap, with the other end of the airline hooked into the truck's air supply, and pressurize the fuel tank, forcing fuel through the system. Once you get fuel coming out of the bleed valve, you close the bleed valve, then start the reefer. In the second process, you open the bleed valve, then use the thumb-pump to manually pump fuel, about one teaspoon at a time, through the system until you get fuel coming out of the bleed valve. Then close the valve and start the reefer. The problem with option two is that you need to pump about four gallons of fuel to fill the fuel filter and the fuel line. At only a single teaspoon per pump, it takes a very long time. It is also very hard on your thumb and arm working at that angle. I always carried the modified fuel cap and airline, but I thought this would be a good lesson for the driver. I highly doubt he would ever run a fuel tank dry again. I had to learn the hard way myself. Trust me, it's a lesson you won't soon forget.

Lot Lizards
Avoiding "Wildlife" at the Truck Stop

With the large amount of traffic constantly moving through truck stops, along with some rest areas, a certain type of "wildlife" is attracted to the bright lights and opportunities for "employment". These (mostly) female prostitutes often target truckers whom they are certain must want a little "relief" from their long day on the road. Many openly advertising over CB radios while other just walk from truck to truck, (usually) knocking on truck doors. Other lingo for these "ladies of the night" include: sleeper leaper, mattress maiden, and pavement princess. I'm not sure of what their personal reasons are for the business they are in, but I do know I'm not interested. Some long-haul truckers declare this brand of wildlife is just an urban myth. I, however, know first hand that they exist.

On one occasion, my partner joined me for a trip. The exact details and location escape me, but one night we were sound asleep in the bunk, when I was awakened by someone knocking on the side of the truck. I opened the vent, and asked what they wanted. To my mild surprise, and great annoyance, it was a lot lizard. I told her I wasn't interested, mentioning that I had my partner with me, hoping she'd take the hint, and go away. Instead, she offered her services to both of us. By now, my partner was awake. She wasn't impressed. I told my partner to settle down, and not do anything foolish, as the woman's "employer" was no doubt close by, armed with a hand cannon. This wasn't the first, or last issue I'd have with these working women.

I had one approach me at a truck stop in New York State, offering, very matter of factly, that she could "finish" me, before I finished fuelling the truck. I politely declined, finished my fuelling task and left, never to return.

One of the more interesting exchanges I ever saw with a lot lizard was in Gary, Indiana, just outside of Chicago. This area was, at the time, crawling with lot lizards. To combat the issue, some of the truck stops had started charging for parking as a way of generating revenue to pay for security personnel to halt the "wildlife encounters". This truck stop, however, didn't have security. The lizard-problem was almost out of control. I was getting ready to leave, just updating my logbook (pre-elog days), when I heard yelling. Across the driveway, was a lot lizard, hanging off the driver's door of a truck. He was yelling at her to leave him alone, in far more explicit language, but she wasn't taking no for an answer. This went on for about five or six minutes, with the driver loudly becoming more and more vulgar. I just kept my head down, drawing my log book lines. I wanted to get out of there before she saw me and wandered over. I had just finished my paperwork when I heard "WHOOSH!". I looked up to see that this woman had literally gone from black as night, to white as a ghost. The driver had finally had enough, blasting her full in the face with his fire extinguisher! From 75 feet away, I could see from her totally stunned expression. I left the truck stop immediately, not wanting to be in the same area code when she reported back to her "employer".

Sharing the Road
Encounters with Non-Truckers.

There are miles and miles of highways stretching across North America. These roadways are enjoyed – or just tolerated, in some cases – by millions of people in all sorts of vehicles. Truckers see the highways as their workplace and are fully aware of the necessary measures to keep them, their loads, and civilian travelers safe and alive. We have, however, no shortage of encounters with those we share the road with.

Quite often I see people tailgating me. Please, do yourself a favour: stop doing this! It's very dangerous for a number of reasons. One, you're almost invisible, especially if it's a dry van, container, or reefer. Second, if a tire blows, and the tread comes off, it can literally go through the windshield and decapitate you. That's about two lbs of vulcanized rubber moving at about 60 mph with about 100 PSI (about triple the tire pressure in your car tires) of air propelling it. Third, if the brake chamber lets go, the parking brake spring will do about the same damage as the tire. If the trailer has drum brakes (and 90% of trailers have them) that spring is oriented front to back. Disc brakes are oriented side to side.

If you're driving a "civilian" vehicle, you may not have given any thought to the braking system of a transport truck and trailer. Understanding this may enlighten the public as one of the reasons why a long-haul driver doesn't hit the brakes like you do, nor do they stop like you do when you drive your car.

An air brake system on a truck and trailer consists of two interconnected air systems: the service (when you step on the brake pedal) and the emergency (when the air is released from the system). On the service side, the brakes are applied with air pressure which is released by a spring. On the emergency side, they are applied with a spring, then released by air pressure. If you've ever been around a truck, and heard "PSHHHHhhhh", that's the sound of the air being released, applying the parking brakes. You may also hear a metallic clunking sound as well, as the spring is forcing the brake shoes again the brake drums. The force exerted by the parking brake spring is considerable. You MIGHT be able to move an empty trailer with the parking brakes applied, but you'll never move a loaded one, unless the brakes are way out of adjustment, or malfunctioning. The braking process is not a fast one, especially with upwards of 105,000 lbs hitched to the cab and pushing from behind. Remember this when you expect a transport truck to quickly stop for you. Simply put, we don't do fender benders.

Life on the road can be very dangerous. Not just from traffic, but some people seem to find great enjoyment from stupid stunts that put everyone one else on the road at risk. There are way too many incidents of people throwing rocks, pumpkins, and other items from overpasses. These items then come crashing through the windshield, potentially injuring or killing someone. At the very least, this surprises the driver, who could easily lose control of their big vehicle and trailer. I've seen the aftermath of people committing suicide from overpasses, too. Thankfully, this has never happened to me. The worst I had was some kids (I assume it was kids, I never saw them, and doubt they were ever caught) just north of St. Louis at six in the morning. They were taking shots at vehicles with a pellet gun. I heard a few impacts, but never saw anything, and just kind of forgot about it. When I later stopped at a truck stop, I noticed a few dents down the side of the truck and trailer, along with a couple of what looked like stone chips in the driver's side window.

One incident on the New Jersey Turnpike just burst its way into my memory. A woman in a midsize car decided to "force" me to change lanes, much to her loss. The Jersey turnpike at this point, is 12 lanes wide: Six lanes in each direction. Three truck lanes, a median barrier, then three car-only lanes. I was in the centre truck lane, staying away from the right lane, where people merge on and off. She was in the far-left lane, right about where my trailer tires were, and wanted to get over to an exit. She had her right turn signal on as she edged over into my lane. I couldn't get into the right lane, due to traffic, so I just carried on, keeping a close eye on her. She could easily have slowed down a bit, then pulled in behind me, making her way over to the right lane, instead, for whatever reason, she was determined to change lanes right where she wanted. This went on for about two miles, getting old very fast. I just carried on in my lane while she kept edging closer. As I was checking my mirror for the umpteenth time, she edged a little too close, brushing the trailer tire with her passenger side mirror. One second it was there, the next, it was gone. It did serve a good purpose however, as she finally slowed down, pulling in behind me to make her exit.

Honestly, some of the people I encounter on the roads aren't qualified to drive a nail. The average person in their personal vehicle, I can understand. They have no idea how much room large commercial vehicles need to operate, make turns, back in, etc. I've had people is cars, and even a few on foot try and sneak behind me while backing in, sneak up on the passenger side while I'm trying

Trying to save time driving behind a truck backing up is never a good idea. Bronx NY.

to turn, with my turn signal on, almost as if they can't see it, or me turning. A word to the wise for driver's of personal vehicles. Pay attention when you see a tractor trailer with a turn signal activated. Even if he's not in a designated turning lane, chances are he's still turning, and he's leaving sufficient room for the trailer to make the corner without hitting anything close to the corner, like a fire hydrant, telephone pole, or perhaps an illegally parked vehicle on the other street that you can't see. Getting yourself beside a turning truck, especially a truck turning right, you're putting yourself in serious danger. Down the passenger side, you become invisible very quickly. Drivers who have a licence class beyond a personal vehicle (taxi, city or school bus, ambulance, etc) should have a better understanding, but, alas, not all of them do. More times that I can count, I've had cars, mini vans, and pick up truck turn onto a highway in front of me so close I've had to hammer the brakes to avoid running them over. It's almost a daily occurrence. One that was a (thankfully) one off incident almost cost a few dozen lives.

Just east of Mattawa ON, there's a fairly long, steep downgrade when you're headed west. I'd estimate it's about a mile long, and about a 7% down grade, with a 56 mph speed limit, with a passing lane for east bound traffic. I was descending the hill one lovely June morning, at about 7am, when I saw a school bus approaching from a side road on the left. When I was about 300 feet from the intersection, the school bus turned left onto the highway in front of me, travelled maybe 50 feet before pulling onto the shoulder, and activated the flashing red lights for all traffic to stop while they loaded school kids. No way in hell I was going to come to a stop before getting to the bus. I did all I could, standing on the brakes, and sounding the airhorn. Since there was no traffic east bound, I crossed into the oncoming passing lane, and just hoped for the best. I was still moving about about 15 mph when I passed the stopped bus. Thankfully, my nerves were the only victims of this hair raising incident. At the next town, I reported the incident to the police, just in case the school bus driver decided to file a complaint with either my company, or the police, but I never heard another word regarding the incident.

SIGN LANGUAGE

LEADING TRUCKS ACROSS NORTH AMERICA.

One aspect about trucking many don't think about is, signage. We are often in unfamiliar areas, relying on proper signage to avoid getting into situations that might be difficult to get out of. When I first started trucking, my instructor drilled into my head: "Read every road sign you see. I don't care if you've seen it 1,000 times, read it again. Things can change, but if you read all the signs, you have a better chance of getting yourself sorted out if you get lost, or make a wrong turn." Sage advice, that I've always passed along to those I have trained.

Alas, signage has caught me a few times. The worst occasion was on a trip through Detroit. The signage for the border crossing at the Ambassador Bridge is much improved, as is the infrastructure between the interstate to the bridge. Back in the 1990s, it was, to put it mildly, a bad joke, creating a dangerous situation. There was no direct access between bridge and the three nearby interstates (I-75, I-94, and I-96). To reach the bridge, you had to exit the interstate then travel on city streets anywhere from a few blocks to a few miles. These streets were NOT in the best part of the city. Signage to help us get to our destination was basically nonexistent. Possibly the signs were stolen, however, for whatever reason the missing signs bit me in the butt. Big time butt bite.

I was coming in from the west on I-94, faithfully following the signs to the bridge. Until they vanished. I ended up by the old Joe Louis Arena at three in the morning. Definitely NOT the place I wanted to be. I could see the bridge from where I was, but couldn't find a truck-accessible route to get there. Don't forget. The truck is 75 feet long, 13 feet 6 inches tall, and 8 feet 6 inches wide. Unlike your average vehicle, it can't just make a u-turn then carry on. I managed to get away from that area. Instead of the bridge, however, I found the entrance to the Detroit-Windsor tunnel. Good enough for me. Paid the toll, and headed towards the tunnel. There's a tight right-hand turn to enter the tunnel. The big rig couldn't make the turn. A string of colourful expletives followed along with a tunnel employee who jumped in front of the truck, waving his arms frantically. I wasn't really going anywhere, nonetheless he really wanted me to stay where I was. He came to my window, asking what exactly I was doing there. I explained the night's adventures. He gave me a crooked grin before telling me: "Your night just got even worse".

It turned out that the tunnel guard was right! Not only could I not make the turn towards the tunnel, the truck was too high to fit in the tunnel. Just freaking great! By now, it's about 4:30 am, just at the beginning of the Detroit morning rush hour. Here I am, almost wedged on a corner, blocking the entrance to the tunnel. Probably the most popular trucker in Detroit at this moment, but for all the wrong reasons. It took about an hour to clear the traffic backed up behind me, so I could back out, then head to the bridge (with good directions from a tunnel employee). I did get my toll money back. The one thing that saved my butt from a huge fine, was the fact that the toll booth person knew I wouldn't fit. Instead of directing me away from the tunnel, they took the toll, allowing me to continue. Today, as I said, there is now direct access from all major interstates right to the bridge. With the advent of GPS and Google Maps, it's now pretty simple. But there are still some drivers who either can't read, don't know their vehicle's dimensions, or just don't care.

Not long ago, I crossed from Windsor into Detroit, headed west to Idaho. I cleared customs, took the ramp, and I was off. Except, there was a detour on the city streets. UGH! Just what I didn't need. I followed the detour, with a line of trucks behind me. I made a turn along the detour route and saw a sign warning of a 13 ft 4 in bridge. Remember, I'm driving a rig that is 13 ft 6 in. tall. I stopped to access the situation. There was a street off to the left, so I put on my turn-signal, checking traffic in preparations of making my left turn. Sure enough, here comes "Billy Bigrigger" passing us all. He didn't turn to avoid the bridge, he just carried on. He made it about four feet under the bridge before coming to a screeching (literally) halt. I just made my left turn, improvising a truck-friendly detour back to the Interstate, with my convoy following. I have no idea what happened to Billy.

BRIDGE OVER TROUBLED WATERS

LONG-HAUL TRUCKING OVER AND UNDER BRIDGEWORKS

Most of long-haul driving is about long distances over the open road. There is, however, one roadway infrastructure that can be the bane of the long-haul trucker. Bridges. Driving over them and driving under them, especially the low ones. We are limited by the height of our units 13 feet 6 inches as to those bridges we can actually travel under. There is a way to get under low bridges. By lowering the air pressure in the tires, then deflating the air suspension you can lower your height enough to sneak under some structures, but it's not guaranteed, and not a good habit to get into.

In all my years of driving, including four or five years of steady runs to New York City, home of the low bridges, I have only ever hit one low bridge, and that was under a direct order from a New York City police officer.

A NYC police traffic cop told me to hit the bridge. This was the result. Note the light hanging from the top corner.

I was travelling between Brooklyn and the Bronx with a delivery, when there was an accident on the Triborough bridge. Everyone was being detoured around that location. A traffic police officer told me to turn right, and head in that direction. I looked, saw the sign clearly stating the clearance under the bridge was twelve feet eight inches. I told her I couldn't go that way as my truck was too tall and I'd hit the bridge. The officer told me that the sign's wrong, trucks do it all the time. I could actually see (never mind the sign) that there was no way I was going to fit. I told her again that I'd never make it under the bridge. She told me to move it, or she'd have the truck towed. I told her, I'll hit that bridge! She told me to hit it. Okay. Off I went. Very slowly, no more than about two mph. I crept up to the bridge until I felt the trailer hit the bridge. She was not happy, as now her detour was also blocked. One of her coworkers who had heard our exchange advised her she had better not even think about writing a citation for me being on a non-truck route, (she didn't), but she did have to reroute a lot of traffic so I could back out, then get turned around to detour around on proper truck routes.

New York, New York
Still Not Sure I Want to be a Part of It

In early 2001 my marriage fell apart. They say it takes two people to make a marriage work. Well, it also takes two people to allow a marriage to fail. I can't speak for her, but I was devastated. There's an entire two or three-week period that I have no idea what I did, except in a few cases where there is photographic evidence of my being someplace. About six months after the breakup of my marriage, I met someone online in one of those old chat rooms they had at MSN and Yahoo. This was long before Facebook or dating websites gained popularity. The only problem was, I lived in Winnipeg, while she lived in southern Ontario. Not exactly in the same neighbourhood. We lived about 1,200 miles away from each other. I managed to get down to see her once or twice a month. Things were starting to get a bit more serious. But getting to see her on anything close to a regular schedule was near to impossible. One day while I was in the office in Winnipeg, they offered me a load to New York City. I flat out refused. No way in HELL was I going to New York. Another driver, who I was friends with, spoke up telling me it wasn't all that bad. He had a load going the same place. Doing a steady run to New York would get me to the southern Ontario area almost weekly, meaning that I could spend more time with my new girlfriend. After some thought, I agreed to take the run. I told the planner this may be a single shot. If everything went fairly well, I'd consider doing a steady New York run. Well, everything ran smooth as silk. So there I was, on a steady New York City run which lasted for five solid years. And yes, there were some interesting stories. (Some I've already related, the bridge-hit being one.) I can divide those New York runs into two periods. Part 1 occurred prior to the 9/11 terrorist attack on the city. Part 2 looks at the job following that terrible day.

PART 1: BEFORE 9/11

West bound on thr Cross Bronx Expressway,
just heading under the apartments.

Times Square, at about 4 pm on a Sunday,
southbound on Broadway Ave, Manhattan, NY.

The first run I had to New York was to Fancy Foods, in the Hunts Point Meat Market in the Bronx. Just getting to Hunts Point was enough to spike my blood pressure. To enter the Bronx, you first cross the George

Washington Bridge. The GW (as it's called) is a two-level suspension bridge on I-95 that connects Fort Lee, New Jersey, to Washington Heights, New York. The bridge is 4,760 feet in length, and carries seven lanes of traffic in each direction: four lanes on the upper level; three lanes on the lower level. Tolls are only collected on the trip into New York, creating a MASSIVE bottle neck. For the upper deck, which all trucks are required to use, there are twelve toll booths. Once you've exited the upper level toll booths, you'll see that – within a space of only 1,000 feet traffic is now funnelled from the multiple toll lanes into four traffic lanes. Before you even get off the bridge, all lanes from both the upper and lower levels merge into four lanes. In another 1,000 feet, there are exits to the Major Deegan Expressway and 178th Street. These take you to upper Manhattan (Harlem) and Broadway Ave. From there, you drop down, and go under four apartment buildings.

The clearance under the apartments is such that they have a hard time maintaining the road surface. In order to redo the surface, they have to shave off a few inches before laying fresh asphalt, as the clearance is JUST enough to allow trucks to pass under. If your trailer is empty, I suggest you keep your speed down, or you might bounce the trailer into the ceiling.

At this point you might be saying: "Wait a minute ... did he just say the Expressway goes under apartment buildings???" While I haven't actually been in one of the apartments, people have written about the experience. Evidently, 4,000 people live in the Bridge Apartments which are four high-rise buildings that are lined up like dominoes over the Expressway. To those that travel the area, they are just called "the apartments". Those living there report that they can hear the traffic even on the middle floors. It can be so loud that they need to raise their voice to talk over the noise. On windy days, vehicle exhaust is carried upwards which is not great for those with balconies. The vibration of the big trucks (along with any construction equipment) can be felt through the whole building. Supposedly, however, the fantastic views make up for what it means to live over the top of a highway.

Back on the road, travelling out from under the apartments, you're on the Cross Bronx Expressway. To get from here to Hunts Point, you now exit onto the Sheridan Expressway, taking the first exit. This brings you to another interesting area of New York. The lights at the top of the exit control a real dog's breakfast of an intersection. From here you continue straight, driving under the subway line. The overhead clearances gradually diminish. At the last minute, however, the road jogs right (out from under the subway), then jogs left over the subway, putting you onto Bruckner Avenue. From there, it's a relatively simple trip along surface streets to Hunts Point Market. It's almost impossible to accurately describe this area of New York City. During daylight hours, it's bustling with commercial activity, some of it being dubiously legal, but not what I'd call dangerous. Auto repairs being done of the side of the street, double and triple parking, parking on sidewalks, driving on sidewalks to get around trucks backing into loading doors, or out of parking lots.

We finally managed to get to Hunts Point, checking in with the receiver at Fancy Foods. Like most New Yorkers, he had an attitude with little time for anything other than business. We told him we had appointments to off load the next morning, but we were here, in case he wanted it early. "No, go park in the staging area." Then he turned away. So off we went to the staging area, which can hold 20 or 30 trucks, and parked.

Hunts Point Meat Market is a massive facility. It covers more than 60 acres, has seven huge buildings housing 52 companies that process and distribute meat products using approximately 700,000 square feet of refrigerated space. Each building has businesses on both sides, with a commercial common area in the middle. One of these common areas was a pizzeria. Another had a small convenience store. On the second floor of each common area were public restrooms, which were a God-send. The market is the largest of its kind in the world. It serves all of the tri-state (New York, New Jersey and Connecticut) area. It truly is a place that has to be seen to be appreciated.

I've been to the meat market suppliers' countless times, delivering mostly to Fancy Foods, Westside Meats and Nebraskaland Meats. There are many other meat-processing companies. Between them all, they process just about any kind of meat you could imagine. I always carried beef products headed for the Market.

One issue with the Market, similar to many places in New York City, is maneuvering room. Being an old city (nearly 397 years old!), most loading facilities were built for the equipment of an earlier period: short wheel based cabover trucks along with 40 foot long, 8 foot wide trailers, usually with a total length of about 55 feet at most. When I started servicing the New York area, it was with a 53 foot long, 8 foot 6 inch wide trailer, and a conventional truck with a total length of about 75 feet. The workers at Hunts Point parked their personal vehicles between the buildings, making the space even more cramped. Considering that modern trucks are a good 10 feet longer, as well as additional six inches wider than those the space was designed for creates a truly challenging job, to say the least. Other places in New York City, however, were even worse!

After a few months, my relationship with the woman in southern Ontario fell apart. While I had no personal reason to be heading that way, the run itself became a very stable, dedicated trip. I would leave Winnipeg on a Friday morning, clear USDA meat inspection at Pembina, North Dakota, then drive to New York, for a Monday morning delivery. From there, I'd get a daytime reload on Monday (usually Cool Whip from Avon NY) heading

These menacing posts and fire hydrant were eventually removed by a driver who didn't see them.

for Toronto or Montreal. From there, I had a LTL load leaving that night for Winnipeg. I'd get back into Winnipeg on Wednesday, then take 24 hours off. Under the rules from those days this allowed me to switch to the 120 hours in 14 days driving cycle. I'd then spend Friday, Saturday, Sunday and Monday running back and forth between Winnipeg and Calgary, pin to pin (drop a loaded trailer, hook to another, and leave, no more than an hour between arrival and departure). This was followed with having Tuesday, Wednesday, and Thursday off for some home-time before heading out again on Friday morning for New York.

On occasion, there was nothing to reload, so I'd dead head (run empty) to Toronto. Very seldom did I dead head to Montreal. Since I got paid the same, empty or loaded, running empty was a bit of a blessing. Nice and light, no slowing down for hills. In time, I developed a good working relationship with the receiver at Fancy Foods in New York City, to the point he would occasionally call me Friday to see what load I was bringing. If it was blade steaks, he'd ask if I could deliver it Sunday when I arrived. No problem. Not once did I ever have any issues with Fancy Foods. The first time I went there solo probably helped. I arrived on the Sunday about noon, and was surprised to see trucks backed in, and activity on the dock. I stopped and went in to see if they wanted the load early. The receiver was gruff, and none too polite. I just said "Okay, I'll be in the staging area, come get me in the morning." I turned to walk out. He said: "You're not gonna yell, scream, and demand to be unloaded?" I said: "No, I'll just go wait. Look at me. I'm 280 lbs. I'm not about to jump up and down yelling and screaming, if it's not gonna do me any good! If it'll get me unloaded today, fine, I'll jump and yell, but if it's just gonna be a waste of time, I'll save my energy." He gave me a somewhat crooked smile, telling me to go ahead and back in, and they'd get me unloaded. I backed in, asked the lumper (a laborer who unloads cargo) how much it was going to cost to get unloaded. $200.00. I contacted the company, got an express code for a $200.00 T-Chek (a method of payment used in the trucking industry) and gave it to the lumper, who gave me my receipt, so I could get reimbursed. In short order, the lumper was busy unloading the trailer. On average, it takes them about two hours to unload a trailer by hand, so a lumper can easily unload four trailers in a day, pocketing $800 cash, more than likely tax-free. Good work, if you can get it, but it wreaks havoc on your body. Some of those cases of meat weigh in at over 80 lbs and an average full load of meat is 45,000 lbs. These guys, along with some women, are moving upwards of 180,000 lbs. of meat each and every day. Have at it, I'm not interested.

One trip, I had a full load going to Westside Meats at Hunts Point. Usually a sweet load, due to its location in the market. It's off to one side, away from the other buildings, with a small awning. When you're backed in, any rain, snow or ice sliding off the roof doesn't fall between the truck and the building. With the exception of doors four through eight, it is a very simple place to back into. This time, I had door ten. A first-year rookie driver could back in there with no issues at all. I swung around, opened the doors, backed in, then walked into the office with the paperwork. Got the price from the lumper, walked to the truck to get the T-Chek, then headed back into the building. While we were getting everything all settled, we heard a crash, and the trailer shook. Oh great! Some fool just backed into my truck! I ran outside, hoping to catch the guy before he took off. I looked around. No truck in sight, except those backed in. I walked to the truck to see how bad the damage was. I was shocked. There wasn't so much as a scratch on the truck. Or the trailer! Then I noticed some wreckage on the ground, and looked up. A portion of the awning had broken free. Some of it was on the ground, some of it was on the trailer. I hadn't been backed into; I'd been hit by the building! I used the one-use camera from the accident reporting kit to submit to the company. I wish I had gotten copies of the pictures. I'm fairly certain there aren't all that many instances of a building hitting a truck.

One incident, which may seem quite trivial, caused a whole lot of headaches that could have been easily avoided, except for laziness at the meat plant. I had two drops in Hunts Point: Fancy Foods, and Westside Meats. After they unloaded the drop at Fancy Foods, the order came up one box short. The receiver, the lumper, and myself recounted all the boxes, and checked the certificate numbers on the wall of boxes for Westside to see if it was there. It wasn't. When they load multiple drops, they load the trailer in reverse. Last drop goes on the trailer first. Generally, they load the boxes six across, and five cases high. At the end of a drop, they place coloured tape to denote the end of an order. There was the tape, and all the boxes we could see had the certificate number for Westside's order. Now the fun began. Called the CSR (Customer Service Representative), who has to get the CSR from the meat plant on the line. A million questions need to be answered. Was the load delivered with the seal intact? Yes. Did you confirm the piece count with the receiver? Yes, three times. Did the piece count on the meat certificate match the piece count on the bill of lading and the customs invoice? Yes. Did you check the next row of boxes for the missing piece? Yes. So now the meat plant has to contact Customs and USDA to report the missing case, arrange adjustments (customs fees, taxes, etc) for the missing case. Took about an hour. Then off I went to Westside, all of about 150 feet. Got backed in, took in the bills, arranged the lumper, the whole nine yards. An hour or so later, he came out handing me the bills, telling me that there was an extra box on the floor in the front of the trailer. I said: "You gotta be kidding me. One extra case. I bet its flank steaks". He asked how I know that, and I explained the whole situation. He just laughed. I climbed in the trailer, and checked the certificate number. You guessed it. It matched the missing box from Fancy Foods. Now, here I had two options: First, I could just take Fancy the missing case, and forget about it. Second, I could go through the whole process, and create more headaches to the meat plant, as they would have to sort out the taxes, customs fees, and all that with customs and USDA all over again. I made the call. The CSR at the meat plant tried tearing a strip off me, until I told her that the people who loaded the trailer should do a better job loading the trailers. Why would they load a case for the first drop right in the nose, then load the last drop around it? Of course, she didn't have an answer. She was probably just annoyed at all the extra work the loaders had created for her.

One other time, the loaders created a problem, which turned into a hugely expensive problem. For me, it was a simple load. A full trailer of mixed products, all going to the same place in South Windsor, Connecticut. Nice! Just a single drop. Getting backed into the place is a bit of a challenge, but not much. I left Winnipeg, stopping at the meat inspection house in Pembina. Phil (the inspector at the time) told me to break the seal (applied after they finish loading) and back in. I did what he asked. A few minutes later, Phil was at the driver's door, asking me to come in and have a look. Someone at the plant, after they had loaded the trailer, walked all over the load with muddy boots. There was muddy footprints, along with caked mud, on all the boxes. Since the boxes were no longer pristine, they were rejected, and left at the meat inspector for later disposal. I don't recall all of the product refused, but I do recall five of them were 80 lbs. boxes of Prime Rib. When I got to the receiver, he saw where the meat inspector had noted those refused entry. He asked me why, and when could expect them to be delivered? I told him why they were refused. As for when they would arrive, that was up to the meat plant, as the cases in question had been deemed unfit for human consumption, and would be destroyed. He wasn't happy, telling me he would never order from that plant again.

In addition to the three places in Hunts Point Market that I serviced, I also ran to places in Queens, Brooklyn, and Manhattan in New York State;

Philadelphia, Pennsylvania; Boston, Massachusetts; along with South Windsor (Connecticut), Jersey City (New Jersey), and too many other places to recall.

One place in Queens I delivered to quite frequently was 98 Packing, located on (as I recall) Third Street. Being the cautious type I am, before going in, I called to ask what this area of the city was like. The gentleman who answered the phone (the owner) spoke no English at all, but he handed to phone to someone who did speak very good English. I asked what the area was like, and if it would be safe to get in on Sunday, then sleep in the truck. He chuckled, and said: "You'll be safer sleeping here, than you are in your own bed." I asked for, and was given, instructions on how to get to the facility. I decided to get there about noon on Sunday, eyeball the place, and the neighbourhood. If I didn't like what I saw, I'd head back to the service plaza in New Jersey, then go back the next morning.

The directions were flawless, and I was soon at the address. The gentleman I had spoken to, a rather large black man named Andre, was working. I told him who I was, and that I had come in to see the area for myself before deciding to stay the night. He laughed almost hysterically, pointing down the street in the direction I had come from. I looked. Walking up the street, carrying lawn chairs, were six of the tallest, widest, most tattooed guys I had ever seen. The smallest was about 7 feet tall; maybe 350 lbs. Andre informed me that the gentleman who owned the business I was delivering to, owned all the buildings on the block on that side of the street. This included the club house for a motorcycle club. These six "gentlemen" were members of the motorcycle club. They would ensure I wasn't disturbed overnight. I slept like a baby. Even the garbage men refrained from emptying the bins.

Unloading at 98 Packing in Brooklyn, NY.

One interesting aspect about 98 Packing was the unloading process. You unloaded on the street. Andre, the receiver, did it all. He was receiver, lumper, everything. After he finished unloading the trailer, he would bring out a pair of 45 gallon plastic garbage cans. One had warm soapy water, the other just warm water. He would hoist them into the trailer, man handling them to the front where he tipped over the can with soapy water using a broom to "wash" the floor of the trailer. Next, he dumped the other warm-water one, rinsing out the trailer. And he never charged for the washout service.

The owner of 98 Packing also owned another facility in the Flushing area of Queens, called "SDJ". I mis-read the bills once, going to 98 Packing, when I was supposed to go to SDJ. I handed Andre the bills. He informed me of my mistake. As I had never been to SDJ, I asked him how to get there, and instead of giving me directions, he said something to the effect of: "I'm not letting that SOB at SDJ rip you off! I'll unload it here, and they can move it later with their city truck." He then proceeded to unload me at 98. Apparently, he caught hell for it. One time I had drops at both 98 and SDJ. Andre unloaded the 98 Packing portion, then climbed into the truck with me. We drove over to SDJ where he unloaded the rest of it before catching a ride back with someone headed to 98 Packing.

Getting into 98 Packing was a bit of a challenge, due to tight corners, as well as the narrowness of the street. It was essential that you either get in on Sunday, when everything was closed, or before 6 am. Anything after that, and forget it. To make the right turn onto Third Street, you have to start from the wrong side of the road, then jump the left curb on Third Street, or you run the serious risk of hitting the fire hydrant, or telephone pole on the corner. I explained this to the company's meat planner, asking him to relay it to the plant, so they could load trailers accordingly. The meat plant obviously ignored the information, as on one trip, they set it up as the second drop of the day. As soon as I saw that, I called Andre to see if we could come up with a plan. Maybe deliver it to SDJ, and shunt it back on their city truck? No, the owner wanted it delivered to 98 Packing. I made the first drop in Hunts Point, heading to Queens as soon as I was done. As I expected, far too many parked cars to make the corner onto Third Street. I stopped, then called Andre, telling him that I was at the corner, but there was no way I could make the turn. Cars were parked on both sides of the one-way street, right to the corner. I would have had a hard time getting just the truck onto the street, never mind the fifty-three-foot trailer. He said to hang on, he'd be right there. A couple of minutes later, I saw him bouncing down the street (the wrong way) in his forklift. He turned, put the forks under a BMW, picked it up, moved it to the sidewalk, gently put it down, with the back end on top of the fire hydrant. The two cars in front of the BMW were also moved the sidewalk. He then moved to the cars on the left side of the street near the corner. Three cars were quickly moved to the sidewalk. Right on the corner was a U-Haul cube van. As Andre he was lining up to move the van to in front of the cars, we saw a guy running down the street, waving his hands, and yelling: "Don't touch the truck! I'll move it right now!" He moved it. Probably didn't get the additional insurance, and even if he did, I doubt it would have covered any of the damages.

Illegally parked cars in New York were (and still are) a city-wide issue, causing truck drivers a LOT of headaches. One occasion in particular had a rather humorous conclusion for me, but was costly for the vehicle's owner. I was leaving Hunts Point, for the Cross Bronx Expressway. To get there you needed to turn right onto Bruckner Boulevard. This is no trivial matter. Bruckner Boulevard, at this point, consists of five lanes in each direction, BUT! …there are two lanes, then a median where they have the supports for the elevated Bruckner Expressway, which is above Bruckner Boulevard. On the other side of the median, are the other three lanes of Bruckner Boulevard. In order to get to the Cross Bronx, you have to turn into the near two-lane part. And it's a tight right turn. On the occasion I'm recounting, I tried to make the right turn to discover that someone had decided that right on the corner was a good place to park their car … and facing south in the northbound lanes. There is no parking along Bruckner at all as it's a VERY busy street. How they managed to get down a one-way street in the wrong direction in New York is totally beyond me. It looked like I had the room to make the corner, but nope. I came up about two feet short. There was no backing up, as traffic was already backed up behind me. I just stopped where I was. I knew the police would soon be along to help sort out this mess. They showed up about three minutes later. I was told to "get the (expletive) truck outta here." Told them I couldn't, as I was unable to back up due to the traffic behind me. I couldn't go forward and avoid the illegally parked car. The police officer repeated that I move the truck now, or I was getting a bigger ticket that the illegally parked car. I said the only way I'm moving, is to run over the car. He said: "Then run it over!" Having been given "official permission" I proceeded to use the trailer tires to push the car out of the way, doing significant damage. As I drove off, I looked in the mirror, and saw the officer stick a ticket under what was left of the windshield wiper.

One of the semi-regular reloads I had, in the beginning, anyway, was at Tropicana in Jersey City, New Jersey. 99% of the time, these reloads were perfect. Load at about noon, take it to Toronto, then drop it in the yard for a city truck to deliver later. No problem at all. Except one time, which turned out to be the last time I ever went there. I was delivering a full load to Fancy Foods at four in the morning. The previous afternoon I was told that I had to get to Tropicana as soon as I was unloaded as they had a rush load for Toronto. Okay, no sweat. It's about an hour's drive from Fancy Foods to Tropicana, maybe another hour to load, then an easy eight hours to Toronto for six a.m. delivery the next day. Ought not to be a problem. I delivered to Fancy Foods, got the trailer washed out at the trailer wash in the market, and off I went to Tropicana. Checked in, and was given a door to back into. Once backed in I waited to be loaded. And waited. And waited. And waited some more. Went in to see the shipper every two hours. I was always told the same thing: "You're next in line. We had some issues, and everything is running a little late." To cut a long story short, I was finally loaded at midnight (15 hours after arriving for the "rush load"). I told them: "The six-a.m. delivery in Toronto isn't going to happen. It's an eight-hour drive. Right now, I'm heading to the closest truck stop, and I'm going to bed, since I've been here all day trying to get loaded, and getting nothing but the run around." Their response? "Nope, this load has to deliver at six a.m. tomorrow." We went back and forth with the discussion for about 20 minutes, until I finally told him to just get this "stuff" off my trailer. He refused, and said again it has to deliver at six. Another 15 or 20 minutes along this useless path, and I told him to unload it, or I was going to unload it. He told me I wasn't allowed on the loading dock, and I had to get going, or the load would be late. I told him it was already going to be late, and get it off my trailer, or I'd get it off the trailer. Again, he said I wasn't allowed on the loading dock. I told him I didn't need a loading dock, or a forklift for that matter. He again refused to unload the trailer.

I pulled ahead about 20 feet, backed up, and hit the brakes. Four pallets of Tropicana hit the pavement. Pulled ahead another 20 feet, backed up, and hit the brakes. By this time, he was at the driver's window, just screaming! Told me to back into the dock. By the time they had the trailer unloaded, the local police were on scene to escort me off the property. The shipper told me I would never be allowed to load there again. I already knew I'd never load there again. My boss wasn't too happy, until he heard the whole story, especially when he saw via the satellite that I'd been held up there all day. Of course, Tropicana filed a complaint, so to smooth ruffled feathers, I was told my three days off were being reported to Tropicana as a suspension. Whatever, tell them what you want, I couldn't have cared less.

There were three places I delivered to in Manhattan, Two of them far down, around 10th or 11th Streets, the other a couple of blocks off Broadway in Harlem. To get to them with a truck, requires a trip down Broadway Avenue, through Times Square. If you ever get the chance to visit New York City, I highly recommend the trip from the Cross Bronx Expressway down Broadway. It's hard to describe the changes as you drive along Broadway. Harlem is not what you'd expect. It's a fairly clean area, nice buildings, and I didn't feel any dangers at all.

My delivery in Harlem was a partial load, 250 cases of ground beef, each case weighing about 50 lbs for a total of approximately 12,500 lbs of ground beef. I called the place for directions. This was pre -GPS and Google Maps days. Even with today's technology, it's a good idea to call, as the address on the bills may be for the office, not the warehouse, there may be low bridges, non-truck routes, and all other kinds of mis-direction. The directions this time, however, were flawless. Before long I was at the customer. Then the fun began. Someone, somewhere, had made a minor error turning the whole process into a huge mess. The meat place sent 250 cases of ground beef. The customer, a small mom & pop type place, had ordered 250 lbs of ground beef. 245 cases too many. To make matters worse, they had signed the bills, accepting the order before they, or I, realized the error. They took the entire 250 cases, and I have no idea where they put it all. For all I know, they had to go buy another walk-in freezer to store it all. As cold and heartless as it may sound, it's a them-problem, not a me-problem. When you're in New York, you pretty much have to adapt to their mentality, or the place will eat you alive.

Of the two places in Lower Manhattan, one I delivered to semi-regularly, the other I delivered to once. This one was also my first deliver in Manhattan. As was my practice for first-time New York deliveries, I called for directions, inquiring about the neighbourhood. I received the directions along with a report that it was safe to stay the night on the street. I drove in at about noon on Sunday to check it out. There were a few other trucks waiting to deliver the next morning, no bars on the windows, not a lot of graffiti, along with nice looking cars parked on the street. All in all, a nice-looking area. Okay, cool. I'll just stay here the night. Nightfall came, nothing untoward going on. About 2 a.m. I was awaked by the sounds of gun fire. I could see bright lights streaming in around the truck's privacy curtains. Police and ambulance sirens pierced the silence. After a stream of expletives, I jumped up, got dressed, crawled into the driver's seat, lit a smoke (first things first!), then opened the curtains a sliver to see what was happening. To my great relief, they were filming an episode of the television show Law & Order at the end of the block. Blood pressure and pulse returned to a somewhat normal state, and I opened the curtains more to watch.

The other place I delivered to in Lower Manhattan was one I went to five or six times. It was, by far, the worst place in Manhattan I ever delivered to. According to Google Maps, it's now called "Interstate Meats" on 10th Avenue. It was a real horror story to back into. You have to do so from the street while traffic continues to just go around all the while you're trying to maneuver your truck in backwards. It's like a giant game of Frogger. Not hitting anyone is a challenge. Again, you have to just relax, and back in like you're a local. If you politely wait for an opening (like a good Canadian), you'll wait forever. Just put it in reverse, and back up. They'll get out of your way. If not, well, it sucks to be them (again, with the New York attitude). Fortunately, they start receiving at midnight, so traffic isn't usually that big of a problem. If you try and back in any time after four in the morning, however, it gets interesting.

One time when I was at the earlier version of Interstate Meats, I asked to use the washroom. The receiver told me that they didn't like drivers using the washroom, as the drivers tend to leave a mess. Nonetheless, he told me where the washroom was. I have only seen a single worse bathroom in my entire life, and I have seen some real disastrous bathrooms. Missing tiles on the floor and walls, ceiling tiles missing, the light was hanging by a single wire, there was blood everywhere, dirty work clothes hanging on nails in the wall, the toilet was stained a variety of colours, the hand towel looked crusted in some unidentified dried liquid, and the toilet bowl was leaking onto the floor then spilling down a hole drilled in the floor. And they don't want drivers making a mess? The WORST bathroom I ever saw wasn't in New York. It was in a small Ontario town, at the customs facility. I had cleared customs, and asked the officer for the key to the washroom, which is located in a separate building. He told me it was closed for the indefinite future, for deep cleaning. I was puzzled, but a bit curious. As I walked back to the truck, the washroom door was being held open by a 4 inch hose, with a blower on it. There was a customs official standing guard, in what appeared to be a hazmat suit, complete with hood and face shield. Now I was REALLY curious. I asked, and was told someone had had an "accident" in the washroom. The odor was quite pungent, but I was still curious enough to want a look. Just then, the door opened, and a person in a similar suit emerged from the bathroom. Before the door closed, I had a good look at the interior. The polite way to describe the interior, is that it looked like a full septic tank had exploded in the washroom, spreading the contents to all walls, corners, and even the ceiling.

One place I reloaded in the New York area was a pet supply company on Long Island. I was there twice. Each time was a major hassle getting in. To get backed in, you have to blind side in off the street at 90 degrees, then turn the trailer 90 degrees to the left across the front of the building, then another 90 degrees blindside around the corner of the building to the loading door. During this whole procedure, you have to avoid parked cars. You can't see the door until you hit it. A good way to spike your blood pressure.

In all the years I ran to New York City, only once did I experience any crime or violence directed at myself. Thinking back, I guess I was pretty lucky, considering some of the horror stories I've heard. Mind you, some of those stories may have been exaggerated. The one time I had a run in with a robber, luck and quick thinking were on my side. I was in the Bronx headed to Hunts Point Market on a one-way street, three lanes wide, at about 11:30 on a Sunday morning. It was a warm, sunny day and I had my window open. As I pulled away from a red light, this guy, maybe 20 years old, appeared out of nowhere, jumping onto on my running board with a pistol in his hand, demanding money, and whatever else I had. I just kept going, cutting close to a hydro pole. He never saw it coming. Him and the mirror left the truck at about 25 mph. Scared the tar outta me, but I managed to escape that run in.

To me, New York City was a great place to deliver. Jersey City, about four miles away, just across the Hudson River, was a whole different ball of wax. I've already told the story of Tropicana. That was more an issue with the shipper. Porky Products, however, was an issue with the area. I went there once, and vowed never to go there again. I did return, but only after they had changed locations to a much safer area. As usual, I called Porky Products for directions. This time they were pre-recorded. The recording was slow enough that you could write them down, without any trouble. Including the warning at the end. I'll remember this recording for the rest of my life: "Follow these directions to the letter.

Do not stop for any reason. You have been routed around all traffic signals and stop signs. Do not speak to anyone. When you arrive, if the gate is closed, sound your airhorn, and continue around the block, making right turns only. Again, do not stop for any reason. If the gate is still closed, sound your horn again, and circle the block. When the gate is open, drive in, and remain in your truck with the doors locked. When the gate closes behind you, we will come to the truck. Again… Do not stop for any reason whatsoever.

A little over the top? NO! On my way in, at two o'clock on a Wednesday afternoon, I passed a Jersey City police car, siren screaming, lights flashing, up on blocks with the wheels removed. That's an area I'd choose to stay away from!

PART 2: 9/11 AND AFTERWARDS.

This was close enough for me on 9/11

Tuesday, September 11, 2001. I, like everyone else who lived it, will remember this day for the rest of my life. I had just delivered a load of toilet paper to Krasdale Foods in The Bronx at six o'clock that morning. I was comfortably parked at the Vince Lombardi Service Plaza in Rahway, New Jersey.

I was in the bunk, with the curtains closed, watching M*A*S*H on a DVD while I awaited a reload, completely oblivious to everything happening around me. I heard the satellite "beep", signaling a new message had arrived, but instead of a single "beep", it was 3 rapid beeps, signifying a priority message. I pulled up the message from my dispatcher. It simply said: "Are you caught in the terrorist incident, or are you clear to go?" At this point, I was still clueless, so, being the smart-ass that I am, I replied: "I'm good, no one saw me do anything, there's no evidence." My dispatcher replied back; "Can you see the World Trade Centre from where you are?" I was puzzled, and opened the curtains to have a look. Holy Mother Of God! I had a direct line of sight to the World Trade Centre. I felt like the wind had been sucked out of my lungs.

I grabbed my camera, snapping two pictures, neither of which turned out worth a damn. I sent a message saying I was clear and not directly impacted by the events unfolding around me. I was told: "We want everyone out of the area. Head to Montreal, we'll find something there." I hauled ass to Montreal.

It wasn't until later that night that I learned the total extent of the attack. Of course, the radio stations were relaying any and all information, some of it was just wild speculation others were only rumours, and some, just plain gossip. The border line up to exit New York State, and enter Quebec faced a three-hour delay, as they were checking everyone on both sides of the border. Border delays usually ruffle truck driver's feathers pretty badly, but there weren't any complaints and no whining this time.

From Montreal, I was given a load of bicycle helmets going to Rantool, Illinois. The border crossing between Sarnia, Ontario and Port Huron, Michigan was another story altogether. I hit the back of the US customs line about 15 miles from the border. The Ontario Provincial Police (OPP) were moving all the trucks to park on the shoulder of the road, telling the drivers to just be patient, and stay in line. They said that once we run out of hours, or get too tired, sleep where we are, and they (the OPP) will make sure no one jumps ahead in the line. It took two days to get to, and then clear, American customs.

At the USA customs, every single driver was questioned at length regarding everything from place of birth, to ancestry. Every trailer was unloaded. Each box, bundle or stack was separated, then hand inspected before being reloaded onto the trailer. I really felt sorry for the guys hauling tarpped loads on flat decks. What most drivers experienced was pretty intimidating, but I can only imagine how bad it was for the drivers with South Asian or Arabic heritage. Some of them have said it was almost a living hell.

In the years following the event now-called "9/11" I continued to deliver into and out of New York. New York after 9/11 was a completely different place. Best way to describe it was, the city "mellowed out". People seemed more eager to help, and in general, they seemed friendlier.

On one trip I was on my way to Toronto after delivering in New York when I got a satellite message from the Toronto terminal manager. He asked me to call him as soon as possible. I knew the manager personally, from when he was a driver, so I found a rest area, then called him. He asked if I was up to recovering a load in Manhattan. "Sure," I said. He told me to come see him the next day in Toronto. I arrived the next morning He told me to find the oldest, hunk of junk trailer I could find, reefer, dry van, heated trailer, it didn't matter. I was to double check with him that it was acceptable, then head to police impound yard in Manhattan. I was a bit confused, but whatever. I found an old reefer in the yard, that was probably due to be retired and sold off. The reefer unit had over 7,500 hours on it, along with a trailer that was about 10 or 12 years old. Definitely past it's prime. He confirmed that it was a good trailer to take. I asked him what was going on. He just gave me a cockeyed smile, saying I'd figure it out when I got there. So off I went with the old clunker of a trailer. The next morning, I found the impound yard. One of our trailers was in the yard, as well as a truck belonging to an owner-operator. I went it to see what was what, and the yard workers told me to drop the trailer I had, handing me the bills for the loaded trailer. While I was dropping the empty, they removed the pin lock (which prevents anyone from hooking to the trailer), I hooked up to the loaded trailer, then headed off to make the delivery. What had happened was that the owner-operator (a team) were on their way to deliver in lower Manhattan when they decided to pick up a street walker. Turned out, she was an undercover police officer. They were immediately arrested. Truck, trailer, and cargo were impounded, and towed to the impound yard. The company successfully pleaded the case that the company shouldn't be penalized for the actions of a non-employee. Owner-operators aren't legally employed by trucking companies. They are their own business, operating under the authority of their company title.

A deal was made to replace the impounded loaded trailer with a similar empty trailer. Because the load was under USDA regulations, transferring the load to a new trailer wasn't feasible. Instead, we just exchanged the empty unit for the loaded trailer. I heard later through the grape vine that said team was of the Muslim faith, where infidelity is a HUGE no-no. More than in western culture, so there were sure to be cultural penalties as well as legal ones. I never learned what the outcome of the court case was, but I never did see that truck again.

Alas, the New York runs came to a rather abrupt end when a meat plant in southern Ontario purchased the Alberta-based meat plant that was shipping the New York loads. Being based in Winnipeg, I lost out on the nice New York load along with the, on average, 13,200 miles a month. My disappointment was to be short lived. The New York trips had proven I was a hard runner, capable of cranking out over 13,000 miles a month on a regular basis. Based on this record, I was given a dedicated run of a lifetime: Texas here I come!

The Laredo Triangle
The Truck Driver's Lament

With a proven record of being able to run long distances for a long period of time, I was rewarded with a dream run. The prestigious "Laredo Triangle" was the envy of all long-haulers. No messing around waiting for shippers or receivers. These loads were all drop and hook. Drop a loaded trailer, grab a preloaded trailer, and off you go.

Laredo, Texas, is on the USA-Mexico border. This community is the largest inland port on the border, with an economy that depends on international trade with Mexico, the United States, and Canada. The city is filled with commercial and industrial warehouses as well as importing and exporting facilities. It is the ending point for Interstate 35 which travels all the way north into Minnesota. As far as the size of the city, it has about a quarter-of-a-million residents. The people here overwhelmingly have Mexican heritage (95.6 % Hispanic and Latino). In an average year, cross-border trucking here moves $79 billion worth of goods, some destined for other points in the USA and some for Canada. As you can imagine, this is a very busy place, especially as more trucks are northbound with Mexican cargo than those southbound with goods heading to Mexico. More than 75% of the goods crossing the border are moved by truck.

The result of overloading trailers going into Mexico. Minor as the damage looks, the trailer is total write-off

The "Triangle Tour" began on a Wednesday with a load from Winnipeg to Calgary. I'd drop it in the yard, then take an empty trailer 120 miles back east to Brooks, Alberta. Sometimes it would be an empty from Winnipeg to Brooks, but not very often. Once the empty trailer was dropped at the meat plant in Brooks, I'd grab a preloaded meat trailer bound for Laredo, Texas. At the Alberta-Montana border, I'd stop at the American Customs office where I could initiate a T&E (Transport and Export) bond to Laredo. Once clear of US Customs and APHIS (Animal Plant Health Inspection Service), I was on my way to Laredo, 1,945 miles south.

I'd get into Laredo Sunday afternoon then report to the Freight Forwarder. Most of the freight forwarders have US Customs officials on site who checked the trailer's seal number against the seal number on the T&E bond, then cancel the bond. The forwarding house would sign the bills, and I'd drop the trailer, then I was off to our local drop yard where I would grab a trailer loaded with produce from Mexico that was headed north. With the north-bound bond was already in place, I'd head to the truck stop to start a logbook reset. The logbook rules had changed a few years before I began the Laredo run. Under the old rules, we were allowed 70 hours of work (driving, and non driving work time) time over 8 days.

If you ran VERY hard, you could hit the seventy-hour limit in five days. Then you were parked until reaching the 9th day. Under the new rules, once you hit the 70 hour limit, you could do a "reset". This translated to 34 consecutive hours off duty (36 hours off duty under Canadian regulations) before your hours reset to zero, thus providing you with another 70 hours driving time. This meant I'd sit in Laredo until Tuesday morning, when I'd have my 36 hour reset done, then I was off again. I'd clear the T&E bond, and Canada customs, dropping the trailer in Toronto Thursday evening. My load home to Winnipeg was usually ready to go. I'd try to get a few miles out of Toronto to avoid the morning rush out, usually stopping for the night at the King City Service area. From there, I'd drive Saturday and Sunday, getting into Winnipeg Sunday evening. I would then be off until Wednesday, when I'd turn, and do it all again. This worked out to just over 13,000 miles a month. No time wasted waiting for shippers and or receivers to load and unload. Almost all my time was spent driving, which is what drivers are paid to do. When I started this run, I was driving what was, and still is, the most comfortable, and dependable truck I've ever driven: a Freighter Cascadia with a Mercedes Benz 500 HP engine into a thirteen-speed Eaton Fuller transmission. That truck was a dream. Other than regularly schedule maintenance, the only time it was every in a repair shop was when the serpentine belt broke.

Eventually, the Laredo Triangle run also disappeared. That put me back on regular line-haul runs. While the run ended, the adventures in long-haul trucking, however, did not.

The Last Laugh
Getting a Chuckle on the Road

The life of a long-haul trucker is not just one of frustration, crazy loads, wonky weather, insane traffic, and silly (and often stupid) people. We get our laughs when we can, where we can. A couple of my homeward bound trips from Toronto provided a few laughs.

One good time involved a driver I'll call Henry. This episode occurred in Longlac, a previously-mentioned small town on Highway 11 in Northwestern Ontario. Generally, I avoid running Ontario's northern route (Highway 11) after two friends were killed in a collision on this highway in January 2000. Compared to Highway 17 (the southern route of the Trans Canada through Northwestern Ontario), Highway 11 takes a bit more time when travelling from Toronto to Thunder Bay. It is, however, a lot flatter with fewer corners and less hills. This, naturally, attracts less-experienced drivers (of all vehicles). Highway 17, which follows the northern coast of Lake Superior has its own challenges. This very scenic route has some mountainous regions hugging the coast, long steep hills, winding sections, limited places to pass, and a lot of tourist traffic during the summer. In the winter, this highway sees massive snowfalls coming out of the north and the west, as well as nor'easters blowing off Lake Superior. Dense fog is possible anytime of the year. Even with those challenges, I prefer this route.

Henry and I, each in our own trucks, were running together from Toronto to Thunder Bay, stopping for the night in North Bay, Ontario. We left North Bay after a good night's sleep. This meant that making Thunder Bay legally was not an issue. There we were, cruising along, chatting about anything and everything, as drivers tend to do. As we approached the town of Hearst, I asked him if he was planning on stopping to use the facilities, grab some food or whatever. He said he wasn't, but he'd stop if I wanted to run in. Since the next place to stop would be Longlac, some 130 miles, or a good two hour run away. I always stopped to use the facilities. That's too long to try and ignore the messages my bladder would soon be sending. When I got back in the truck, I asked him, again, if he wanted to use the restroom before we left. He said he was good, heading back out on the highway. Sure enough, about an hour later, he called back saying he should've made a pit-stop in Hearst. This stretch of highway is what you'd call desolate. Safe places to pull over are few and far between. If you don't know exactly where they are, you'll pass them before you realize they're there. It was about four in the afternoon and we were driving into a setting sun, making it even more difficult to spot these turnouts. By the time we got to Longlac, Henry's teeth must have been floating. He wheeled that cabover onto the service road, popped the parking brake, opened the door and jumped to the ground, all in one motion. But he never made it to the ground. He hooked the waistband of his jeans on the door handle, and there he hung. I couldn't help him much, as I was doubled over laughing at the sight of him struggling to free himself. By the time I managed to stop laughing, and help rescue him, he was some angry at me, as his bladder had long since won the battle. Once he cooled down, he finally saw the humour in the situation, and chuckled about it himself.

One driver I have a lot of respect for was "Indian Joe". His real name is Joe Nayanookeesic, but he insisted on being called "Indian Joe". Joe was quite a character. At an annual awards dinner one year, the ladies asked his name as they looked for his name tag. They were new to the company, and obviously didn't know Joe on sight. He replied "Indian Joe." They were speechless. They knew that couldn't be his name, so they asked again. He replied again, "Indian Joe". The welcoming committee called one of the women who had been with the company a few years to come to the desk.

She said "His name is Joe Nayanookeesic, but he goes by Indian Joe." They found his name tag with his proper name, handing it to him. He tossed it in the garbage, grabbed a marker, and a blank tag, wrote: "Indian Joe" on it, stuck it to his shirt, handed them back the marker, and walked into the room. As God is my witness, if you ever addressed him as "Joe", or "Mr. Nayanookeesic", or another name, he would correct you by saying: "It's Indian Joe."

If you ever had the pleasure of meeting Joe, you know exactly what I'm talking about. He loved practical jokes, both playing them, and having them played on him. If you caught him with one, you could bet your last dollar he'd find a way to improve it, then play it on someone else. I was witness to a few Joe stories, but I've heard from credible sources many other stories. One I heard about, but wasn't around for the actual event, was the time his truck was stolen. Joe was famous for pulling pranks, and other mischief to get a laugh. This backfired when he called into dispatch once to report his truck and trailer had been stolen, no one believed him! As the story goes, he had to call the police himself, and it wasn't until the police called the office to confirm that, yes, Joe was at the truck stop, but the truck and trailer were not, that the office took him seriously. As the story goes, they located the truck and trailer, and arrested the culprits as they were unloading the trailer. Knowing Joe, I can believe it actually happened.

One time I was in the Toronto yard trying to slide the 5th wheel on the truck. The 5th wheel can move forwards or backwards to adjust the weight on the steering and drive axles. The axles on the trailer can also move, adjusting the weight on the trailer and drive axles. The general idea is, when the truck is brand new, slide the fifth wheel to allow your steering axle to be just below the legal limit, then you seldom have to slide it again. This fifth wheel was gummed up something bad. I couldn't get it to slide to save my life. Joe wandered over to see what the problem was, and I was happy for the help. I know how to slide a fifth wheel, but having someone else help makes life easier. He might catch something I missed, or he may have a few tricks I don't know about. Joe double checked everything I'd done to facilitate the sliding of the fifth wheel. Unlocked the locking pins, lowered the landing gear on the trailer and dropped the air bags on the truck. These last two steps aren't necessary, but they take the weight off the 5th wheel, making it easier to slide.

We both lit a smoke and scratched our heads. A minute later, I got a typical Joe response. "Did you check the oil in the reefer?" Of course, this would have nothing to do with sliding the 5th wheel. I slowly turned, and with a quizzical look on my face, I asked him: "Are you on glue?", a typical "me" reply when asked a stupid question. Joe just gave me a blank look, and with a perfectly straight face said: "No, Lysol!" A typical Joe response! He would poke fun at anyone, no matter their race, colour, gender, religion, age, whatever. Everyone was in danger of a Joe-joke. Even himself. We finally got the fifth wheel to slide, and my weights were good to go. Joe's load was ready about the same time, so I hung around in case he needed help with his. He did, and it was sorted out quickly, and off we went.

I couldn't tell you any of the stories or jokes he told me on that trip. I was laughing so hard my stomach and jaws hurt. He could keep you in stitches for days. As we travelled along, more and more trucks fell in behind us. Some heard him carrying on and slowed down to let Joe pass, others caught up, and stayed behind to enjoy the stories. When you ran with Joe, there was never a dull moment. When Joe pulled in to fuel, or use the washroom, or sleep, the entire convoy followed like lemmings going to the sea. The one I distinctly remember, was when we all left the now closed Tower Hill truck stop in Ignace, a small Trans-Canada Highway town in northwestern Ontario. By now, there were about 19 or 20 trucks in the convoy. By the time the last truck was out of the parking lot, Joe was up around the corner, therefore he couldn't see if we had all gotten out. He called on the CB to see if everyone had gotten on the highway. A chorus of confirmations followed. Once everyone had checked in, Joe came back with: "Just like the old days… White men chasing an Indian!" And the laughter and silliness returned until we reached Winnipeg.

One time, I left Toronto about two hours after Joe did. I hustled to catch up. I asked every truck I could reach on the radio how far ahead of me Joe was. I got a few replies, so I just kept moving as fast as I could. All the way to Winnipeg, I was hustling. Never did see him, either on the road, or in any of the truck stops. When I got to Winnipeg, I asked trip arrivals (whenever you got to a terminal, you always checked in with trip arrivals, turning in your paper work) "When did Joe get in?" Wouldn't you know it, I had passed him about 90 minutes out of Toronto. Here I was, running hell bent for leather trying to catch someone I had already passed!

At one of the company awards dinners, in 2000 if memory serves, the owner of TransX was giving his speech when Joe just stood up and said: "Louie, when do I get my new truck?" Dead silence in the room. Louie looked at Joe for a minute and said: "Come see me Monday" then continued on with his speech. With that one question, Joe started a new company policy. Once you reach 30 years of service with the company, they will order you a truck to your personal specifications regarding make, model, engine make, horsepower, colour, sleeper size, etc. Joe being Joe, ordered a canary yellow Peterbilt with a Caterpillar engine. Why? Because he knew the shop manager hated Peterbilt's as well as hating Caterpillar engines. I guess somewhere along the line the shop manager had managed to annoy Joe. Evidently, Joe had finally succeeded in getting his revenge. I got my proof when I asked Joe why he went with that truck and engine combination. He replied: "Because the shop manager hates Peterbilts and Cat engines."

With Joe's penchant for practical jokes, you always had to be on guard, lest you fall victim to one of his pranks. He would never do anything to endanger anyone, but you still had to be on guard. One time, he got a two-for-one, and I was one of them. As discussed earlier, the brake systems on the trailers have two separate circuits. Joe had a little prank where he would disconnect the red supply line, remove the seal, pop in a coin, replace the seal, then reconnect the line. When you pushed the button to charge the trailer's air supply, the coin would prevent the air from reaching the trailer, and the parking brakes wouldn't release. You're not going anywhere. Had he done that with the blue (service) line; you'd have no trailer brakes. Well, he caught me with the old "quarter in the red (supply) line prank." Knowing Joe was around, when the brakes wouldn't release, I did some checking, and found the quarter. I also kept it, just out of spite. The other driver he caught, should have known not to turn your back on Joe. He didn't get the quarter in the air line. Joe got him good. As we were getting ready to leave, Joe, with a huge grin on his face, told me to let the other truck go first. I knew something was up, because with Joe around, something was always up. We left the yard, heading into Winnipeg. About five minutes later, it was obvious what Joe had done. He had dumped two jars of hot air popcorn down the stack of the other truck. That driver was busy trucking along, oblivious to the fact that he was blowing black popcorn out the exhaust stack. The show lasted about five or ten minutes, but it's a sight I'll remember until the day I die.

It's been said more than a few times that trucking is more than a job, more than a career. It's a lifestyle. Once a trucker, always a trucker, and even on those rare vacations we're still truckers, all day, every day. Once a year, my ex-wife and I used to travel back east to Thunder Bay to visit family. On one trip back, I gave her ample reason to laugh hysterically at me for a couple of hours. We were cruising along in our mini-van, headed back to Winnipeg. As we crossed into Manitoba, I saw the lights flashing for all trucks to enter the West Hawk Lake weigh station. From force of habit, I pulled in. As I crossed the scale, the scale master, with a chuckle, said over the load speaker, something to the effect of: "Carry on, we don't make a habit of scaling minivans." I dropped my head in embarrassment. My ex laughed, ribbing me about it all the way to Winnipeg. I hope I'm not the only one who has ever done this! I'm sure other truckers on auto-pilot in their personal vehicles has done this too.

In 2002 a rather humorous incident occurred. The ever present, seemingly unavoidable brain-fart. That winter, shortly after my divorce was final, I finally took my first vacation to take a break from Canada's cold weather. I love flying, and had always dreamed of seeing Australia since a Grade Two project, when I made a relief map of Australia from salt ceramic. But I wasn't sure how I'd handle the long flight to Australia, so I decided to start small, with a trip to Puerto Plata in the Dominican Republic. The best deals I could find, departed from Toronto. I booked a week of fun in the sun for the last week of March. I finished a run to Toronto, then got ready for my mini-vacation. Since I was going to be gone for a week, I arranged for the dock to send a clean, empty meat-combo box on a pallet out to the truck. I unloaded all my trucking worldly belonging into the box. They put a tracking sticker on the box, showing the box's origin and destination terminals. The dock worker's next task was to scan the tracker's bar code. The code tells them where the pallet is going along with the expected date of arrival. They entered all the information on my box, with Toronto being both the origin and destination. The "arrival" date was the day I returned. This way the box would be easy to find and we wouldn't have to dig it out from a pile of cargo. Everything from the truck was in the box, except for a week's worth of clothing.

My plan was that on my return, my truck would be back in Toronto. I'd move everything back in, grab a shower, and do all my vacation-laundry. Well, the best laid plans, usually fall apart. Upon my return, sunburnt from falling asleep on the beach, I got to the Toronto terminal to find NOTHING! Someone had seen my name on the box, knew I lived in Winnipeg, and was on vacation. Ever-so-helpful, they sent my box to Winnipeg the night before I returned. There I was, a duffel bag full of dirty clothes with every-thing I else I owned on a trailer headed to Winnipeg. I did my laundry in Toronto so I at least had something clean to wear, then called the night dispatcher in Winnipeg to explain the situation. He had a good chuckle. He sent me a purchase order number for a taxi along with another for a hotel room. The next morning, I called my daytime dispatcher to tell him what was going on. Another chuckle was heard. Because I had nothing but a duffel bag full of clothes, they split up a team in Toronto to bring my truck back, and flew me home. As it turned out, I arrived in Winnipeg before all my gear did. The truck arrived the next day.

On one of my first trips across Ontario on highway 11, I was driving the night shift. It was an overcast night, no stars, no moon, very dark. One of the small towns along the way is called Moonbeam, and they have a very appropriate display outside their visitor information building. Said display is well lit internally at night, and the first time I saw it, it scared the pants off me.

The Moonbeam ON. UFO, outside the tourist information center.

As you come around the corner, there it is. A six foot tall replica of a flying saucer, lit up internally. It made me jump to the point that it woke up my partner, who came out of the bunk like a rocket to see what the hell was going on. After I told him, he had a good chuckle at my expense. I have since returned the favour to some of my former students.

If I may pass on a little sage advice that once provided me with a good chuckle, if you see a cattle truck stopped at a traffic light, railway crossing, or anywhere on a street, don't get too close. That's not mud on the sides and rear of the trailer. A number of years back, I was a lane over, and slightly behind a cattle truck at a railroad crossing. In front of me, and beside the cattle trailer, was a young woman in a Ford Mustang convertible with the top down. It was a nice, warm, sunny day, and she had her music blasting away from the stereo. I guess Ol' Betsy on the top level of the trailer wasn't impressed with the music, because all of a sudden, cow pies were falling, and the bladder was draining. And the poor young lady in the Mustang got it all. Just over a gallon from the bladder, and four of five good sized cow pies. Really felt sorry for her. One, that's guaranteed to ruin your day, and secondly, that will affect the car's resale value.

TRUCKERS ARE PEOPLE, TOO

LIFE WHEN WE'RE NOT IN A TRUCK

In November of 2004, I finally fulfilled a life-long dream I'd had, taking a three-week and two day vacation to Australia. Australia had always been a dream vacation spot for me, ever since I had made that salt ceramic relief map of the country back in Grade Two. Back in those days, long before Facebook, Instagram, and other social media platforms, we had chatrooms on MSN and Yahoo, along with messenger services. In one MSN trucker chat room, I met quite a few people, including four from Australia. Of all the people I met in the chat room, I still maintain contact with four of them. One here in Canada, and three from Australia. I had planned, booked and paid for the trip in March 2008. The plan was to stay with one of my Australian friends for the duration with a quick visit the other two on my last day before flying out.

The journey was not the most direct, but it was the least expensive at $1,590.09. The routing saw me fly out of Winnipeg heading to Calgary followed by legs to Los Angeles, Taipei, and Kuala Lumpur before arriving in Brisbane. Air Canada took me to Calgary, and Los Angeles, and Malaysia Airlines carried me the rest of the way, including a 21 hour layover in Kuala

Lumpur. Malaysia Airlines put me up in a hotel, giving me three meal tickets while I was there. One thing that really struck me in both Taipei and Kuala Lumpur were signs as soon as you exit the plane: "ILLEGAL DRUGS ARE A DEATH PENALTY!"

On the way to the Kuala Lumpur hotel, the shuttle bus stalled. The driver wasn't familiar with driving a standard transmission. Not being a local, I wasn't sure what to expect. Almost everyone on the bus exited, and started pushing the bus to get it started again. Another interesting event in Kuala Lumpur involved a bit of shopping. I had neglected to get a pair of sandals before I left Canada (in the almost-winter). The hotel was in a district with a lot of shops and street vendors, so I wandered down to see what they had. I found a decent pair of sandals at a street vendor, but, of course, had no local currency with me. The cost was 33 ringgits (the local currency). I found an ATM, withdrawing 50 ringgits then returning to the vendor to purchase the sandals, which, by the way, I still have, and wear to this day. Back in the hotel room, I started wondering: "Exactly how much did I pay for these sandals?" Of course, this was before internet access was readily available, so I had no way of finding out until much later. Turns out the exchange rate was quite favourable. They cost me $3.30 Canadian.

Lunch and supper at the Malaysian hotel were unremarkable. Can't really remember them, so they must have been decent. Breakfast the next day was another story. And it was my first real experience with "culture shock". Malaysia is mostly an Islamic country, therefore following the rules of Islamic law, including dietary ones. For breakfast, I had a choice of meats: turkey bacon or chicken sausage. Neither appealed to me in the least. The scrambled eggs could have been served in a glass with a straw. No thanks, I'll pass. The toast and coffee, though, were first class. The service was exemplary, it was just the food choices that didn't thrill me. The locals I met were decent enough folks, as interested in me and where I was from as I was in them and their country.

From Kuala Lumpur, it was a 9 hour flight to the Brisbane airport, where my friend was waiting. After customs and immigration clearance, I walked into the Arrivals Hall, spotting her at once. Respecting her privacy while sharing our adventures means giving her a name – in honour of the country – I'll call her "Matilda". It was as if Matilda was standing in an area with no one around. We were, and still are, strictly platonic friends. When I was planning the trip, I told her, in no uncertain terms, that our friendship was too important to me to risk destroying by becoming "more than friends". We caught a taxi to the hotel (two queen-sized beds). During the taxi ride, wouldn't you know it, we were delayed by a truck accident! Half way around the world, one of the first things I see, is a truck accident!.

After checking in, we headed across to street to a local restaurant chain that advertised Texas-style food. Matilda had never tried Texan-styled foods whereas I, after much time spent in Texas (especially Laredo) had a good idea of what we'd be eating. Right above the door, as soon as you walk in, there was a stuffed moose head (although I don't think I've seen or heard of a Texas moose!). Again, here I was, half way around the world, and I'm greeted by something I can't avoid seeing at home! I commented on the moose head to our waitress, and she said "Yeah, they're pretty big, aren't they!" The look on her face when I told her that head came from a calf, maybe two years old was priceless. It was a small moose head. The next day we took the bus to the small town where Matilda lived, settling in for a greatly-anticipated vacation.

Being November, it was quite warm, and the sun was blazing hot. The season's are opposite in the southern hemisphere. I was treated to some good Australian cooking along with some foods that were pretty foreign to me. Like Vegemite and Marmite. Australians eat Vegemite like we eat peanut butter. The best way I can describe Vegemite is: salt paste. To me, it was one of the worst things I had ever tasted. Fresh fruits and vegetables were plentiful, however, some of the vegetables they consider "normal", us North Americans probably wouldn't consider ordinary food. Like pumpkin. They cook it up so that it comes out like mashed potatoes. Pretty tasty, actually. I'm sure we've all heard the Australian term: "Throw another shrimp on the barbie!" I was thinking: "That's a damn small barbecue! No, it was actually a very large shrimp. I was never a big fan of seafood, so I passed on the shrimp, sticking to the snags (sausages), which were excellent. While I was there, we took a few side trips to some local attractions. Bundaberg was a personal favourite. This was where (in no particular order) I got a tattoo, and was introduced to my "liquid love" - Bundaberg rum. Nectar of the Gods as far as I'm concerned. We took a tour of the distillery, which included a taste testing session, with a maximum of two taste tests. It was heaven, in my opinion. The best rum I had ever had, and is still my favourite to this day. It is probably a good thing that brand is not available at home. Another side trip Matilda had planned was a drive to Beerwah, to visit the Australia Zoo, home of the world-famous Steve Irwin, who almost ran me over on his motorbike. I was lucky enough to see him doing one of his crocodile shows at the zoo. A memory I'll never forget.

On the trip home, I stayed the evening with a couple I had met in the chat room. He was a driver in Australia, she worked for the local government. We had dinner, then I grabbed a shower before heading off to the airport for my midnight flight to Kuala Lumpur. Problem was, I had been up all that day, the night before at my going-home party, and all day the previous day. All without a nap. When I got to the airport, I was still pumped up, and didn't realize just how exhausted I really was.

I'm an aviation nut, loving all things related to planes. One of the reasons I had chosen this route, was the chance to fly the "Queen of The Skies". A Boeing 747-400. Going to Australia was in the 747-400 from Los Angeles to Kuala Lumpur, and it was supposed to be a Boeing 777_200 (a newer wide body) from Kuala Lumpur to Brisbane. Alas, they switched aircraft, and it was a 747-400 from Kuala Lumpur to Brisbane. Not bad, but I was disappointed as I had looked forward to the 777-200, too. When I checked in for the first leg of my homeward-bound journey I discovered that that the flight to Kuala Lumpur was a Boeing 777-200! A nice surprise. I boarded, found my seat, and settled in. Next thing I remember, a flight attendant was waking me up in Kuala Lumpur! I'd slept through the safety briefing, taxi, take off, the entire 9 hour flight, meals, landing, and awoke to seeing everyone getting off the flight. The next leg was from Kuala Lumpur to Taipei. In Taipei, everyone had to deplane while the craft was cleaned, fuelled and serviced. While this process took place, everyone must go through US Customs for pre-arrival clearance. The process took just a few minutes. On the way to the gate, I spotted an indoor smoking area. Left turn, bro. The smoking room, as I recall, was about 100 feet long, and 100 feet wide. The exterior wall was filled with huge fans sucking the smoke outside. They were fighting a losing war, though. The leg from Taipei, to Los Angeles was uneventful, except for having a row of three seats to myself. In Los Angeles, I again had a hotel room paid for, this time by Air Canada. Upon check in, I was shocked when they asked if I wanted a smoking or non-smoking room. Smoking it was. The rest of that journey was uneventful. Soon I was back in Winnipeg, and back to work.

While on my second Australian vacation in 2008, I had the first inkling of something interesting awaiting my return to Canada. After my marriage disintegrated in 2001, I had spent five years dating people for all the wrong reasons. Each relationship ended in disaster, usually after three or four months. The last one fell apart just after my father passed away in 2006. I vowed I'd stay single forever-and-a-day. In my opinion (at the time), women were more trouble than they were worth. I later learned, after much soul searching, and self examination, that it was me, not them that was the problem. Just before I left for my Australian vacation, I decided that when I got home, I'd give the dating scene one more attempt. This time I'd set myself some "rules". The primary rule being that women with certain "interests" would not be considered. Or, to put it politely, the big head will make the decisions. A few days before I was to return to Canada, I received a message on the dating site. My handle was, in reference to my driving job, "redy2run". The message was from "Eros64". Total anonymity on this site. I checked her profile, and saw she was a non-smoker. Usually, smokers and nonsmokers don't get along too well, but I realized if she was "worth my time", she'd better have read my profile, were I specifically stated I was a smoker. It also said I was looking "kick my old life to the curb". This statement apparently intrigued her. Her message was a simple one. "Where are you running to? Or from?". That day in Australia, it was blazing hot. The asphalt was bleeding oil it was so hot. Me being the smart ass that I am, replied: "I'm running to the air conditioning". November in Canada, and especially Manitoba gets quite cold, so I knew this would pique her interest, and prompt some kind of response. She asked me where I was, and I told her I was in Australia, and that I'd be home soon. It intrigued her that I would take such a vacation by myself.

Twice the Fun
Running Turnpike Doubles

Long combination vehicles (lcvs) operate across Canada and the United States under special permits. These units consist of a truck (tractor) and two or three trailers, depending on the specific combination.. There are various types of lcvs: Turnpike Doubles (two trailers, either 48 or 53 foot long), Rocky Mountain Doubles (a 48 or 53 foot tailer with a 28 foot trailer behind it), Triples (three 28 foot trailer), Reverse Rocky Mountain Doubles (a 28 foot tandem axle trailer with an empty 48 or 53 foot trailer behind it) and Queen City Triples (a 48 or 53 foot trailer pulling a pair of 28 foot trailers behind it). Turnpike doubles (known simply as "pikes"), Rocky Mountain doubles (known as "Rockies") and triples are by far the most common. I've seen very few reverse Rocky Mountain doubles, and I've yet to see a Queen City Triple. Alberta ran a pilot (test) program a few years back with triple 53 foot trailers, but I believe it never came to be. It is up to each state or province to determine what is allowed on their public road-ways along with the regulations governing them. This means there may not be consistency for your entire route if you are crossing provincial or state lines. Pikes are common across Canada's prairie provinces (Manitoba, Saskatchewan, and Alberta) where the Trans-Canada is a divided highway and the landscape is primarily flat hills are low and gentle. They are also permitted along the 400 series highways in southern Ontario, and along the Trans Canada Highway in Quebec, as well as over the Coquahalla Highway in British Columbia between Kamloops and Hope. Yes, the Coquahalla is the highway most viewed on Discovery's "Highway Thru Hell". Drivers need to have additional certification and maintain certification on a regular basis to pull lcvs. The loads themselves can be a challenge as the trailers need to be properly loaded, with the heaviest trailer hooked to the tractor. One benefit with hauling lcvs is, it's all pin to pin. From one terminal yard to another.

When I first returned from my Australian vacation, the company didn't have a pike route set up for me yet, so it was back on the line haul for a while. I was okay with this, on one condition: I didn't care what truck they gave me, so long as it wasn't a Mack. The truck I was given was the oldest truck in the fleet, one registered to CoolX which was one of TransX's sister companies. CoolX was eventually merged into a future TransX acquisition, CanX. As I recall, the truck was a mid-2000's Freightliner Cascadia flat top sleeper (no standing up in the truck) but I couldn't care less. After the issues I had with the Mack's before my vacation, this was a welcome change. I ran this truck from mid-December until mid-March, when I was informed that I'd be filling in on the turnpikes for an injured driver.

The temporary turnpike run I was assigned would take me from Winnipeg to Grenfell, Saskatchewan, and back. It was a Monday to Friday run, meaning I'd have weekends off. The pay rate was $.52 per mile, for 564 miles a day, plus $20 to hook up, and another $20 for the spilt up. I'd be earning $313.28 each day. The only downside was that due to Saskatchewan's regulations involving the turnpikes, as well as all lcvs at the time, there was a maximum speed 55 mph driving through the province. Saskatchewan also had a maximum overall length for the pikes of 125 feet meaning we could not use highway trucks. We needed to use day cabs (trucks with no sleeper) to stay under the length requirements. Thankfully, the regulations have since been changed to allow the use of trucks with sleepers. The allowable speed was raised to 62 mph.

Just as the planner was informing me of the particulars of the run, another planner joined the conversation. He said he was wanted me to cover for a different turnpike driver who was injured. This new run was a far more important contract. There I was, caught between two planners trying to sort out what run I would cover, and for how long. In the end, I covered the more important contract until that driver was ready to return. Then I moved to cover the Grenfell switch run. Both paid the same, but the important contract was 60 miles less each day. Worked fine for me. I found out later why they wanted me on the more important contract. It involved some city driving including two or three very tight corners. Remember, trucks always have to swing wide when turning to allow for the offset turning radius of the trailer. The further the rear tires are from the steering tires, the greater the trailer offset. With turnpikes, the offset can be as great as 25 feet. You can imagine just how wide you have to "lead" the turn, all the time making sure you've swung wide enough (no backing up these very long turnpikes). You also have to make sure another vehicle has gotten inside of you as you make the turn.

Believe me, this happens a lot more than you think, hence, the "button hook" turn.

I'm sure most of you have seen a button hook maneuver and wondered "what the hell is this clown doing?" To make this turn, a truck starts in the right turn lane. Once we get to approximately one truck length from the corner, we swing wide into the next lane (or however far is needed in order to make the turn safety and successfully). This places the truck well away from the curb to allow room for the trailer to make the turn without hitting anything, yet leaves the rear of the trailer in the right turn lane, thus blocking access to other traffic that might sneak up on the inside. Someone who does this is virtually invisible from the cab of the truck. When the driver is able, they pull as far as possible into the intersection, then start their right turn. The trailer(s) will then swing left, following the tractor around the corner. Hopefully, Joe Motorist will see that the truck is turning right, then stay out of the way. But not always. I've seen more than a few accidents where someone has gotten in beside a truck turning right, and has paid a hefty price. At 135 feet long, and weighing up to 140,000 lbs, turnpikes don't do fender-benders. Trust me, you will lose that argument.

On this particular run, there was a right-hand turn from a three-lane road (including the right turn lane) onto a two-lane road, and an almost immediate left turn into the plant. It was so tight, that when you made the left turn into the plant, the truck was on the plant property before the rear trailer had gotten off the three-lane road. It was hairy, along with being quite stressful the first few times. Coming out was even worse. We would turn right out of the plant, swing all the way to the left, blocking the entire street, then make another right to get to the highway. I covered this run for about two weeks until the driver was able to return. Then I started the Grenfell switch run that I was mine until December of 2014.

In the early years of lcv use, there were quite a few restrictions surrounding their use. Speed, length, and travel time restrictions, weather restrictions, horsepower restrictions, and many others I'll cover if they come up. To explain all the restrictions would take another book entirely. Most of the restrictions were because the highway from Winnipeg to Calgary (the Trans Canada) still had some sections that were two lane highway. The 55 mph restriction was the worst. The posted speed limit was 62 mph, meaning cars and other trucks required a lot longer to overtake the slower-moving LCV. As a result, we were required to display a "LONG LOAD" sign on the back of the rear-most trailer. Of course, there were a few who had issues with the long load sign. More than a few drivers didn't understand the placement requirements, and displayed them upside down. Others displayed the wrong side (the signs were two sided: LONG LOAD on one side, OVERSIZE LOAD on the other). Some put it on the back of the front trailer (who would ever see it?). One driver even placed it on the front of the truck.

In the beginning, we were using Peterbilt day-cabs (no sleeper) equipped with 600 HP Cummins engines with an 18 speed transmission. These trucks were a dream. They had an abundance of horsepower needed to move the 140,000 lbs unit. These units were much more maneuverable than a full-length bunk truck. All the trucks were also equipped with onboard speed monitoring devices (another requirement at the time for lcv operations). These devices were either electronic (GPS) or manual (using a tach card to record engine RMP and truck road speed). Back then, Saskatchewan had a zero tolerance for speeds over 55 mph. Today, however, all prairie jurisdictions allow a maximum speed of 62 mph for lcvs.

By the time I started the run to Saskatchewan, there was a divided four-lane highway all the way to my destination. Nonetheless, the run had been set up to depart at four in the morning according to the two-lane restrictions. I had no issue with the early start, as it meant I'd be finished my day earlier. At the time, there were only four or five LCV runs. My run left at four a.m. The next left at six am, both loads bound for Calgary. The other two runs left at eight am, with one going to Calgary, the other to Edmonton, while the fifth was a dedicated run (that I had earlier covered) between plants for the same company. The Calgary and Edmonton runs ran Monday to Friday while the other was Tuesday to Saturday.

The Calgary runs were a "triple switch". On run one, I'd take the trailers to Grenfell, about 282 miles west of Winnipeg. In Grenfell, I'd switch with another truck that had travelled 80 miles eastward from Regina. Then I was homeward bound, back to Winnipeg. Run two had the Regina switch driver taking up the load I had delivered, turning back west for a 260 mile to Gull Lake, Saskatchewan. Here, the third run and another switch occurred. A driver from Calgary took the load further west on a return trip to Calgary 260 miles. At each turning point the old driver headed with a load back the way they came, switching as they went.

A tandem axle, 'A' type converter dolly.

As you can imagine, any issues in Calgary or Winnipeg that delayed departure, would throw the whole sequence into a tailspin. This could make the whole week a mess. The list of potential issues is long and varied. Bad weather in eastern Canada could delay the arrival of west-bound trailers. Mechanical issues with trucks and/or trailers were amongst the most common delays. Another issue often occurred on the first day of the week. The eastbound truck from Regina might not have any loaded trailers headed for Winnipeg. He had to wait for the planners to get to the office at eight a.m. to get assigned two empty trailers to haul east. Hopefully, there were two empties, one of which being equipped to pull a second trailer, as well as there being a converter to hook the two together. A converter is a small type trailer that is used to hook two trailers together.

As the switch time for the Grenfell run was 9:30 a.m. the Regina driver had to leave that location by 8:15 a.m. to make it to Grenfell by 9:30. He was seldom on time the first day of the weekly run, unless there were trailers in Regina ready to go. Another issue he had with having to bring two empties were weight considerations. Under the regulations, for safety reasons, the heaviest trailer must be connected to the truck. If the trailers are empty, no issues, right? WRONG! An empty refrigerated trailer weighs more than an empty heated trailer, which in turn is heavier than an empty dry van. Additionally, a tri-axle trailer is heavier than a tandem-axle trailer. I have been required at a scale to break the unit up, then scale each trailer individually, to make sure I had the heavier trailer hooked to the truck.

My first switch-run, two drivers from Regina didn't last very long. The first one lasted maybe a week. As the other Winnipeg switch driver running this route in addition to me, was a non-smoker, whereas I smoke. My switch driver from Regina was also a non-smoker. The other Regina switch, on the other hand, also smoked. It only made sense to flip it around so that a smoker switched with a smoker, and a non-smoker switching with a non-smoker. It was only a week, but worth the change to someone with similar smoking (or non-smoking) habits.

My smoking switch-driver, however, didn't last too much longer. Within a few months, he was gone. This guy was definitely NOT a team player. On occasion, he would call me, saying that since he had gotten away early, he would meet me in Whitewood, Saskatchewan to make the switch. This little Trans-Canada highway town was 30 miles closer Winnipeg. While this might have seemed like a small thing, since we were paid mileage, this resulted in more miles and money for him, less for me. I'd agree, being the easy-going type that I am, only to arrive at the truck stop, then end up waiting for up to another hour for him to show. I learned later that he was doing the same with the Calgary-based driver. After a few of these games of his, I decided "enough was enough". Instead of leaving at 4:00 a.m., to switch at 9:30, I left at midnight. He, predictably, called me at 6:00 am saying that he was getting away early so we could switch in Whitewood. I told him that I, too, had gotten away early. I was already in White City about

30 miles from Regina, so he'd best get out here ASAP. Coincidentally, the Calgary-based driver had had enough. He had left early as well, driving 35 miles beyond his original Gull Lake, Saskatchewan drop to Swift Current, Saskatchewan. This was just 167 miles from White City where I was dropping my load. Mr. Regina's day (and mileage) was considerably shorter that what he was expecting! After that, dispatch decided that there would be no deviations from the company-approved switch locations. The Regina driver was NOT impressed. The Calgary driver and myself couldn't have cared less.

On occasion, there wasn't enough freight to fill two trailers, so we would leave with either a single trailer, or a single trailer and a converter. One day, I left with a single. The Regina driver was to stop in Regina on his way to Gull Lake, pick up a converter and an empty trailer, then carry on. Well, he wasn't happy with this. During his walk-around inspection in Grenfell, he swung his hammer at the air connections in an effort to damage the service connection. Damage would take time to repair, and Mr. Regina hoped that the company would then abandon the converter and second trailer. Bad idea, made worse by his bad aim. He ended up knocking the supply glad hand off the trailer. The glad hands control the air supply to the converter and to the back trailer. The service line (blue in colour) only supplies air when the brakes are applied. The supply line (red) supplies full air system pressure (120-150 PSI) to release the parking brakes. Both glad-hands have a valve, that you open when the converter and back trailer are attached, closed when they are not. When he swung his hammer to knock off the blue valve, he took the red one off instead. That meant he was not going anywhere until it's repaired, since he was losing air pressure faster than the compressor could replace it. He called the shop to arrange for repairs, claiming that I had brought the trailer from Winnipeg in this condition. Of course, everyone who heard this explanation knew it was a lie. With an air leak of this size, there's no way that trailer was going anywhere. These were just a couple of run-ins he and I had. I think he assumed (without really knowing me or asking anyone) that I was a new driver and he could "pull the wool" over my eyes. Sorry. I quickly learned to double-check every piece of equipment he brought me. I found more than a few safety issues, along with one huge goof, which I took great pleasure in watching him fix.

If you look at the side of a 53 foot trailer, near the axles, you will see that almost all trailers have a mark of some kind showing the 41 foot mark. This is because all trailers of this size can have a maximum distance of 41 feet from the king pin (that hooks into the fifth wheel) to the centre of the rear axle assembly. The centre of the axle assembly can be ahead of the 41 foot mark, but not beyond it. There are, however, a few exceptions. With lcvs, on the front trailer the axles can be at, or behind the 41 foot mark, and on the rear trailer, the axles can be at or ahead of the 41 foot mark. Mr. Regina showed up one day with a set of empties, both dry vans, so at least the weight difference wasn't an issue. But he had the axles on the front trailer all the way to the front, and the axles on the back trailer all the way to the back. Definitely not legal. I told him, flat out, that I wasn't dropping the trailers I brought him until he fixed it. Otherwise, he would have just hooked up, leaving me to fix his mess. I'm pretty sure he had done it on purpose, but whatever.

If you know what you're doing, sliding the axles on a set of lcvs is quite simple. This can be done in a matter of minutes. By opening and closing the valves that supply air to the rear trailer, you can shut off the supply line from the converter, disconnect to red line, and exhaust the air, which will apply the parking brakes. You then release the axle locking pins, then back up a few feet to position the axles where you want them, followed by connecting the red line, and opening the valve. The system pressurizes, and the brakes release. To adjust the axles on the front trailer, close the blue line to the converter. Release the axle locking pins on the lead trailer, then drive forward. All parking brakes are released. When you apply the dashboard hand trailer valve the axles on the front trailer stop. The trailer moves forward on the slider. Once the axles are where you want them, release the locking pins, open the blue line to the converter, and off you go.

Apparently, Mr. Regina didn't think the necessary scenario through. He split the trailers, slid the axles on each, one at a time, grumbling: "You happy now?!" I said: "No, put them back together. Why should I have to do it?" Well, that really set him off. Meanwhile, I unhooked from the trailers I had brought while he huffed and puffed, storming around, hooking the set back together. I gave him the paperwork, which he all but snatched from my hands, and off he went, calling me every name he could think of. Again, I couldn't have cared less.

I don't know all the details of his last "stunt", but I managed to piece together what probably happened. I brought him a single trailer, with the switch going fairly simple. We had already gotten to the point of dropping the trailer(s) with the paperwork included so we didn't have to interact at all. I left with the two empties he had brought while he headed back west with the single trailer. About an hour later, the shop called me, asking about the trailer I had taken him, as there was an issue with it. Apparently, the service glad hand was missing. I told them to check the work orders, as that trailer had just been in the shop the day before for repairs to the glad hands. What Mr. Regina had done upon being told to grab the converter and second trailer, was to take his hammer to the blue glad-hand, so he wouldn't have to stop. This time, he was caught red handed. This wasn't his first attempt to get me in trouble. He once called the shop complaining I had brought him a trailer with three bad tires. A quick check with the shop proved I had two bad tires changed before I left. This time, however, he was suspended for a few days. Another driver was put on the run. Once his suspension was up, they offered him a different lcv run, as the new driver had far more seniority with the company. He refused, demanding his run back. He eventually went to the labour board with a complaint against the company. Once the labour board learned he had been offered a comparable position with the same pay, benefits and everything, they denied the claim. He eventually left, and I neither know (nor care) where he went.

THE PEOPLE THAT YOU MEET,

AND SOME OF THE THINGS YOU SEE,

As you may guess, spending so much of my time on the road, I have had the pleasure, and displeasure, of meeting more than a few celebrities, usually touring musicians, circuses, and the like. Most times, it's on the highway, as they pass me, some times it's in a highway rest area, or service plaza, and sometimes, it's a chance meeting in a truck stop restaurant. More often than not, it's on the highway. I only recall meeting one group on tour in a restaurant, and that was the Rolling Stones in Dimondale, MI. during the Steel Wheels tour, if I'm not mistaken. As you would expect, they had security to keep people away while they were eating. Common courtesy should keep people from bothering them for pictures and autographs while they're eating, but not always. I've met more than a few celebrities away from trucking, and they all hate being "bothered" while busy doing something else.

On the road, other than the Stones, I've seen Alabama, Taylor Swift, Bob Chandler (owner of the Bigfoot monster truck), AC/DC, Metallica, Micheal Jackson, Dale Earnhart Jr, and countless others. Away from trucking, the list is almost endless. Vince Neil of Motley Crue, Frankie Banali of Quiet Riot, Freddy Curry of Cinderella, John Corabi, of Motley Crue, Robert Sweet of Stryper, Mike Portnoy, Billy Sheehan and Richie Kotzen (The Winery Dogs). Girlschool, The Iron Maidens (all female tribute to Iron Maiden), Paradise Kitty (all female tribute to Guns N Roses) The Atomic Punks (tribute to early Van Halen). A word to the wise. If you get the chance to see either of these three tribute acts, GO! They're all awesome

Just a few of the celebraties I've encountered on the road.
And a boat from Hawaii, in Northern Ontario.

In Closing

So there it is. Some of the more interesting stories of my life as a professional driver. With a few exceptions, almost everything in here was prior to December 2014. From then, until January of 2019, I was doing mostly city and local work, and basically home every night, with weekends off, and long weekends as well. But, as I said back in the beginning, running long haul gets into your blood. You can escape it for a while, but not forever. In January of 2019, I returned to the long haul life, this time pulling flat decks. Deck work is so different from vans and reefers, that I still feeling like a rookie sometimes.

A few people who have proofread the manuscript have expressed amazement that I can remember all the stories. The truth is, I can't. I started with a list of maybe 20 or 25 stories. As I typed away, one story would remind me of another, so I'd make a note so as not to forget. Talking with co-workers, I'd be reminded of other stories, and again, notes were made so I'd remember them. What you see here, is about 9 months worth of "Oh yeah! I forgot about THAT!". Sometimes it would be a conversation, other times, I'd be going through old photos to include here, and see one that would remind me of something.

So here it all is, for better, or worse. I hope you enjoyed reading it as much as I enjoyed writing it.

1 million safe driving miles.

2 million safe driving miles.

ABOUT THE AUTHOR

November 2015, on Vacation to Uluru, Northern Territory, Australia

Don Taylor has been a professional driver since 1985. In that time, he has accumulated over 3,000,000 miles of driving, having visited every US State and Canadian provide except for Alaska, Hawaii and Newfoundland. In that time, he has seen, and done it all. Meat loads to New York City and the Mexican Border, and rolls of paper to points all across North America.